V. α. e Fedrus 7

2000

WAR,
RESISTANCE
AND
INTELLIGENCE

WAR, RESISTANCE

AND

INTELLIGENCE

Essays in Honour of

M.R.D. Foot

Edited by

K. G. ROBERTSON

LEO COOPER

First published in Great Britain in 1999 by
Leo Cooper
an imprint of
Pen & Sword Books Ltd
47 Church Street
Barnsley
South Yorkshire
S70 2AS

ISBN 0 85052 689 2

A catalogue record for this book is
available from the British Library.

Typeset in 11/13pt Sabon by
Phoenix Typesetting, Ilkley, West Yorkshire

Printed in England by Redwood Books Ltd,
Trowbridge, Wilts.

CONTENTS

NOTES ON CONTRIBUTORS

K.G. Robertson is a Director of AnalyticA Research Ltd, a company at the forefront of new approaches to intelligence management. During his academic career at the University of Reading he played a leading role in developing Intelligence studies in the UK. He was the inspiration behind the formation of both 'The Study Group On Intelligence' (1982) and the 'Security and Intelligence Studies Group' (1993), a specialist group of the Political Studies Association. They have established themselves as the leading UK bodies for the academic study of security and Intelligence issues. His six books include *Secrecy and Open Government* (1999), *British and American Approaches to Intelligence* (1987) and *Public Secrets* (1982).

John Roberts was Warden, Merton College Oxford and Vice-Chancellor of the University of Southampton. He is the author of eight books, including *History of the World* (1976) and *The Triumph of the West* (1985).

Christopher Woods joined the Army from school and fought in the Italian Campaign, starting in the south with the Eighth Army and finishing in the north with SOE, having skipped the middle by joining No 1 Special Force and being parachuted as a British Liaison Officer with Italian partisans for the last nine months in the Veneto. Having volunteered for further service with SOE in Asia, he arrived to find the war against Japan over, but spent a year in Java and Sumatra attached to British Forces holding the ring as the Dutch East Indies became Indonesia. He studied history and Russian at Cambridge, joined the Foreign Office and fought the Cold War, serving in Persia, Cyprus and Europe East and West. After retirement, he acted as SOE Adviser in the FCO in charge of the SOE Archive. He is now writing the official history of SOE in Italy.

Born in California and educated at Berkeley and Oxford, **Kathleen Burk** is Professor of Modern and Contemporary History at

University College, London. A specialist in Anglo-American relations and economic diplomacy, she is the author of a number of books, including *Britain, America and the Sinews of War 1914–1918* (1985), *Morgan Grenfell 1838–1988: the Biography of a Merchant Bank* (1989) and (with Alec Cairncross) *'Good-bye, Great Britain': The 1976 IMF Crisis* (1992), as well as the Editor of the journal *Contemporary European History*, which is published by Cambridge. Currently completing *The Troublemaker: The Life and History of A.J.P. Taylor*, to be published in 2000, she is embarking on a book on the Marshall Plan from the European perspective.

P.M.H. Bell is an Honorary Senior Research Fellow and formerly Reader in History at the University of Liverpool. He is the author of *Disestablishment in Ireland and Wales* (1969); *A Certain Eventuality: Britain and the Fall of France* (1974); *The Origins of the Second World War in Europe* (1986, 2nd Ed., 1997); *France and Britain 1900–1940: Entente and Estrangement* (1996); *France and Britain 1940–1994: The Long Separation* (1997). He gave the Churchill Lecture at Westminster College, Fulton, Missouri, in March, 1999, on 'Churchill and France during the Second World War'.

Peter Lowe is Reader in History in the University of Manchester. Among his recent publications are *Containing the Cold War in East Asia: British Policies towards Japan, China and Korea, 1948–53* (Manchester University Press, 1997), *The Origins of the Korean War* second edition (Longman, 1997) and (editor), *The Vietnam War* (Macmillan, 1998).

John Lukacs, now retired, is the author of many books and studies in diplomatic and international and cultural history, of which the best known in England are *The Last European War, 1939–1941 The Hitler of History, The Thread of Years*, and the very recently published *Five Days in London, May 1940*.

Ian Kershaw is Professor of Modern History at the University of Sheffield and one of the world's leading authorities on Nazism. He was the historical advisor on the BBC series, 'The Nazis: A warning from History'. His ten books include *The Nazi Dictatorship* (1985), *Stalinism and Nazism* 1997) and most recently the first volume of his biography of the Nazi leader *Hitler 1889–1932: Hubris*.

Sir William Deakin led the first British mission to Tito in 1943. After a distinguished diplomatic career he was appointed Warden of St Antony's College, Oxford. He is the author of *The Brutal Friendship* (1962) and *Embattled Mountain* (1971).

Ralph White is Senior Fellow at the Department of Politics and Contemporary History at the University of Salford. He is the editor, with Stephen Haws of *Resistance in Europe, 1939–1945*, Allen Lane, 1975.

Mark Seaman is a Historian with the Research and Information Office in the Imperial War Museum. Having joined the staff in 1980 he has specialized in the field of Resistance, Intelligence and Special Operations during the Second World War and was responsible for the IWM's 1984 exhibition 'European Resistance to Nazi Germany' and the more recent permanent gallery 'Secret War'. In October 1998 he organized a three-day conference at the Museum on the Special Operations Executive.

He has written extensively on his specialist subjects. His latest published works include an introduction to the Public Record Office's *Operation Foxley, The British Plan to Kill Hitler* and *Bravest of the Brave*, a biography of the Special Operations Executive agent, Wing Commander F.F.E. Yeo-Thomas, GC MC*.

Professor of History at the University of Sussex, **H.R. Kedward** is currently researching a third volume of a trilogy on resistance in the southern regions of France. The published volumes are *Resistance in Vichy France* (1978) and *In Search of the Maquis* (1993). His work features the oral histories of French men and women at the grassroots of resistance as well as national and local archives. In 1989 he received the honour of Officier de l'Ordre des Palmes Académiques, and the Maquis book was awarded the Prix Philippe Viannay – Défense de la France.

David Stafford, an Honorary Fellow at the Institute for Advanced Studies at The University of Edinburgh, is the author of two books on SOE: *Britain and European Resistance 1940–1945* (London and Toronto 1980) and *Camp X: SOE and the American Connection* (London, Toronto, New York 1986). His latest book is *Churchill and Secret Service* (London and Toronto 1997, New York 1998).

Group Captain Hugh Beresford Verity DSO and bar, DFC, MA. Officier de la Légion d'Honneur, Croix de Guerre avec Palme, RAF (ret'd) was educated at Cheltenham College and the Queen's College, Oxford. He was learning to fly in the University Air Squadron in 1938 when he was commissioned in the Royal Air Force Volunteer Reserve. In 1943, he commanded the pick-up flight of No 161 special duties squadron, landing Lysanders and Hudsons on meadows in occupied France. For the rest of the war he was a Wing Commander staff officer responsible for SOE's air operations in Europe and then for all clandestine air operations in South East Asia. The seventh version (including three in French) of his book *We Landed by Moonlight* appeared in 1998.

E.R.D. Harrison is a Lecturer in International History and member of the European Studies Research Institute at the University of Salford. His research and teaching interests focus on Nazi Germany, Communist China, British Intelligence and Anglo-Polish relations. Recently he has held the Anthony de Rothschild Fellowship of the Winston Churchill Memorial Trust, an Alistair Horne Visiting Fellowship at St Antony's College Oxford and is currently Visiting Professor at Wayne State University. Otherwise he lives in Leeds, where one of his main interests is learning languages.

Christopher Andrew is Professor of Modern and Contemporary History at Cambridge University, Chair of the British Intelligence Study Group, Co-Editor of *Intelligence and National Security*, former Visiting Professor at Harvard, Toronto and the Australian National University, and a regular presenter of BBC documentaries on modern history and international relations. His twelve books include *Secret Service: The Making of the British Intelligence Community* (Heinemann, 1985), *KGB: The Inside Story of its Foreign Operations from Lenin to Gorbachev* (with Oleg Gordievsky: Hodder and Stoughton, 1990), and *For the President's Eyes Only: Secret Intelligence and the American Presidency from Washington to Bush* (Harper Collins, 1995).

Peter Hennessy was a journalist for 20 years (mainly with *The Times*, the *Financial Times*, the *Economist* and BBC Radio 4 *Analysis* before returning to academic life in 1992. Since then he has been Professor of Contemporary History at Queen Mary and Westfield College,

University of London. His publications include *Cabinet, Whitehall, Never Again: Britain 1945–51, The Hidden Wiring* and *Muddling Through*. He is currently working on *The Prime Minister: The Office and Its Holders Since 1945*.

Mirjam Michaela Foot, D. Litt., F.S.A., was until recently Director of Collections and Preservation at the British Library. She is a part-time lecturer in Historical Bibliography at University College, London. She has published extensively on the history of bookbinding and allied subjects.

INTRODUCTION

What does the colour of ladies' underwear have to do with British intelligence? Perhaps you may think of Ian Fleming's fictional character James Bond, but this is no work of fiction. Names such as Malcolm Muggeridge and A.J.P. Taylor may also suggest a literary essay, but again the connection with spying is real, not fictional. The link between Winston Churchill, US General Douglas MacArthur and Charles de Gaulle may seem easier to make – the Second World War – but this too is misleading. The essay on Churchill is concerned with his early life and the emergence of his fascination with the world of intelligence, although this experience may help us to understand why, during the war of 1939–45, he was willing to rely on intelligence when so many others of his generation were sceptics, if not opponents, of 'the dirty game'. The essays on MacArthur and de Gaulle are as much concerned with their role as diplomats, with shaping the post-war environment, as with their role as military officers. What then links Soviet espionage, Churchill, the Special Operations Executive, resistance and military history? The answer is the life and work of the distinguished 'warrior historian' M.R.D. (Michael) Foot. All of the friends and colleagues able to contribute were asked to address some of the themes that have played a part in Michael's writing. However, within the chosen themes of war, resistance and intelligence, each author was allowed to select his or her topic. Some were working on topics that could not be discussed without reference to Michael, such is his standing and influence in the field, whilst others' research was taking them in new and different directions. In the editor's view, to provide the opportunity for each to give of their best is the finest tribute to a fellow historian.

However, the volume makes no claim to cover all of the topics that have been important to M.R.D. Foot. As John Roberts states in his foreword there is no reference to Mr Gladstone and yet

Michael's work on Gladstone placed him firmly in the top rank of contemporary British historians. It was a difficult decision to omit the nineteenth century, but, as editor, I felt that coherence required some selectivity in the range of topics to be covered. This was not just to be a book about one man but a contribution to scholarship. By doing so it became even more of a tribute.

I first met Michael in July 1982 at the inaugural meeting of a group of historians, which I had initiated, committed to the serious study of intelligence. Looking back, it is clear that the time was right for such a meeting, since the *Study Group On Intelligence* has gone on to establish itself as a valuable and regular part of intelligence studies. From our earliest discussion of a 'statement of purpose' for the Group Michael insisted that resistance, subversion and sabotage, the type of activities carried out by the wartime SOE, should be included under the heading 'intelligence'. I can only say that I am delighted that it was; it has provided many of our most enthralling and enlightening sessions.

The book is divided into three sections, although they are obviously linked and some topics fall under more than one heading. However, I have tried to provide some sense of moving from the earlier to the later and from the particular to the more general. But no one should let this stand in the way of enjoyment, for the essays are entirely capable of standing on their own. They cover a variety of events and personalities, as well as reflections on some of the 'great debates' associated with the major conflicts of the twentieth century, and there will, I hope, be something new and enjoyable for all those familiar with the work of M.R.D. Foot. And as much enjoyment for those coming to war, resistance and intelligence for the first time.

Christopher Woods provides a dramatic start with his tale of a British SOE officer in Italy who, despite being arrested and interrogated, went on to play an important role during the Armistice. However, in 1944, he was again sent to Italy and was again arrested. Despite finding himself being taken to SS HQ in Verona, a cause, he says, of sudden consternation, he went on to play a vital part in the negotiations for the German withdrawal from Northern Italy. This remarkable character, Major Mallaby, will surely go into the annals of great SOE characters. Kathleen Burk describes A.J.P. Taylor's war as 'useful but unheroic', but the story of his wartime relationship with the BBC and the Ministry of Information certainly involves storms and tempests! On several occasions Government Ministers had to repeat that Mr Taylor was speaking in his personal capacity and not as an official in receipt of remuneration. This shows that they also serve who only stand and speak. Philip Bell argues that 'what men choose to remember is often more important than what actually happened' and this certainly is the case with French memories of Churchill's treatment of de Gaulle. However, Bell argues that the record is far more complex and that Churchill did not 'choose' the United States over and above the interests of France but that he was trying the much more difficult task of balancing between them. The British desire to 'balance' European and US interests continues to this day. Peter Lowe discusses the problems Britain faced in dealing with that most 'political' of Generals, Douglas MacArthur. At times the US feared that MacArthur had fallen under the spell of 'communists and British imperialists', whilst the British government felt excluded from the post-war reconstruction of Japan. However, despite difficulties during the Pacific War it was disagreements over conduct of the war in Korea, and British fears that MacArthur may involve the UN in all-out war against China, that led Britain to argue for his removal. However, as Lowe argues, the debates over MacArthur also symbolized British difficulties in dealing with the reality of its declining role and influence and the rise of a new world power, the United States. John Lukacs provides the most wide-ranging of all the essays, covering as it does great debates over the interpretation of the wars of the Twentieth Century. Determining the origins of war involves more than setting the record straight, since nations wish to blame others or to preserve their national pride as honourable among nations. Lukacs argues that the obligation of the historian is to the evidence and not to the temptations of fads and fashions. In the days of 'new styles of history' the argument that many of these novelties have produced poor history is one that will arouse controversy. Michael Foot will enjoy that! Ian Kershaw, in the midst of completing his magisterial two-volume biography of Adolf Hitler, has produced a miniature portrait of the true nature of the Nazi régime. Kershaw argues that one does not need to find a direct order from Hitler to know who and what was responsible for genocide. Hitler's 'visionary' goals for German expansion and racial purification provided the guidelines within which others did what they believed was required. German policy in the Warthegau area of Poland, (1940–41) with its 300,000 Jews (8% of the population), demonstrates that 'ethnic cleansing' was taken for granted. By the end of 1940 250,000 Jews had been deported as part of a plan to 'make room' for 500,000 ethnic Germans from the Baltic, Bessarabia and Bukovina. However, deportation was neither as quick nor effective as desired and by the autumn of 1941 Himmler, in agreement with Heydrich, had given 'permission' to kill 100,000 Jews 'incapable of work'. This is an appropriate point to remember what Nazism involved and why war was necessary.

Sir William Deakin provides one of the most delightful tales in the volume. I will not spoil it by saying more than that it involves wireless communication, SOE, Yugoslav resistance and ladies' underwear. Read on! The next three essays all focus on important debates on the role of individuals in secret operations. There is no doubt that enormous courage and personal initiative are required for survival, let alone success, as a British agent in occupied Europe, but how significant was their individual or collective contribution to the war effort? Immediately following the war such a question could not be raised; it seemed to say more about the morality of the questioner than about the brave men and women involved. However, as time passes we have become somewhat more relaxed about asking awkward questions and confronting difficult issues. M.R.D. Foot was the first scholar to begin this process, but it is one that continues. The three essays by White, Kedward and Seaman provide different, but complementary, views on current interpretations of the Special Operations Executive and resistance. White assesses the significance and meaning of Foot's work on SOE; Kedward, in a brilliant, learned essay, examines the whole debate over the significance of the personality in 'heroic' situations and Seaman assesses the degree to which memoirs provide a reliable source of historical fact for those wishing to add colour and detail to their understanding of events.

There is no doubt that Churchill was fascinated by intelligence, but where and when did this fascination begin? David Stafford traces the roots of Churchill's experience of intelligence back to his watching Spanish efforts to crush the 1895 revolt in Cuba. Later, in the Admiralty, he became familiar with the growing interception of communications war, Sigint, that so revolutionized intelligence in the Twentieth century; people were liable to error and weakness, whereas technology gave 'hard' and untainted facts. Such a view dominated the intelligence war for the next eighty years. Hugh

Verity returns to an earlier theme in that his focus is on the bravery and courage of members of the resistance, the Royal Air Force, SOE and the British Secret Intelligence Service, more commonly known as MI6. The hair-raising experience of pilots and their 'clients' once again provides the human background to great events. There are wonderful stories of Lysanders being stuck in fields and people pushing rather large ladies into the backs of rather small aircraft! Malcolm Muggeridge seems to have enjoyed an infinite capacity for reinventing himself but few of his critics or admirers will be familiar with his experiences as an intelligence officer with MI6. Ted Harrison's story of kidnap, bribery and diplomatic furore is worthy of any novel! Muggeridge was rather scathing about his time with British intelligence and Graham Greene described him as a 'bit of a flop', but Harrison shows that Muggeridge was, if anything, rather too cavalier for his own or anyone else's good. During his period in Mozambique he was enthusiastic, if rather irresponsible, and Harrison concludes that he would have been rather more suited to SOE than to SIS. You can judge after reading Harrison, Verity, White, Kedward and Seaman! The controversy surrounding communist penetration of western institutions during the Cold War still rages but all such debate must now make reference to VENONA. Venona was the name given to the decrypts of Soviet telegrams and led not only to the discovery of Soviet spies but provided the crucial, but often secret, confirmation of suspicion. So secret was VENONA that its very existence was kept hidden from those responsible for tracking Soviet espionage. Christopher Andrew assesses the significance of VENONA and its role in reassessing the period we now call McCarthyism. The US was trapped by its desire to alert the public to the danger of espionage and yet to preserve its success in breaking Soviet codes; this was the gap that McCarthy so ruthlessly and shamelessly exploited. The volume of essays ends by looking forward. There is no finer commentator on Whitehall than Peter Hennessy. His understanding of the Whitehall village gives him the ability to place intelligence in context; what is its role in the next century and why is it worth spending about one billion pounds to obtain it? Hennessy demonstrates that there are threats aplenty and that the relationship with the US, the impact of technology, and the quality of analysis means that intelligence has an even brighter future in the next century than it had in the last.

However, this introduction would not be complete if it failed to give credit to Mirjam Foot, Michael's wife, who not only inspired us all with her enthusiasm for the project but provided much valuable support. It is only fitting that she has the last word, the bibliography, since Mirjam was the beginning.

K.G. Robertson

FOREWORD
by
JOHN ROBERTS

After more than fifty years my memory is far from exact, but it was in my first or second term as an undergraduate, Hilary or Trinity, 1946, that I first met Michael Foot. I am sure that it was at a class in political theory held by Donald Mackinnon, then Keble's philosophy tutor, and I know that I was strongly impressed by this new acquaintance. Here was a fellow-undergraduate (my first impression was that this was his status, though it was in fact not the case, since he had already taken his first degree under the wartime regulations of the university), about ten years older than the very callow seventeen-year old straight from school that I was, evidently learned in matters still closed to many of us, experienced in the ways of men in war, with a slightly romantic aura about him. As I got to know him better, my initial impression was confirmed and deepened: here was, too, a young man already master of much recondite information, a curious enquirer possessed of a sharp intelligence who phrased his questions with great precision and some subtlety, and with access to almost legendary academic figures who thought well of him.

That impression never quite faded, though, of course, its details took clearer and harder shape on further and closer acquaintance (and one that did not really begin to grow until I had gone away and come back from my own National Service stint to the Oxford of late 1950). One of those details was a very distinctive conversational style, even a particular voice. It was always quiet and measured, and tending to the clipped, but with never less than a hint and sometimes an occasional surge of intensity. Often it was interrogative in mode (it was not necessary to answer the rhetorical questions which studded it, but more enjoyable to let them build up by implication the steps to the point he wished to make) and enthusiastically decorated with apt quotation (in those days many from Mr Gladstone – it was already always *Mr*), illuminating allusion and the evidence of a well-cultivated mind. His leg could be pulled, though. Sometimes he would, unaware, extend it for the purpose: he artlessly reminisced one day, I recall, of 'reading – or, rather *re*-reading Proust . . .'. Michael was already prodigal in his helpfulness and generosity to other young historians, too, and clearly could look forward to a successful scholarly future.

I sometimes thought that the characteristic voice and presentational style was something learnt at Winchester; other Wykehamists seemed to me sometimes faintly to echo it. Whether that was true or not, the Wykehamist strain was certainly of the first importance in shaping the boy and the man. His father, a mining engineer, had been a Wykehamist too, and must have been proud of his son's successive scholarships, in college at Winchester and then at New College, to which Michael went up in 1937. Through his fellow-schoolboy, Christopher Seton-Watson, he had come to know an almost legendary contemporary historian and public figure, Robert Seton-Watson, Christopher's father. To him, in later tutorials at Oxford, Michael owed two invaluable lessons: instruction in how to skip irrelevant matter in reading and the first hint that Gladstone was a figure of absorbing historical interest.

While still an undergraduate Michael joined the Territorial Army, a step which no doubt reflects the influential examples of a grandfather and great-uncle, both of whom had been regular soldiers. He read PPE and was taught by (among others) John Wheeler-Bennett, whom he recognized as the major influence in making him a historian. Then came the war, and in retrospect it is easy to see that wartime experience was decisive for the future shaping of his historian's career. From the Royal Artillery he transferred in due course to the Special Air Service, and finished the war with the rank of Major. By that time he had extensive experience both of staff work and planning – at Combined Ops HQ and, notably, for the ill-fated Dieppe raid – and of operations in the field. These he entered first as an observer accompanying flights to France, then as a principal on a special mission which ended, unhappily, with his capture by a German unit. His personal captor, perhaps intent on souvenirs, cut off the SAS insignia on his tunic, a circumstance probably very fortunate for the new prisoner of war, who was marched off to interrogation and imprisonment near St Nazaire. A number of attempts to escape resulted in success, though only temporarily; Michael broke free of his German captors only to be re-delivered to them after a disabling attack by an enraged French peasant with a pitchfork, who left him with a broken neck and cracked skull. From then until after D-Day he was tended in a German field hospital, to be exchanged in due course for a German major with an Iron Cross and sent home.

Undoubtedly seeds were sown by these experiences – and the value of his military service was duly recognized by decoration – which were to fructify in his later academic work (as this volume notably demonstrates). On his return to Oxford, though, equipped with his wartime degree, he eked out his resources by teaching, at first mainly for Keble and Trinity. In the British Museum, meanwhile, he began to immerse himself in the study of Gladstone. There, in 1947, he met the veteran scholar J.L. Hammond, who at that time might be regarded as the first – and virtually only – Gladstone 'revisionist'. His book on Gladstone and Ireland, published just before the war, had just begun the rescue of the GOM from scholarly neglect and the condescension of a public attuned to the 'debunking' of Victorian biographies (or, in this particular case, of Morley's Edwardian one). Hammond was old and died in 1949, but before that he had recommended that Michael be asked to finish the volume which appeared under their joint names in A.L. Rowse's admirable and useful series of *Teach Yourself History* books in 1952. This was the first fruit of the younger man's Gladstonian study and he had taken great care, and pride, to produce so seamless a text that nobody should be able to distinguish Hammond from Foot within it. It is said to have caused him some irritation, therefore, when his mother was able to identify all his own contributions to the text at first reading.

Although not devoting himself solely to Gladstone immediately on returning to Oxford, he had (like other young and promising graduates about Oxford in those days of an overcrowded university) a fair amount of occasional teaching of undergraduates to do, which was welcome as a way of earning a little money. Thus he soon acquired an evidently justified reputation as a stimulating and conscientious tutor. He also worked for a time with Stanley Morison on the *History of the Times* and even found time to win election and serve as City Councillor, an experience of practical politics which had a happy outcome in a decision that it was not the life for him.

The Hammond relationship proved in the end to have been decisive. In 1956 he was asked by the Delegates of the Oxford

University Press to advise them on a proposal to publish the Gladstone diaries. Soon, after his report had been digested, he was invited to undertake their editorship for the OUP. Like that of so many important historical enterprises at the outset, the scope of the task was underestimated; Michael himself, with better knowledge than the Delegates, appears to have envisaged an eventual publication of only six volumes, half what proved in the end to be necessary. The manuscript diaries had been transferred on loan from Lambeth to the Manuscripts department of the British Museum Library. The new editor soon established in the North Library a constantly replenished 'Foot shelf', the envy of lesser mortals, and a source of bibliographic wonder to them and celebrity to himself. Its ample traffic provided daily and continuous evidence of the huge scope of the project he had undertaken. The first two volumes appeared in 1968. There followed two more before he left the task, their editing completed by Colin Matthew, who had been appointed two years before to succeed Michael as editor after an earlier appointment to a special lectureship at Christ Church to assist with the editorial work.

His last work on the Gladstone project appeared in print in 1974. In the previous decade there had been two other key developments in Michael's professional formation. One was his successful application for the chair of Modern History at Manchester, the other a shift in the focus of his studies to what might be called the recent history of subversion, sabotage, undercover warfare, topics until then too easily dismissed in jocular fashion as 'thud-and-blunder' history. The appointment in 1965 to Manchester, where he took up his post in 1967, was a striking one. He had not followed the *cursus honorum* of research fellowships, junior lectureships and lectureships which mark most advances to the sunlit professorial uplands, but had depended on the precarious support provided by teaching – Keble remained a frequent employer and he did a spell at Southampton – and his involvement with the *The Times* project. At the moment of his arrival, the Manchester Department of History, much aware of (and perhaps even a little encumbered by) consciousness of its long distinction and success, was beginning to engage in strongly contested debate about the undergraduate syllabus. It was soon felt that the new professor was in favour of change. A number of retirements at senior level led to the appointment also of John Western to a chair in Modern History, and the partnership which ensued – all too brief, for Western died in 1971 – seemed to many to augur well for a balanced future development of the department, given the seemingly complementary qualities of the two men. Michael was, a colleague has remarked, 'an arresting lecturer', and students found him fascinating. His personal influence, too, extended beyond the university in the encouragement and friendship he offered to colleagues at other institutions less ancient and perhaps less regarded in those days. Within his own institution, it was a time of contention in many respects, and Michael soon won a reputation with student representatives for his speeches in the Senate as those of a friend at court with progressive views, and among his junior colleagues as a sensible proponent of change. One of them has recalled that 'Michael believed in talking to students, discussing problems frankly, and arriving at reasonable solutions'. It was not a time when all professors gave that impression.

Nevertheless, Manchester was not to hold him for long. In 1973 he resigned his chair to become Director of Studies at the Foreign Office's European Discussion Centre at Wilton Park. The decision to leave Manchester had been the outcome of a complex set of reasons and circumstances. Work on the Gladstone Diaries had proved increasingly demanding and required his presence in London for some considerable part of each week. The burden of commuting was heavy and intensified domestic and personal pressures. In the early 1970s, too, universities were making heavy demands on professors which were all the more distasteful then, because they were so unprecedented. Not a few of them at that time felt that they were being distracted from teaching and research to rebarbative administrative and political debate. At any rate, for reasons complex but persuasive, Michael stepped out of the institutional mainstream of academic life and did so, it was to turn out, for good. Yet it was not to be permanently into the world of the civil service. Of his new post his tenure was to be only two years, even briefer than that of his professorial chair. It was evidently not a satisfying transition. The Foreign Office post had looked, as the grass next door sometimes does, more comparatively attractive than it turned out to be, for it was far less of an academic than an administrative post.

By then, though, it was beginning to be clear that SOE in France, published in 1964, had been the public announcement of a new academic era in turning professional attention to a number of topics until then relatively neglected in this country. The invitation to write it had come from the mysterious recesses of Whitehall in 1960 and by the end of 1962 a draft was ready. The book appeared in the year before he moved to Manchester, and after he had published two other books. *SOE in France* announced the opening of a new historical seam whose exploitation was to be the preoccupation of more and more of his subsequent scholarly career. There followed in the next twenty years several more specialized studies as well as books addressed to the general reader. The historical profession had henceforth to take account as a major academic activity, alongside the study of intelligence activities such as were also being advanced by other scholars, of British involvement and success in stimulating resistance in occupied countries, of reprisal and prisoner-of-war history, of secret operations of all kinds. Inevitably, this had a significant international dimension, too; foreign scholars already at work on what were often highly delicate topics because of their continuing political and social resonance in many countries soon came to recognize the importance of what British scholarship could reveal. Another part of his service to international collaboration in this field must be reckoned to be Michael's successful organization of a conference in London on Dutch resistance as part of the events associated with the centenary of the Glorious Revolution. It will hardly be news to most of his colleagues to know also that he has just completed and submitted for publication the text of *SOE in the Low Countries*, a second volume in the official series.

There is enough said in other pages of this book on the historical significance of his work to leave it to others better equipped to judge it. The steady work Michael has done in his chosen area of specialization was, nevertheless, accompanied by manifold other scholarly and intellectual activity. The cultural awareness and sensitivity to experience which he showed as a young man (he had won a prize for English verse at Winchester) bore fruit, for example, in a book for the Imperial War Museum on art and war which has achieved the discreet but remarkable distinction of finding a place among the set books prescribed for a Special Subject in the Oxford Final Honour School of Modern History – a crown won by few indeed. Besides other books, too, articles and reviews have poured from his pen, and both in scholarly journals and newspapers. No volume of the DNB since 1960 is without contributions by him. Elsewhere, signed or unsigned, according to the conventions of the host journals, his obituary notices alone form a massive archive of biographical accounts of spies, resisters, politicians and secret agents. Since 1972, in addition, he has represented the Royal Historical Society (of whose Council he was for many years a member) as its appointed representative to the Advisory Board of the *Annual Register*. He served, too, on the committee of the Society of Authors between 1968 and 1970, writing a number of articles for its journal, *The Author*.

So creative but so unconventional a scholarly career resists easy summary. Its continuing threads, though, are not difficult to discern, nor are its enduring achievements. The launching of the great enterprise of *The Gladstone Diaries* would alone make the Foot *oeuvre* memorable. Few scholars, though, can be said to have achieved so much in the definition and establishment of a new branch of historiography as followed the publication of *SOE in France*. It seems above all likely, though, that Michael will be best remembered by those who know him in a very different way. His greatest impact has always registered at a personal, not easily categorizable level, especially on the young. It was well put to the present writer by one historian whose own doctoral work Michael encouraged and stimulated though he was not his supervisor: 'The scholarship was – is – always accompanied by warmth. . . . He personifies for me the idea of academic activity as part of a civilized and humane way of life, in which people cooperate as friends in doing things in which they believe, for their own sake.'

A TALE OF TWO ARMISTICES

CHRISTOPHER WOODS

Cecil Richard Dallimore Mallaby, the hero of this tale, was born in 1919 in Newara Eliya at the heart of the tea country in Ceylon, a pleasant place which still retains (or at least did when I visited it a few years ago) some of the atmosphere of a typical British colonial hill station. His father had been born in India and was himself a tea planter, but in 1926, at the age of 40, having inherited via his second (Italian) wife a property in Tuscany, he abandoned Asia for Europe and tea-planting for the attractions of living on his Tuscan estate. As a result Dick was to spend his formative years between the ages of seven and twenty mostly in Italy, receiving the greater part of his education there and becoming fluent in Italian.

The outbreak of war found him in England and in October 1939 he enlisted in the Devonshire Regiment. He was sent on a five-month signals course, a chance which was to affect his future career. Being an adventurous type (while still a student he had made a solo bicycling tour of Europe), he volunteered for parachuting but was posted instead to a Commando training school in Scotland. In February 1941 he sailed for Egypt with No 8 Commando, part of Layforce. This provided him with his first taste of action, at Tobruk, but in August Layforce was disbanded and he remained for some time at the Commando depot in Egypt. Although recommended for a commission, he preferred to remain in the ranks, now being a corporal.[1]*

Just how he first came to SOE's notice, or SOE to his, is not recorded. His SOE file mentions simply his recruitment in Cairo on 15 January 1942 as a 'Conducting NCO and Interpreter'. We may surmise that, following the break up of Layforce and becoming bored with life at the Commando Depot, he was on the lookout for a more

* See notes p16 et seq

1

active, preferably adventurous, role in the war. What is known is that SOE Cairo were at that time in urgent need of extra Italian-speaking staff to handle their first group of Italian volunteers. Who then in the Middle East theatre better qualified to meet this requirement than the bilingual radio-trained commando Corporal Mallaby?

The Italian volunteers were newly arrived from East Africa, recruited from among Italian PoWs and civilian internees in Abyssinia and Eritrea. After initial training in Egypt some of the more promising were sent early in February in the charge of Corporal Mallaby to the SOE Middle East Training Centre (STC 102) at Haifa in Palestine, for more advanced training, including WT. This sort of work was to engage Mallaby for the next few months, during which he himself absorbed SOE training in sabotage and WT at STC 102, as well as completing a parachute course.[2]

By midsummer the Italian Section of SOE Cairo had begun planning their first operation to put a radio operator into Italy. Their general idea, submitted to London for approval on 8 August, was to attach one of the Italian volunteers to a party of Slovenes which the Yugoslav Section hoped to infiltrate soon into North-West Yugoslavia. The Slovenes were to help him across the border into Italy and thereafter transmit his messages sent to them by courier. London refined this plan by getting SOE Berne not only to provide a safe address in Trieste but also to send in a radio set for his use.

The Italian chosen for this operation, to which Cairo allotted the codename PALINODE, was a single man in his early 30s, who had done 18 months' service in the Italian Air Force and then worked for 6 years as a clerk in Asmara and Addis Ababa. He was informed early in November that he had been selected for a special operation and was sent back to STC 102 for 'a progressive operational course' in WT, accompanied by Mallaby, who already knew him well and was keen to lend him a helping hand.

But the despatch of the party was held up, and by the end of December the Italian was showing signs of nerves and Cairo judged him no longer fit for such an important operation. Mallaby, who had spent the last three months with him (and reckoned he knew more about WT than the Italian), now volunteered to take his place. With no other suitable trained Italian WTO available, his offer was accepted, his blond hair and Nordic appearance notwithstanding, and on 6 February 1943 he was given a formal detailed briefing for the operation.[3]

2

Since the German occupation of Vichy France in November, the only already tried land route via Switzerland into northern Italy, SOE London attached increasing importance to establishing a new line of entry through Yugoslavia. But when Cairo's operation continued to be subject month after month to air transport delays, and with future military operations in Europe becoming imminent as the campaign in North Africa drew to an end, London began to look for other and quicker means of getting Mallaby into Italy.[4]

And so at the end of June Mallaby (a sergeant since September, though Cairo had planned to get him commissioned) found himself flying from Cairo to Algiers, where he was given temporary employment in the MASSINGHAM signal section, while alternative plans for his despatch were laboriously worked out between MASSINGHAM, London and Berne. Various options were considered and rejected, and it was not until 6 August that a final decision was reached on a blind drop with an inflatable dinghy into Lake Como (Operation NECK).

The plan was that he would paddle himself ashore and make his way (in civilian clothes) to an address in Como where he would be expected. He would then be provided with a radio set (for which he would carry with him in a concealing device the crystals, signal plan and ciphers) and a safe house for transmitting. He was given an alternative address in Milan and a further fall-back one in Genoa. The addresses were of contacts of SOE Berne who were to put him in touch with resistance groups. The radio set had already been sent in by Berne.[5]

Scheduled first for the night of August 12/13, NECK was not flown until the following night – Friday the 13th. This augury did not deter Mallaby: it was now just over a year since his first involvement with Operation PALINODE, and eight moon periods that he had been standing by in Cairo and at MASSINGHAM signal section to go in himself. But this final 24-hour postponement was to prove critical. On 12/13 August Milan was subjected to a heavy air raid, as a result of which the shores of Lake Como were brightly lit the following night for the benefit of refugees from the city. (It may also be noted that the air raid caused the man in Milan, whose address Mallaby had been given, to abandon the city in panic and to get rid of the radio set which he was supposed to deliver to Mallaby.)

Mallaby, however, was to have no immediate need of a radio, for his parachute descent was clearly witnessed from a lakeside village.

3

He was picked up before he had time to paddle ashore and handed over to the Carabinieri in Como, who after a preliminary interrogation transferred him to Milan for further investigation by the C/S (counter-espionage) branch of SIM (Military Intelligence Service). Under interrogation, and in view of the compromising signals equipment found on him, he admitted to being a radio operator (first giving his name as Captain Richard Norris, though eventually his true identity was discovered), but claimed that the object of his mission was not sabotage but propaganda, working with local groups. Later he was handed over at their request to the C/S Service in Rome.[6]

None of this, of course, was known at the time to London, Berne or MASSINGHAM. The pilot of the aircraft reported a successful drop, but no signals were heard from Mallaby in London or at MASSINGHAM. Soon, however, news began to leak out from Italy. On the 17th Berne told London that the Swiss press was quoting reports of travellers from Italy that parachutists dropped from a British aircraft in the Como area during the night of 13/14 August had been captured. SOE's man in Berne, McCaffery, concerned primarily for his contact to whom Mallaby was to have reported in Como, was keen to initiate enquiries there but was dissuaded by London and advised to discount 'scare stories'.

Saturday the 21st, however, brought confirmation of the capture of Mallaby with a Berne telegram reporting that a full account of the incident, including details of items found on him, had been carried by a Milan evening paper. This, while removing all doubt, nevertheless proved timely news, and it was relayed immediately by London, not just to MASSINGHAM, but also to Lisbon, where the head of the Italian Section in London, Roseberry, had just arrived. To understand the reason for this we need to go back a few days.

On the evening of 12 August – just 24 hours before Mallaby took off on Operation NECK – General Castellano from the Italian Supreme Command, accompanied by Franco Montanari of the Italian Foreign Office, left Rome by rail for Lisbon with a secret mission to negotiate with the Allies for a possible *renversement d'alliances* on the part of Italy. During a stopover in Madrid on Sunday the 15th they contacted the British Ambassador Sir Samuel Hoare. As a result the news was relayed to Quebec where the Allied leaders were gathering for the QUADRANT conference.

So it was that on the morning of 18 August General Eisenhower in Algiers received a signal of instructions from the Combined Chiefs of Staff to send two officers to Lisbon to issue terms of unconditional surrender to the Italians, and also to arrange a clandestine channel for eventual communications with the Italian General Staff in Rome. To meet this special requirement Eisenhower consulted the senior SOE officer at MASSINGHAM who telegraphed at once to London. On receipt of this message Roseberry discussed the requirement with the signals section, who provided him with signal plan MONKEY and a code, and arranged to fly to Lisbon, where the SOE station was instructed to give him an SOE radio set. Before leaving he informed MASSINGHAM that, provided he arrived in time to brief the Italians, and if meanwhile definite news had been received of the capture of Mallaby, he proposed to tell them that a WTO had been dropped into Italy precisely for such an eventuality as this and that they should immediately secure his release and make use of him. He failed to catch the aircraft that night and the following night's flight was cancelled. But he flew on the 20th, reaching Lisbon late that night.

By the time he arrived there had been an all-night session with the Italians, ending at 7 o'clock that morning, during which they had agreed in principle to take back with them a means of clandestine communications between Rome and Algiers. The two Allied Generals had already flown back to Algiers, but the Italians were still there. Roseberry arranged a meeting with Montanari that evening. Before they met, the telegram from London reached him confirming Mallaby's arrest, thus allowing him to offer the Italians not only a means of communication but also the man to operate it, and in so doing to uphold the legendary reputation for foresight of 'British Intelligence'.

The Italians left Lisbon by train on the 23rd. It had been agreed that, as soon as they crossed into Italy on the evening of the 26th, Castellano would telephone instructions to Rome that no action be taken in the Mallaby case before he arrived next day, when he would apply to take immediate custody of him. To establish his bona fides with Mallaby Roseberry had furnished Castellano with messages which Mallaby should recognize as coming only from SOE. Castellano was as good as his word and the first message received on the MONKEY channel on the morning of 30 August told MASSINGHAM that Mallaby had been freed. Installed in a small room on the top floor of the HQ building of the Supreme Command in Rome with a senior Italian WTO, he continued to work on the MONKEY traffic, particularly coding and decoding, and by the time the Armistice was announced on the evening of 8 September some seventy messages had been exchanged.

When the King and Badoglio left Rome on the morning of the 9th Mallaby was included in their party and, a day or so after their arrival in Brindisi on the 10th reported by MONKEY, an SOE signal party sent from MASSINGHAM found him still working the MONKEY link, which he continued to do until it was closed down a week later. This exploit earned Mallaby, whose commission had come through just after he left on Operation NECK, the award of an immediate Military Cross.[7]

This first part of our tale, however, does not end there, for there is a postscript to add another dimension to the story. In November, after two months' operational collaboration with SOE in Brindisi, SIM officers disclosed that most of the Italian contacts of SOE Berne had been working all along under Italian control. These included both the contact through whom the original preparations for the reception of PALINODE had been laid on in Trieste and the two contacts in Como and Milan involved in the plans for the reception of NECK. Thus, even if Mallaby had not been seen dropping into Lake Como, he could have walked into the arms, as it were, of SIM very soon after he clambered ashore – yet not necessarily, for the evidence does not point to SIM being poised to catch him (they were unaware in advance of just who he was). By mid-August they, like most other Italian organizations, were operating, when operating at all, in a state of profound uncertainty. SOE at least was able to act decisively and by flexibility exploit a failure to their advantage.[8].

For the second part of our tale we must move on to the end of 1944. Throughout the intervening period Mallaby (now Lieutenant C.R.D. Mallaby MC) has been in Monopoli at the HQ of No 1 Special Force (1SF), the SOE unit running operations in Italy in support of the military campaign. We may suppose him growing impatient for another more direct share in the action. A first chance came in September, when he was selected as radio officer of a large British Mission to be dropped to work with the CLNAI (Committee of National Liberation Upper Italy) in Milan in anticipation of an imminent German withdrawal. But despatch was delayed, by weather and by competing military priorities for the use of the available aircraft, until eventually, when the prospect of German withdrawal had receded, the party was stood down.[9]

But soon came another opportunity. In November a delegation arrived from the CLNAI for discussions with SOE, the Allied

Military Command and the Italian Government. One of the delegates was Edgardo Sogno, the charismatic leader of 1SF's most active *réseau* in Northern Italy, the Franchi Organization. They had already met on two previous occasions and taken to one another: the first time a year earlier, when Mallaby had taught Sogno coding for a mission in N Italy; the second in midsummer, when Sogno came out on a visit to 1SF HQ and Mallaby was there to help debrief him and prepare him for return to the field.[10]

With Sogno once more in Monopoli, and with 1SF's radio communications with the north in need of repair following a series of recent arrests, plans were laid for Mallaby to follow Sogno back into the field to set up a new radio channel for him and the CLNAI, and to take charge of improving communications generally in the north. On 15 December, accompanied by an Italian WTO with previous experience in the field (Anselmo), Mallaby left by air for Lyons with Sogno and two other returning CLNAI delegates (Pizzoni and Parri). A few days later they all crossed clandestinely into Switzerland. There they separated and Mallaby and Anselmo went to Berne to wait until called forward into Italy by Sogno, who with Parri crossed the border on Christmas Day.[11]

Almost at once plans were set back by the arrest on 2 January in Milan of both Parri and an important member of a 1SF Italian mission who had been working closely with Sogno. News of these further arrests magnified 1SF's already considerable worries concerning the security of both Sogno and the CLNAI. In consequence plans for sending Mallaby in were suspended. But Sogno was not to be deterred from despatching one of his associates to Berne to fetch him and/or Anselmo. The reaction of McCaffery, in charge of SOE Berne, was to detain him in Switzerland, along with other associates of Sogno's already there, until the security situation in Milan should show signs of improvement. Instead the situation deteriorated still further with the capture of Sogno himself on the night of 27/28 January 1945 in an audacious attempt to free Parri.

1SF's critical need to improve radio communications with the north, however, remained, becoming more urgent indeed as the time approached for the awaited Spring military offensive. Mallaby, in Berne, was no doubt also growing impatient to go into action. If Milan was now considered too hot for him, there should be less risk in sending him to a resistance group in the mountains ('Fiamme Verdi') who could send him on later to Milan when the time came.

7

So towards the middle of February an effective plan for putting him into Italy finally matured.[12]

He was to travel in civilian clothes with Italian identity papers. Anselmo would go with him. All their communications equipment was sent in separately to the 'Fiamme Verdi' by courier, so they wouldn't have to carry any compromising material with them. They were to be conducted to their destination by two Italian priests, one of whom ('Don Giovannino') had been chaplain to the 'Fiamme Verdi' and had recently come in to Switzerland to report to SOE. The other ('Don Mario') had long experience of frontier-crossing operations.[13]

Mallaby left most of the practical arrangements for the infiltration operation, including choice of route, to Don Giovannino and contented himself with searching Anselmo before departure (but not the other two). Their documents, prepared partly in Southern Italy and partly in Berne, were sent to Lugano for final completion, when the whole party assembled there on the day of departure, by the acting military liaison contact between the CLNAI and Allied services in Italy, an Italian lawyer. It was perhaps unfortunate that the resident SOE representative in Lugano was absent on a visit to 1SF HQ, while the regular CLNAI liaison contact had recently been detained for a technical infringement of Swiss regulations. Their presence might have ensured more experienced and careful supervision.[14]

The party of four set off from Lugano on the evening of 14 February by car, picking up two smugglers on the way who were to guide them over the border into Italy. This involved five hours' walking in sometimes deep snow, but the actual border crossing caused no problem, and around 3am they eventually reached a house belonging to one of the smugglers, where they rested and decided on the next stage of their journey. (For Mallaby, who had travelled overnight from Berne to Lugano by slow train to avoid security controls usual on the faster trains, this was a second night without sleep.)

The choice lay between Don Giovannino going on ahead to Como, where he might hope to obtain a car from the Bishop in which to drive them to Milan, or all walking the remaining 12 kms to Lake Como and finding some form of onward transport there. They opted for the latter and walked to Menaggio, where, finding no transport to Como, they hired a boat to cross the lake to Varenna, where they finally secured a lift on a lorry to Lecco.

Arriving in Lecco around midday and by then hungry, they went to eat in a cafe before starting on the next stage of their journey. Although having agreed that they had only met on the way, they sat together at a table where the Italian members of the party talked, despite Mallaby's efforts at restraint, increasingly freely and loudly, overheard by a young man who came and sat for a while at the next table and then left. Whether it was due to indiscreet talk then or on the lorry, the young man's departure was shortly followed by the entrance of two uniformed police NCOs. As Mallaby's party rose to leave they were asked for their documents and then searched. Neither Mallaby nor Anselmo aroused any particular immediate suspicion, but both the Italian priests (of whom only Don Giovannino was in clerical dress) were found in possession of Swiss money or goods, while suspicious papers also emerged from Don Giovannino's pockets. This was enough to cause the NCOs to take them all off to the local HQ of the Fascist Black Brigade. There comparison of their identity documents revealed three of them living in the same street in Milan, though they had claimed not to know one another. So they were segregated for separate interrogation in turn, Mallaby last.

While waiting his turn, Mallaby reflected on his situation (caught within hours of arrival for the second time – and in the same area). Realizing that his cover was thin and the risk of exposure critical, he decided to try to bluff his way out, drawing on his experience from the previous occasion he had fallen into enemy Italian hands. When his turn for interrogation came, therefore, he declared himself boldly as a British officer, Captain Richard Tucker, on an urgent and secret mission to Marshal Graziani about which he could only speak to a senior officer. To cover his companions he claimed that the two priests were acting simply as his guides and Anselmo as his body-guard. The attitude of the company commander changed at once, and he put through a call to his superior in Como and had Mallaby taken there that evening.

At Como he was received by the Black Brigade commander. To him he recounted that Don Giovannino should have taken him to the Archbishop of Milan, Cardinal Schuster, through whom he was to seek a meeting with Marshal Graziani. The CO, without subjecting Mallaby to any formal questioning, reported at once by telephone to the Chief of Staff of the Black Brigades in Milan, General Facduelle, and advised that Graziani should be alerted immediately. Then, having assured Mallaby that arrangements had been made for him to see Graziani, he introduced Mallaby to the officers' mess, where he dined with the other officers and was treated as a prisoner of war rather than a suspect under arrest and spent the night there.

The next afternoon the Brigade Commander drove him to Milan and delivered him to General Facduelle who, according to Mallaby, received him most cordially and told him that everyone was very happy with his mission which they felt would be crowned with success. As Graziani could not come to Milan, the General took Mallaby to his own villa on Lake Garda, where, after an amicable evening spent in the company of the General's family, he slept that night.

The following morning (17 February) Mallaby was escorted to Graziani's HQ on Lake Garda, where after a while he was told that the Marshal considered it unwise to receive him there 'as the place was full of Italians and Germans, especially the German SS' and he wished him to be seen first by Colonel De Leo ('head of his intelligence service and his right-hand man') at the Colonel's HQ (at Volta Mantovana), whither Mallaby was then conducted.

Captured Italian documents confirm that De Leo, a regular military intelligence officer and head of the Republican counter-espionage service (SID), was summoned by a call from Graziani at midday, while on duty in Milan, to return at once for 'an important mission'. Told on arrival at Graziani's HQ about the captured British officer claiming to have come on a mission from the Allied Command, he was instructed to return to his HQ to interrogate him. He saw Mallaby that evening and again the following morning and obtained a signed statement from 'Captain Richard Tucker', which he sent to Graziani on the 19th for his attention and 'such action as required'.

Faced with interrogation by De Leo, Mallaby now reached what, in at least the figurative sense, was the moment of truth, when he had to give a more detailed account of his mission. The story he told was that, as a junior officer at General Alexander's HQ who knew Italy well and spoke fluent Italian, he had been selected for a special mission, for which he was briefed personally by Alexander towards the end of December, to reach north Italy clandestinely via Switzerland and there through Cardinal Schuster make contact with Graziani, to whom he was to present certain propositions:

1) In the event of German withdrawal from north Italy the Italian troops under Graziani's command should do everything possible to preserve Italian industrial installations and public services from destruction by the Germans;

10

2) In such circumstances they should also do what they could to maintain law and order in the face of any attempt at disturbance from whatever quarter;

3) Partisan formations, who would carry out similar tasks in the areas controlled by them, would be directed by Allied missions sent in at the appropriate time;

4) These measures were aimed at avoiding unnecessary bloodshed alike between Allied and Italian Republican forces and between the latter and partisan formations;

5) In the event of Italian Republican forces being unable to keep order in difficult local situations, Alexander would send in adequate airborne police forces.

Of these five propositions (as presented by De Leo in his report to Graziani) 1, 2 and 4 were based on Mallaby's spontaneous account, while the other two were drawn out of him by De Leo's questioning about the partisans, and were designed by Mallaby to allay De Leo's expressed fear that they would 'come down fighting from the hills and cause chaos'.

Mallaby further stated that, having presented Alexander's propositions, which he was not empowered to discuss, he was to say that, if Graziani wished to enter into discussions at Allied HQ, Alexander was ready to send an aircraft to fetch him or his representatives or else arrange reception of a Republican aircraft. If his mission succeeded, Mallaby could collect a radio set from Switzerland and with his radio operator provide a channel of communications with Alexander's HQ.

Concluding the interrogation, De Leo assured Mallaby that he would present his statement to Graziani, but he made the point to Mallaby that there had been an unfortunate lack of security in the way in which his mission had been carried out. Whatever Graziani's reactions to Mallaby's statement when submitted to him by De Leo on the 19th – which may have included consultation with Mussolini, since the captured documents show that the Como Black Brigade commander requested General Facduelle on the 16th to inform Mussolini, and subsequently addressed to the Duce 'by request' a statement on the case – Mallaby was left in suspense for the next six days.

Then on the 26th around midday, without warning and to his sudden consternation, he found himself taken off by a German SS

11

Captain to the main SS HQ in Verona. By the time he got there his apprehensions were already somewhat allayed by the German officer's pleasant and courteous demeanour, which persisted throughout the subsequent careful interrogation to which he then subjected Mallaby, showing particular interest in his personal background, the nature of his mission and how he had come to be given it. In his statement to De Leo, a copy of which the German Captain appeared to have in his hand, Mallaby had given a sanitized version of his background and war service, without revealing either his true identity or any previous involvement in clandestine operations (no hint of MONKEY). To the German Captain he stressed that as a young and junior officer in a large HQ he had been selected, on particular account of his linguistic qualifications, simply to open a link and to make certain general suggestions which could be discussed further, if received favourably, through other channels to be decided later. At the conclusion of the interrogation Mallaby was told that he would be taken before a German General (unnamed).

That same evening Mallaby was driven to Fasano on Lake Garda to the private villa of SS General Karl Wolff. Wolff (who had recently, on return from a trip to Germany, called a meeting of military and SS officers, at which he had asked to be kept personally informed of any possible contact with the British or Americans) devoted two hours to interviewing Mallaby through an interpreter and in the presence of the same German Captain who had interrogated him earlier. Wolff presented himself as head of all German police units in Italy and commander of all German troops in the rear areas. Beginning coldly but politely, he said he wished to see Mallaby to form his own impression of his bona fides, especially as he had no credentials. There could be no discussion without first establishing his identity and the authenticity of his mission. After Mallaby, putting on his best show of sincerity, had suggested that to have brought any proof of identity with him could have prejudiced the security of his mission, and that to obtain it now he would have to be allowed to return to Switzerland for the purpose, Wolff agreed to accept the word of honour of a British officer.[15]

Mallaby now repeated his version of Alexander's 'proposals'. These Wolff countered by stating (a) that his friend Marshal Graziani had already agreed that his Italian troops would withdraw shoulder to shoulder with their German comrades, so the question of their helping to keep order in vacated areas would not arise; and (b) that

12

he had already undertaken to Cardinal Schuster that the Germans would carry out demolitions only to the extent of immobilizing industrial plants for up to one year, this so as not to leave unemployed workers too long a prey to communism.

Then, to Mallaby's surprise, Wolff launched into a long lecture on the SS – how it had been formed, its history and development, and its role in the war. Asserting its innocence of the atrocities attributed to it by Allied propaganda, Wolff maintained that the finest chivalrous ideals of medieval knighthood found their modern expression in the German SS. They were a body of picked men whose business it was to uphold truth and honour. This all led up to the proposition that the SS, to which he belonged, was the only body in Germany capable of guaranteeing that any agreement with the Allies would be adhered to and carried out. He continued with a detailed explanation of the importance of his own position, outlining the responsibilities of his various titles and appointments, and adding that, while Kesselring was in charge of military operations at the front, he had control of all the rear areas and had the final say in any decisions taken in regard to Italian affairs.

On this note Wolff, acknowledging that Germany was now clearly losing the war but foreshadowing the likelihood of a defeated Germany succumbing to communist influence whatever demarcation line might be set for the westward advance of Russian troops, offered himself as a link, should Alexander or any other Allied leader see fit to make use of him, to Kesselring, of whom he was a personal friend, or to any other German military leader including Hitler. Mallaby now renewed the offer, as previously held out to the Italians, to arrange for Wolff to travel to southern Italy by Allied or German aircraft. Wolff, however, said he preferred to take the chance of letting Mallaby go back to Switzerland with a promise to return as soon as possible with whatever reply Alexander should choose to give. And, pointing to the danger from communism in north Italy, he asked Mallaby to put the following specific proposal to Alexander: if Alexander would undertake to stop supplying arms to communist bands in north Italy, he (Wolff) would guarantee safe passage to south Italy for all other partisan formations.

At the end of the interview, by which time Wolff's manner had become friendly and cordial, Mallaby was made to give his word of honour to return from Switzerland as soon as possible with an answer. He was then escorted back to Verona, where he remained all

13

the following day (27th), while the German SS Captain made arrangements for his journey to Switzerland. On the 28th there was further delay, with five hours spent in an air raid shelter, before Mallaby finally left Verona to be driven by an Italian-speaking German in civilian clothes to the German SS frontier post at Cernobbio on Lake Como, where the final details of the border crossing were arranged. There it was agreed that a few days before his return he should have broadcast by the BBC a message with the prefix 'Per Giovanni', followed by the day and hour when he would make the return crossing by the same route.

Mallaby entered Switzerland early in the morning of 1 March and reported to the Swiss frontier post at Chiasso. Here things began to go wrong. Claiming to be a licensed contact of Swiss Military Intelligence, he presented himself under an Italian name which he believed to have been registered in his absence by one of Sogno's men (himself accredited by Swiss Military Intelligence) whom he had seen shortly before leaving Switzerland. But the name was not on record nor was he recognized by a Swiss MI NCO summoned to the frontier post. Faced with the alternatives of return to Italy or internment, he chose the latter in expectation that his representations to the Swiss would soon lead to his recognition and release. But by the end of a week his confidence and patience had worn thin, so, meeting a young Italian Red Cross worker, whose father he knew to be in touch with McCaffery, he persuaded him to smuggle out a letter which McCaffery received on the 8th.

Now McCaffery had been aware of the capture of Mallaby and his party since 23 February, when a bare report to this effect had come in from the 'Fiamme Verdi', to whom Don Mario had got word, having escaped under cover of an air raid from his cell in Lecco on the first evening. A later report from the same source revealed their capture at Lecco by the Black Brigade, and that Don Giovannino was held there on a currency smuggling charge, but nothing more on the fate of Mallaby. From the letter which now reached him McCaffery gathered that he was in a Swiss internment camp under a new name, having been sent out with a message from General Wolff, a reply to which he must take back to Italy as soon as possible, and on which apparently depended the lives of his two companions detained in Italy. Apart from seeking urgent release, Mallaby asked McCaffery to have a BBC message broadcast in Italian 'For Giovanni: Detained, continue to listen'. SOE got it included in

14

an Italian Service transmission that same evening.

What neither McCaffery nor Mallaby, however, knew was that Wolff was no longer at Fasano to receive the message, but, since early that morning, there in Switzerland, and moreover that evening in conversation in Zurich with the OSS chief Allen Dulles. How he came to be there has been told by Dulles in *The Secret Surrender*, his account of Operation SUNRISE which led to the surrender of the German armies in Italy on 2 May. The timing is interesting.[16]

Operation SUNRISE began for OSS effectively on 25 February when Dulles, called back urgently from a visit to the American 6th Army in Alsace, sent his assistant to interview Baron Luigi Parrilli, an Italian who had come to Switzerland on a personal mission to get in touch with an Allied clandestine service. He wished to tell them about his relations with German SS officers in Italy sympathetic with his desire to spare northern Italy, in the closing phase of the war, from German vengeance in the form of a threatened scorched earth policy to be activated by the SS on orders from Berlin. Their shared views, so Parrilli claimed, had been represented by a senior German SS officer, Colonel Dollmann, directly to General Wolff himself.

On return to Milan Parrilli reported on 28 February or 1 March (the dates differ in Dulles's and Parrilli's accounts) personally to Dollmann on the line he had established in Switzerland to an OSS officer on Dulles's staff, who had shown interest in the possibility of a meeting in Switzerland with Dollmann or even Wolff himself. Dollmann reported straight to Wolff, who instructed him to accompany Parrilli on his next trip to Switzerland and follow up this line to OSS. Dollmann had a meeting with OSS on 3 March, from which he brought back an invitation to Wolff to pursue the talks in person, and to provide evidence of his good intentions by arranging the release of two important Italian prisoners of the Germans (Parri & Usmiani). Wolff entered Switzerland with Dollmann early in the morning of 8 March, shortly preceded by the two released Italians.[17]

Now it is to be noted that, while Parrilli's initial contact with OSS took place the day before Mallaby was taken into German custody, news of it did not reach Wolff until two or three days after he had interviewed him, when indeed Mallaby was already on his way back to Switzerland bearing Wolff's message to Alexander. Had Mallaby succeeded in delivering this message to McCaffery in Berne on 1 March, two days before Dollmann saw OSS, it is possible that Operation SUNRISE might have taken a somewhat different course –

15

but without necessarily significantly altering the eventual outcome.

As it was, Mallaby did not reach Berne until after the critical first meeting between Dulles and Wolff on the evening of 8 March. News of this meeting was revealed to McCaffery next day by Dulles, who was then aware also of the release of a British officer with a message from Wolff. It was subsequently agreed on the highest level that OSS should have the sole responsibility for the future handling of the case, and McCaffery received instructions from CD (General Gubbins) to intervene only at the request of Dulles. Although Mallaby volunteered while in Berne to fulfil a role similar to the one he had played earlier in MONKEY, it was agreed by all not to send him back to Italy, and in due course 'Captain Tucker' was released from his parole; his other two Italian colleagues were returned to Switzerland by the Germans, who had taken them over from the Italians when Mallaby left.

Thus did history not quite repeat itself and Mallaby was deprived ultimately of what would have been a remarkable personal double of playing similar roles in the surrender of both the Italian and the German forces in Italy. He ended the war with the rank of Captain, but without a bar to his MC.

Dick Mallaby died in 1981. He had worked for many years in Verona as an interpreter and translator for NATO.[18]

NOTES

1. Mallaby's file in SOE Archive plus information from friends and colleagues.
2. Mallaby's SOE file – and HS 6/889 for Italian volunteers with SOE Cairo in 1942.
3. Operation PALINODE in HS 6/869–871. Copy of the brief dated 6 Feb 43 for PALINODE (sic) in the papers of Lieutenant-Colonel Count J A Dobrski [known in SOE as Dolbey: head of the Italian Section in Cairo from March 1942] in the Liddell Hart Centre for Military Archives in King's College London. The plan for PALINODE at this stage envisaged Mallaby being sent to Trieste from Split by ship as a crew member.
4. See also HS 3/127 for a possible submarine operation.
5. Operation NECK in HS 6/869 and 871. A small illustration of the diffi-

culty of planning an operation solely by signal in hand cipher with three parties involved – there being no direct telegraphic link between MASS-INGHAM and Berne, all traffic had to be reenciphered in London – is the fact that MASSINGHAM only received corrected details of the addresses to be given to Mallaby on the day originally scheduled for his departure.

6. Notes dated 1 Aug 44 (on Mallaby's SOE file) made from captured Italian Police papers on the arrest and interrogation of Mallaby.

7. Details of MONKEY on HS 6/779. See also HS 6/775 for Roseberry's account of 'The Olaf Story' (Olaf was the name for Mallaby used in SOE signals traffic). Among the many published accounts in English and Italian of the events leading up to the Italian armistice see in particular those by participants who mention him by name: *Intelligence at the Top* by Major-General Sir Kenneth Strong (Cassells 1968), *Come firmai l'armistizio di Cassibile* by Giuseppe Castellano (Mondadori 1945), and more recently *Per la Liberta* by Luigi Marchesi (Mursia 1995) pp 10–11.

8. Papers on a personal file in SOE Archive.

9. See Operation Instruction to Major M W Salvadori dated 20 September 1944 in WO 204/7293.

10. *Guerra senza bandiera* by Edgardo Sogno (2nd Edition Mursia 1970)

11. Planning of Operation EDENTON BLUE briefly indicated in telegrams on HS 6/785; despatch from Italy recorded on personal file for @Anselmo in SOE archive.

12. McCaffery had long been in regular communication by courier with the 'Fiamme Verdi'.

13. 'Don Giovannino' = Giovanni Barbareschi, mentioned by Dulles in *The Secret Surrender*, p. 188, and described by an Italian member of the Franchi organization who knew him in Switzerland as 'a very young and enthusiastic priest of first-class intellect but somewhat imprudent' (on HS 6/802). 'Don Mario' = Don Mario Zanin whose earlier activities helping escaped Allied PoWs reach Switzerland are mentioned in *A Strange Alliance* by Roger Absalom (Leo Olschki, Florence 1991) p106.

14. Details of the operation (EDENTON BLUE) in this and succeeding paragraphs, including those based on captured Italian documents, to be found mainly in HS 6/873–4, but some in personal files SOE Archive.

15. For Wolff's request to be kept informed of possible contacts with the Western Allies see *The Secret Surrender*, p. 81.

16. *The Secret Surrender* by Allen Dulles (Weidenfeld & Nicolson 1967).

17. Parrilli's account in *La Resa degli Ottocentomila* by Ferruccio Lanfranchi (Rizzoli Ed 1948).

18. See 'Captain Dick Mallaby: A Tribute' by R T Hewitt in Vol II of the proceedings of a conference in Bologna in 1987 on 'No 1 Special Force and Italian Resistance' (published by the University of Bologna 1990).

AN OXFORD DON AT WAR:
A.J.P. TAYLOR 1939–1945

KATHLEEN BURK

A.J.P. Taylor had a useful but unheroic war. Unlike many of his contemporaries he did not decode Enigma intercepts or parachute into Yugoslavia or run a Whitehall ministry. Instead, he wrote and he talked. For almost the whole of the war he remained in Oxford, where he had been a Fellow and Tutor in Modern History at Magdalen College since October 1938. With the coming of the war European history suddenly assumed some relevance. It was vital that the subject be taught to undergraduates, and later to officer cadets, and, as virtually the only European history specialist left in Oxford, Taylor was apparently deemed irreplaceable. In any case the university authorities certified his work as of national importance and he received exemption from military service. Therefore his main work was to teach anywhere from twelve to twenty hours a week. Nevertheless, he made a number of attempts to go beyond this, and over the six years of war he lectured on behalf of the Ministry of Information until he was sacked, he attempted to write guidebooks for the future British Occupation Forces for the Political Warfare Executive until he was sacked, and he broadcast to the forces and to foreigners, as well as to the home audience, over the BBC, from which he was not sacked, but which eventually reined him in.

When the war began Taylor was thirty-three years old. He had been an academic since 1930, when he had been appointed to a lectureship in history at Manchester University. During his eight years in Manchester he had married and had a son, had developed a lecturing style which kept the interest of his audiences, had published three books (one of them a translation from the German),[1] had become a regular book reviewer for the *Manchester Guardian*, and had become a seasoned speaker at political meetings of various sorts.

19

Upon moving to Oxford, he lost his political links, and had to create once more a reputation for public speaking, as he had already done in Manchester. Only with the coming of war did he find his talents of interest to others.

At the outset of the war Taylor, who believed (probably rightly) that he was not cut out to be a soldier, nevertheless joined the Local Defence Volunteers, thereby becoming a founder member of the Home Guard. From his description of his time as a member, it is not difficult to see how the television series 'Dad's Army' emerged: 'We had rifles, but of course no ammunition. Whenever there was an air-raid alert, we turned out to guard the gas works, on the assumption that the entire German paratroop force would descend on Oxford. Failing any Germans, our only function was to demand identity cards from passers-by, and many a time we turned back innocent citizens going home across the fields in the gathering dusk. One night I failed to hear the alert and so missed what would otherwise have been the most dramatic event in my military career. By this time our company had acquired one clip of ammunition which was passed with awe from hand to hand and usually entrusted to a veteran of the first war. When the company stood down in the early morning, Frank Pakenham, its commandant [later Lord Longford], asked whether the rifles had been unloaded. The veteran pointed his rifle at the ground and demonstratively pulled the trigger. The effect was literally shattering. It nearly blew Frank's foot off and peppered John Austin [the philosopher] in the backside.'[2] There was less amusement as the Battle of Britain reached its climax in late August and the outcome hung in the balance: 'Just after eight o'clock on the evening of 7 September, the Home Guard stood to arms, having received the signal that invasion was imminent.'[3] After a short period, however, now certain that the Germans would not invade, Taylor quit the Home Guard, retaining his army boots for use in gardening.[4]

Taylor's more appropriate war work began through the medium of Oxford University's Delegacy for External Studies. Taylor had never been involved in adult education at Manchester, regarding it, as he wrote in his autobiography, 'as a capitalist device for misleading the workers'. But in the autumn of 1939 the tutor of a class at Princes Risborough went off to war, leaving the class in the lurch, and Taylor took it on. This was the beginning of a much larger task, not teaching civilians but teaching soldiers. The Delegacy was in charge of education for the forces, a grandiose scheme, as Taylor

20

wrote, 'deriving from Cromwell's remark that men fight best when they know what they are fighting for.' For the duration of the war he went out three or four times a week, speaking to audiences ranging from 'three men manning a huge naval gun in the Nore estuary to five hundred at an air camp'.[5] He was also enlisted to lecture to the civil officers who were being trained to administer the future conquered territories, Germany and Italy [AMGOT]; his job was to travel to Wimbledon where they were housed and give them lectures on contemporary German and Italian history, with emphasis on the two types of fascism. He later recalled that 'there was a dramatic moment when J.R.M. Butler, the commandant, broke into my lecture and announced, "Mussolini has fallen. You won't be here much longer." Everyone cheered.' Taylor, for reasons which he failed to explain, thought them 'a rum lot'.[6]

His energy must have been phenomenal, because, besides his Oxford teaching and his talks to the forces, he also became a cog in the Ministry of Information machine. As he described its inception, 'among my many romantic notions was the idea that in this great national crisis we should be sending missionaries round the country as the Bolsheviks had done during the Russian revolution, and I aspired to be one. I offered my services to the Ministry of Information, another misguided creation of wartime.'[7] It must be said that it is unclear just what Taylor did and when he did it. His autobiography is a bit opaque on the subject, while he was too unimportant in the scheme of things to figure greatly in the surviving papers of the Ministry. Fortunately, however, he got into trouble often enough and in a sufficiently public manner to have left an intermittent trail of evidence.

The Ministry of Information divided the country into regions, each under a Regional Information Officer, who was responsible for implementing the directives of the Ministry, and for organizing most of the talks and events in his region. Oxfordshire fell into the Southern Region, along with Berkshire, Buckinghamshire, Hampshire, Dorset, the Isle of Wight and the Channel Islands. The Southern Regional Office was at Reading and the man in charge was Sir Arthur Willert, a somewhat elderly ex-journalist who had spent the First World War in Washington, D.C. and was a friend of Franklin Roosevelt. Before the war ninety per cent of the Southern Region had been agricultural, with only five towns in the entire region – Reading, Oxford, Portsmouth, Southampton and Bournemouth –

having populations greater than 100,000. It was a region of small market towns and a largely rural population, but one which saw the transformation of its character with the establishment of war factories, military camps and aerodromes, and the necessary influx of new population to operate them (not to mention American servicemen in due course).[8]

One of the earliest activities of the regional offices was to establish, or to call for the establishment of, Local Information Committees, 'voluntary and advisory bodies' which were intended to have on them 'representatives of every shade of opinion'[9] and particularly of the three political parties. The members of these Committees were intended to provide leadership in keeping up morale, partly by transmitting propaganda but also by providing information on the war and its associated affairs as far as the service departments, the politicians and the Ministry itself thought it wise to provide it. The Oxford Borough Information Committee was inaugurated on 2 October 1939, although it is unknown whether Taylor was a founding member; he was certainly a member of the Committee a year later. What he was in any case was a speaker for the Committee from the early days of the Ministry.

The Ministry had three categories of speaker: Category A, which included Party leaders and others with a national reputation; Category B, which included peers, MPs, candidates 'and others of national repute, although not so outstanding as those in category A';[10] and Category C, speakers for smaller meeting who were to be chosen locally. Category A (or Class A, as it was sometimes termed) speakers were to be utilized at great national and regional rallies, and their appearances would be organized from the Ministry's Headquarters at Senate House, the once and future administrative centre of the University of London. Category B speakers were to speak at town meetings and local demonstrations, while Category C speakers would be sent to open-air and factory-gate meetings and smaller indoor meetings and lectures. Taylor appears on no Class A or B list and, judging from his own description of what he did, he was clearly a Class C speaker.[11]

Taylor explained that while the nominal head of the Reading Regional Office was Willert, 'an easy-going elderly man, rather resentful at being consigned to Reading', the working head was 'a former Congregational minister who had become a travel agent. Willert's explanation for employing him was that as a travel agent he must know about Europe. In fact the former clergyman had never been abroad in his life and merely wanted some job when his travel agency collapsed with the war. At least he knew how to arrange my travel schedules. There he was, eager to raise morale and with no one qualified to do it. I was manna from Heaven to him. I was given a free hand. I went to the principal towns in the southern region, contacted the local information committees, which were run by the agents of the three political parties, and offered my services. The party agents, though not very keen, usually acquiesced. I went to the main shops and offices, secured a ten minutes' break and addressed the staff on the war and what it meant. . . . I never received any instruction as to what to say. . . . The important thing was to turn in as many reports as possible. I always exaggerated the numbers of those attending and sometimes invented a meeting where I had drawn a blank. In the section marked "public opinion" I put in whatever appealed to me at the moment: "Resolute determination to go on until victory" or later: "Strongly-voiced demand in Aylesbury for the immediate opening of a Second Front".'[12]

At some point Willert suggested that, instead of preaching, Taylor should explain. He found this very much more congenial and spent the remainder of his time with the Ministry giving war commentaries. Although it is not possible to know for certain, since very few of the Southern Region papers appear to have been kept, it seems possible that Taylor actually became one of the Ministry's staff speakers. Staff speakers received a salary of about five guineas per week plus minimal expenses, while voluntary speakers usually received no fee. Taylor also received fees for his forces education work, although how much is not known. What he does say is that C.S. Lewis, his colleague at Magdalen where Lewis was Fellow and Tutor in English, was also engaged in a different form of forces' tuition, religious education, and, agreeing that they should not profit from their work, they gave their fees to Magdalen for a charitable fund which by the end of the war amounted to nearly £10,000. If Taylor earned half of that huge sum then it is likely that it came from more than one source. Secondly, a Ministry of Information Minute of April 1943 refers to 'the trio of speakers, Taylor, Wehl and O'Neill, who between them have been responsible for a large proportion of the meetings, many of which tend to be arranged at regular monthly intervals at the same place and time.'[13] Finally, according to the final report on the activities of the Southern Region during the war, 'The War Commentaries of one of the Ministry's staff speakers proved very popular in Oxford, and there was much regret when his name had to be removed from the panel on account of an indiscreet statement which he was alleged to have made during a talk.'[14] This was exactly what happened to Taylor.

This indiscretion was not his first. In October 1940, as he described it in his autobiography, 'At Oxford I remarked one day, that, with the Mediterranean closed, the loss of Egypt and the Suez canal would be of little importance. There was a tremendous outcry that the Ministry of Information was defeatist or preparing the country for a compromise peace.'[15] Quintin Hogg, the MP for the City of Oxford, was outraged and asked a question in the House of Commons:

'Mr Hogg asked the Minister of Information whether his attention had been drawn to a public speech in Oxford by Mr A.J.P. Taylor, a member of the local Information Committee appointed by the Ministry of Information, to the effect that a withdrawal from Egypt would not be a disaster; and whether he is prepared to take steps to prevent members of committees from committing themselves to irresponsible public statements of this nature without consultation with the Ministry?

'The Parliamentary Secretary to the Minister of Information (Mr Harold Nicolson): Yes, Sir, the gentleman to whom the hon. Member refers is a member of the local Information Committee of the Ministry of Information, but, as he was careful to make clear at the time, he was speaking entirely in his personal capacity and not as a member of the local Information Committee. Mr Taylor is neither a civil servant nor in receipt of remuneration from the Government, and he therefore enjoys the same right as any other British subject to express his private opinion on public affairs. [If Taylor did become a staff speaker, and therefore in receipt of remuneration from the Government, it was clearly after this date.]

'Mr Hogg: Is not the Minister aware of the very grave public disquiet which was caused in Oxford by the irresponsible and ridiculous statement made by a person in a public position? Is he not aware that it led to a very grave misapprehension as to the intentions of the Government?

'Mr Nicolson: I am aware that Mr Taylor's statements led to a considerable controversy at the time, but Mr Taylor speaking as an independent person.

'Hon. Members: No.

24

'Mr Hogg: Does not the Minister recognize some responsibility for the people whom he appoints to these committees?

'Mr Nicolson: I think my hon. Friend is under some misapprehension as to the functions of these Information Committees. They are not administrative sections of the Ministry of Information. They are voluntary and advisory bodies, and we have taken very great care that they should have on them representatives of every shade of opinion, even if those opinions are not such as to commend themselves to every member of the community.'[16]

Hogg was not satisfied and insisted on raising the question of government responsibility for local Information Committees during the Debate for Adjournment, during which Taylor got lost in the larger question.[17]

Taylor was unlucky that this particular indiscretion gained so much unfavourable publicity. Indeed, he recalled in his autobiography that he had slipped up even worse in Southampton, although no one seemed to have noticed: 'I remarked that it would take years of bombing by the entire German air force to kill all of the inhabitants of Southampton. This, though true, did not look so good when the Germans obliterated the centre of the city only a few nights later. I did not go to Southampton again for some time.'[18] What he did was concentrate on war commentaries, surveying what had happened in the war during the previous month and sometimes speculating on what would happen during the next. He made quite an impression with his first talk at Oxford in May 1941, when he finished by saying, 'Before we meet again Hitler will have attacked Russia'. Willert had come to listen to the talk and he told Taylor, as they walked out, that the Regional Office would have trouble over that particular comment, since someone was bound to accuse Taylor of revealing secret information. No one did, but Taylor achieved a local reputation for prophecy. He developed a regular round, covering Oxford, Banbury, Aylesbury, Wolverton, Reading, Bournemouth, Swanage and a few other towns. He enjoyed the work. He liked talking about the war and wrote later that it taught him to look at the war as history in the making.[19] But in June 1943 it all came to an end when his rhetoric ran away with him.

In February 1943 the Tunisian campaign came to life again once the winter rains had ceased and the ground was dry enough for planes to land and troops to move. On 14 February the German General Rommel attacked the US 2nd Corps at Faid and quickly advanced through them, although the Corps fought back strongly, and by 3 March Rommel's troops were back where they had begun. In one of his war commentaries in April Taylor apparently remarked that the Americans were still inexperienced and bound to make mistakes. This remark, coming on top of comments he had made some months before about the major British ally, the Soviet Union, seems to have decided the Ministry of Information that he was too dangerous to remain on its speakers' list. (Willert had warned him the previous year that 'up in London they don't like anything that draws attention to the Ministry of Information. Never take a line on anything. Otherwise you will be in trouble.') In June he announced in Banbury that he was giving his last war commentary.[20]

The result, according to the *Oxford Times*, was a 'storm of criticism' in several places where he had given his talks. Taylor had told one of his students that 'I won't go quietly' and he tried his hand at stirring up the press, agreeing to give an interview to an *Oxford Mail* feature writer who had been trying to interview him for some time with no success. The result was his appearance in the regular feature 'Drawn and Quoted', in which the usual long and sometimes humorous interview was capped with a drawing of the interviewee. Taylor was interviewed as he gardened, surrounded by wife, children, visitors, including A.L. Rowse, and the odd student. He did indeed emphasize that what was required was not a propaganda ministry, which by implication was what the Ministry of Information was, but a ministry which stimulated the public to think, which by implication was what Taylor had been trying to do. At the end of the interview Taylor asked to see the drawing of him which had been sketched whilst they had been talking. '"Hmmm, yes," he decided. "Now only one thing remains to be done." He took a sheet of paper and neatly pasted it over the features. "Banned by the Ministry of Information," he scrawled in his characteristic hand.' And that is how the picture appeared.[21]

The local Information Committees protested, and the Mayor of Aylesbury went up to London in person to argue for his reinstatement. The contretemps raised real issues for the Ministry, which had to walk a thin line between provocation and boredom. Certainly it was felt by a number in the Ministry itself that 'the Ministry's policy of "playing safe" would result in its losing its following in Oxford.' But the fear of raising the ire of the House of Commons was always greater in the Ministry than that of losing its influence in any single locality, and the order was not countermanded. Taylor's career as a Government spokesman was ended.[22]

Taylor also tried to write for England. During the First World War the Foreign Office had set up within itself a Political Intelligence Department, heavily staffed by historians, including Arnold Toynbee, Lewis Namier, Charles Webster and E.H. Carr. In 1922 a number of those who had worked in the PID established the Institute of International Affairs, later the Royal Institute of International Affairs, more popularly known as Chatham House. At the outbreak of the Second World War Chatham House moved to Balliol College, Oxford, and reconstituted itself as Political Intelligence Department, whose duty was to write reports for use by the government. Taylor offered his services, but was turned down for a regular position; however, he was 'grudgingly given unpaid work and set to write a report on British war aims. This was an instructive exercise [he later wrote]. I read all the ministerial statements both before the war and after its outbreak, reaching the conclusion . . . that the British government had no war aims nor indeed any idea of what they were doing. I was in the process of writing a report on these lines when I was abruptly told to cease work: orders had come from on high that war aims were not to be discussed.'[23]

A second opportunity along these lines came in 1943, ironically enough in the month before he was dismissed by the Ministry of Information. In May he was summoned to London, where a retired colonel read him the Official Secrets Act and inducted him into the Political Warfare Executive (PWE), 'yet another body pronouncing on foreign countries. The accumulation of information was now enormous. The Foreign Office was doing it; Chatham House was doing it. The Ministries of Information and of Economic Warfare had their research staffs and so had the European and overseas services of the BBC. The PWE now entered the pursuit, its control disputed between the Foreign Office and the Ministry of Economic Warfare, to say nothing of its claim to control itself. PWE presented itself as more practical than the other departments, actually doing things as well as accumulating information. . . . It was perhaps more relevant that PWE prided itself on being Left wing whereas all the other bodies veered to the Right.'[24]

In 1941 Taylor had published his fourth book, *The Habsburg Monarchy 1815–1918: A History of the Austrian Empire and Austria–Hungary*, which had been very well reviewed. This is probably what led PWE to call him in, because they wanted a left-wing authority on Hungary. It was necessary to produce a handbook on Hungary for the autumn, when, it was assumed, British troops would be in occupation and would require guidance. It was also necessary that it be a left-wing handbook, because otherwise 'the reactionaries of the Foreign Office would write it and Horthy the Regent would be given a clean bill.' Taylor took four months' leave from Magdalen, receiving the enormous salary of £5,000 – tax free because the work was too secret to be revealed to the authorities – and moved to London. He worked in Bush House, which PWE shared with the European services of the BBC. 'Suitable Hungarian refugees provided me with detailed information on Hungarian administration and economics which I merely turned into good English.' He drew on his burgeoning friendship with the Hungarian democrat Prince Michael Karolyi to help him compose a chapter on Hungarian politics, although Taylor relied only on himself for the chapter on Hungarian history.

He completed his work by the autumn of 1943, with copy sent off to the printer each day as he completed it. The proofs were sent to the Foreign Office, whence they returned with his chapters on history and politics deleted and a right-wing version (which Taylor thought had been written by the historian C.W. Macartney) substituted. Taylor assumed that the PWE protested, but to no avail.[25] It is impossible to tell, since no papers relevant to the case survive. He also assumed that the handbook was never issued; this was probably the case, as no British troops ever entered Hungary.

The PWE authorities were dismayed at what had transpired, evidence perhaps that the issue had been taken out of their hands. In any case they tried again, asking Taylor to write a chapter on the Weimar Republic (1919–33) for the handbook on Germany which they were in the process of preparing. According to Taylor, 'I duly wrote my chapter only to learn that I had hit the wrong note again. This time the objection came from PWE itself. I had taken the line, perhaps somewhat exaggerated by wartime feelings, that Germany had not been firmly democratic even in Weimar times and that Hitlerism, far from being an aberration, grew out of what had gone before. This did not suit PWE which with its Left-wing outlook believed fervently in a strongly democratic Germany groaning under Hitler's tyranny. My chapter, I was told, was too depressing to be given to British officers.'[26]

Again, there are no papers remaining in the Public Record Office

28

archive which refer to this case, but it is now known what happened. F.L. Carsten had been an active member of an underground socialist group in Germany from 1933 until 1939, when he fled Germany and came to Oxford. In 1942 he completed a D.Phil thesis on early modern Prussian history, looking at the development of the manorial system. He then had to find a job. Duncan Wilson offered him a job in PWE. His task, as he later recalled, was to help draft the handbook on Germany. 'I was still an "enemy alien", but for the next two to three years I wrote chapters on German administration, local government, the Nazi organizations and ranks, and German politics in general.' But, he adds, 'the contribution of A.J.P. Taylor on earlier German history, which he wrote as an outsider, was so one-sided and partisan that it was rejected on my initiative.'[27] PWE agreed that he could take his rejected chapter with him, and this later formed part of *The Course of German History*, published in 1945 and, as a book which met the needs of the time, Taylor's first best-seller.[28]

By the end of 1943, therefore, Taylor had failed in his attempts to speak and to write for England. He remained in only one official outlet: this was the BBC, where his attempts to broadcast for England were still continuing. In February 1942 he had written offering himself to the BBC, and in response Trevor Blewitt, a producer in the Radio Talks Department, wrote inviting him to London to audition as a speaker in the series 'The World At War – Your Questions Answered', which was to go out on Forces' Radio.[29] He was successful and made his first appearance on 17 March 1942. According to Taylor, although 'in theory the questions came from bomber pilots, soldiers in North Africa and naval ratings in the Atlantic' . . . in fact 'they were made up by Guy Chapman, later a professor of history at Leeds.' He clearly enjoyed himself, although he later claimed that he did not think the work very important but that it taught him radio technique.[30]

Such technique did not come easily. An internal BBC memorandum dated the day before his first talk indicates what was involved: 'Here is Taylor's script. We are asking him to re-write the introduction: he stresses "guessing" too much. We are also asking him to introduce a breathing space into the script – at present it is tough going for our audience. The script also is too long: cuts will be made.'[31] He would soon learn how many pages of script were required for a programme of ten minutes or fifteen or twenty, a very useful skill for the future.

Taylor made seven appearances from March to June 1942, all on the same programme, 'Your Questions Answered'. He then ceased to appear until 1944, when in August of that year Blewitt wrote to him that he had now taken over the talks on foreign affairs in the Home Talks Department and that he and his colleague would very much like to meet Taylor to 'talk about things'. 'How admirable is your willingness still to contemplate the trouble I should cause you!' Taylor responded eagerly. 'Of course I should like to see you and even to smell the dust of the microphone.' It was agreed that he would join three other speakers for a talk on 'The Future of Germany',[32] broadcast on 26 October 1944, and this indeed might be said to mark the real beginning of his broadcasting career: three appearances that year, but twenty in 1945.

Taylor broadcast on the Home Service now and again, but he broadcast much more often for the Overseas Service. One series in which he appeared was 'Freedom Forum', which, as Taylor described it, 'demonstrated to non-existent American listeners our democratic virtues. People like Harold Laski and me wrangled over supposedly controversial subjects. I soon became an expert at the game.'[33] Another series was 'London Calling Europe', for which, in a series of twelve seven-minute talks, he set out 'The Pattern of the News', putting events of the war in context. There were programmes on, for example, Poland and France, and Europe Under Hitler.

The BBC had continuing difficulties with Taylor. He gently ridiculed their bureaucratic procedures, but more serious for the Corporation was the increasing concern that he would upset people by what he said – the listeners, the Foreign Office, later the political parties.[34] This concern would in due course become acute and in mid-1946 he was taken off one of the Home Service's current affairs series, 'World Affairs: A Weekly Series'. But this belongs to Taylor's postwar history: suffice it to say that, on balance, from 1942 through 1945 Taylor pleased more than he displeased the powers in the BBC, an interesting contrast with his relations with government departments.

During the Second World War, then, Taylor served his country according to his own lights, attempting to use his strengths – a knowledge of foreign countries and foreign affairs and a way with words both written and spoken – to help people to understand events and to encourage them to think about what they meant. In the process he ran up against individuals and institutions who disliked and distrusted his approach, and more often than not he was silenced. Yet he also honed the skills which would enable him to develop a career in public speaking and writing which would, for some years, be unique for an academic, but which were largely responsible for his becoming the most famous historian in the United Kingdom.

NOTES

1. A.J.P. Taylor, *The Italian Problem in European Diplomacy 1847–49* (Manchester: Manchester University Press, 1934); Heinrich Friedjung, *The Struggle for Supremacy in Germany, 1859–1866*, translated by A.J.P. Taylor and W.L. McElwee, Introduction by Taylor (London: Macmillan, 1935); and Taylor, *Germany's First Bid For Colonies, 1884–1885: A Move in Bismarck's Foreign Policy* (London: Macmillan, 1938).
2. A.J.P. Taylor, *Personal History* (London: Hamish Hamilton, 1983), p. 154.
3. Adam Sisman, *A.J.P. Taylor: A Biography* (London: Sinclair-Stevenson, 1994), p. 141.
4. Taylor, *Personal History*, p. 156.
5. *Ibid.*, p. 152.
6. *Ibid.*, p. 166.
7. *Ibid.*, p. 159.
8. 'Survey of Activities of the Southern Region No. 6, Ministry of Information, 1939–1945', INF 1/297/54303, Ministry of Information papers, Public Record Office, London.
9. Hansard, *H.C. Debs, 1939–40*, Vol. 365, 24 Oct. 1940, col. 1144.
10. Ivison Macadam, 'Public Meetings', Ministry of Information Regional Administrative Division Regional Circular No. 37, February 1940, INF 1/294A, p. 2.
11. Ministry of Information Home Publicity Division, 'Public Meetings. Instructions to local Information Committees Enclosure with Regional Circular No. 12', 17 Sept. 1939, INF 1/294A; list of Class A and Class B speakers, Appendix A of George Meare to Mr Rhodes, 5 Dec. 1940, INF 1/294C. The Leader of the Opposition, Clement Attlee, who was one of the three speakers on the Class A list, had his name spelled Atlee.
12. Taylor, *Personal History*, p. 159.
13. S.S. Semneer, 'Public Meetings Expenses', 23 April 1943, INF 1/301.
14. 'Survey of Activities', INF 1/297.

15. Taylor, *Personal History*, p. 159.
16. Hansard, *op. cit.*, cols 1143–44.
17. Hansard, *op. cit.* 5 Nov. 1940, cols 1293–7.
18. Taylor, *Personal History*, p. 160.
19. *Ibid.*, p. 160.
20. *Ibid.*, p. 165 for Willert's comment; Stanley Parker, 'Drawn and Quoted: A.J.P. Taylor or My Waterloo', *Oxford Mail*, 17 June 1943, p. 2; *Oxford Times*, 11 June 1943, p. 4.
21. *Oxford Times*, 11 June 1943, p. 4; Stanley Parker, 'Drawn and Quoted: A.J.P. Taylor or My Waterloo', *Oxford Mail*, 17 June 1943, p. 2.
22. Taylor, *Personal History*, p. 165; 'Survey of Activities of the Southern Region', INF 1/297/54303, p. 4.
23. Taylor, *Personal History*, p. 153.
24. *Ibid.*, pp. 170–1.
25. *Ibid.*, pp. 171–2.
26. *Ibid.*, p. 172.
27. Francis L. Carsten, 'From Revolutionary Socialism to German History', in Peter Alter, ed., *Out of the Third Reich; Refugee Historians in Postwar Britain* (London: I.B. Tauris, 1998), pp. 31–2. Carsten later became Professor of Central European History at the School of Slavonic and East European Studies of the University of London.
28. *The Course of German History: A Survey of the Development of Germany Since 1815* (London: Hamish Hamilton, 1945), 229 pp.
29. Blewitt to Taylor, 19 Feb. 1942, Radio Contributors, Talks, A.J.P. Taylor, File 1, 1942–46, BBC Written Archives, Caversham.
30. Taylor, *Personal History*, p. 165.
31. Lloyd Williams, 16 March 1942, Radio Contributors, Talks, A.J.P. Taylor, File 1 1942–46, BBC Archives.
32. Blewitt to Taylor, 21 Aug. 1944, Taylor to Blewitt, 23 Aug. 1944, Boswell to Taylor, 27 Aug. 1944, all Radio Contributors, Talks, A.J.P. Taylor File 1, 1942–46, BBC Archives.
33. Taylor, *Personal History*, pp. 165–66.
34. See Blewitt to Taylor, 9 March 1945 and Taylor to Blewitt, 10 March 1945 for the ridicule, both in Radio Contributors, Talks, A.J.P. Taylor File 1, 1942–46. For a fracas over his views on Trieste, see Record of telephone conversations between Massey and Barnes, 24 Sept 1945; memo by Rendall re telephone call by Grubb, 24 Sept. 1945; memo by Barnes re complaint by Cunard, 1 Oct. 1945; and memo by Rendall re interview with Taylor, 30 Oct. 1945, all Radio Contributors, Talks, A.J.P. Taylor File 1, 1942–46, BBC Archives.

BRITAIN BETWEEN FRANCE AND THE UNITED STATES, 1944

P.M.H. BELL

On 3 June 1944 General de Gaulle said farewell to the *Comité National de Libération* in Algiers to fly on a momentous journey to England, where the Allied invasion of Normandy was about to be launched. *'Il faut regarder loin dans l'avenir,'* he said, *'celui des relations franco-britanniques.'*[1] As often, he spoke prophetically. 1944 was indeed a crucial year for relations between France and Britain, with protracted effects on the triangular relationship between Britain, France and the United States which was so important for all three.

It has often seemed that in 1944, under the leadership of Churchill, Britain leaned so far towards the United States and away from France that the choice could not be altered for many years. When Churchill and de Gaulle met on 4 June 1944 they exchanged bitter words which were to echo down the years. Churchill exclaimed vehemently that 'no quarrel would ever arise between Britain and the United States on account of France,' to which de Gaulle replied that 'he quite understood that in case of disagreement between the United States and France, Great Britain would side with the United States.'[2] De Gaulle never forgot that conversation and it has come to appear that relations within the British-French-American triangle were fixed at that moment for years to come. Yet the reality was very different. Relations within the triangle were far from fixed in 1944, and Churchill's severe remarks to de Gaulle on 4 June did not convey his full thoughts or his settled policy. In the wider context of events in 1944, we find a difficult and uncertain situation, in which the position of Britain between France and the United States remained fluid, and the future quite undecided. Let us examine that context and review the uncertainties.

To understand the situation in 1944 we must go back to 1940. In May 1940 the British government confronted the possibility of an imminent and total French defeat by Germany. Churchill, who had just become Prime Minister, requested the Chiefs of Staff to assess Britain's chances of immediate survival and ultimate victory in the event of a French collapse. On 25 May 1940 they duly reported to the War Cabinet on 'British Strategy in a Certain Eventuality'. Two fundamental assumptions of that crucial document were that American financial and economic support were necessary to continue the war, and that the active co-operation of the United States was essential to win it.[3] In June the 'certain eventuality' came about. France concluded armistices with Germany and Italy, and dropped out of the war, with the gallant exception of a small group led by General de Gaulle – *France Libre*. Within a short time the government of Marshal Pétain at Vichy embarked on a policy of collaboration with Germany, designed to secure France a place in the German 'New Order' in Europe. The *Entente Cordiale*, which, despite many ups and downs, had formed the basis of British policy since before 1914, was broken.

To replace it there was no alternative to the assumptions made by the Chiefs of Staff in May 1940. Only the Americans, with their economic and eventually military power, could ensure survival and final victory. Churchill therefore set himself to build up an American alliance to replace that with France. He developed a personal relationship with Roosevelt which achieved an intensity and depth unusual among statesmen. On Churchill's side at any rate there was an abiding affection, respect and loyalty, which by no means excluded calculation. Churchill regarded his personal contacts with Roosevelt as being of the highest political importance. As the war went on, and Britain's material contribution declined in relation to that of the United States, the Prime Minister relied increasingly on his personal influence to redress the balance, deploying information, argument, exhortation and flattery as he judged best. But he recognized that the key to his influence was to use it sparingly, reserving it for particularly grave issues. For some time these methods served Churchill well. His powerful personality, his experience of war and the resources of the remarkable British war planning machinery gave him an advantage in a series of conferences and strategic debates in 1941 and 1942, culminating at the Casablanca Conference in January 1943.

The result was a wartime alliance which met British needs. American supplies, provided under Roosevelt's characteristically flexible system of Lend-Lease, sustained Great Britain. Vast American forces accumulated for the invasion of Europe. The British and Americans conducted the war together through the machinery of the Combined Chiefs of Staff and a system of integrated commands which produced much closer co-operation than had been achieved with the French in the war of 1914–18. But that was not all. Churchill believed that the American alliance was vital for peace as well as war. He wanted to keep the Combined Chiefs of Staff in being when the war ended. He sought to consolidate an enduring political co-operation, speaking sometimes of some kind of Anglo-American union. His *History of the English-Speaking Peoples*, begun before the Second World War and finished after it, emphasized the common heritage of Britain and the United States and was an enterprise close to his heart. Churchill was aware of the many problems in Anglo-American relations, but he looked to a permanent association with the United States for the salvation of his country in war and as the firm foundation of future peace.

In 1940 it seemed unlikely that relations with France would ever return to a degree of importance which would approach that of relations with the United States. But as the war went on France assumed an increasingly important role in British policy and calculations. This owed little to personal chemistry. Churchill's relations with de Gaulle were of a very different nature from those with Roosevelt and showed a very different side of Churchill's character – fiery, abrasive, arbitrary and sometimes petulant. The disputes between Churchill and de Gaulle were often explosive and left deep scars on both sides. On 10 December 1942 Churchill told a secret session of the House of Commons that 'the House must not be led to believe that General de Gaulle is an unfaltering friend of Britain. On the contrary, I think he is one of those good Frenchmen who have a traditional antagonism ingrained in French hearts by centuries of war against the English.' In 1941, on his way back from Syria, 'he left a trail of anglophobia behind him'.[4] In June 1943, at a time when Churchill came very near to a complete breach with de Gaulle, he took the highly unusual step of issuing in his own name a formal 'memorandum of guidance' to the British press, stating flatly that 'De Gaulle owes everything to British assistance and support, but he cannot be considered as a friend of our country. Wherever he has been he has left a trail of anglophobia behind him' – the very same words which he had used in the House of Commons six months earlier.[5]

Yet Churchill also recognized the greatness in de Gaulle. At Marrakesh in January 1944 the two men had one of their difficult encounters, but when it was over Churchill said to one of those present: 'There is no doubt about it! *C'est un grand animal!*'[6] Moreover, whatever his changing feelings about de Gaulle, Churchill always held France in deep affection. In that same secret session of 10 December, he said: 'I have lived myself for the last 35 years or more in a mental relationship and to a large extent in sympathy with an abstraction called France.'[7] This was very true, though the word 'abstraction' rings strangely. Churchill knew France as a reality; he felt at home in France, was familiar with French history, moved easily among French friends, and had a confident if sometimes erratic familiarity with the French language. He had a steadfast faith in the French Army which had been deeply ingrained during the 1914–18 war and which was ready to be revived even after the disasters of 1940.

Such feelings counted, because Churchill was often moved by instinct and swayed by emotion. But he was above all a statesman, and as such he was convinced that France must be restored as a great power. As early as 7 August 1940 Churchill undertook 'to secure the full restoration of the independence and greatness of France'.[8] From this purpose he never wavered, despite much exasperation against de Gaulle, whom he refused to equate with France. Anthony Eden, Foreign Secretary from the end of 1940 to July 1945, pursued the same objective with great tenacity and with more consistency than Churchill, because he was less buffeted and distracted by personal quarrels with de Gaulle. This policy owed something to sentiment, but much more to calculation. The restoration of France as a great power was necessary for British interests in two respects: Britain needed the French Army and the French Empire.

The French Army would be needed in the first place to take part in the defeat and subsequent occupation of Germany, because the British were convinced that American forces would leave Europe shortly after the end of the war. Next, there was the further question, much less avowable at the time, of the Soviet Union. Churchill's views on Stalin and on Soviet policy were far from consistent, and in 1944 and early 1945 he was still at times optimistic, but in his bleaker moods he foresaw with anxiety a time when there would be nothing

36

'between the white snows of Russia and the white cliffs of Dover'.[9] The French Army would offer at least some protection in such dire circumstances. The French Empire, on the other hand, offered a defence, not against the Soviets, but against the United States. Churchill was well aware of Roosevelt's anti-imperialist sentiments, though he rarely chose to tackle the issue openly. In this situation, the French Empire served as an outer line of defence for the British, and Churchill was glad to take note of American statements of support for French imperial possessions. As he wrote to Halifax, the Ambassador in Washington, in February 1943, 'I do not at all mind the various statements that have been made by the President and others near him about restoring the French Empire and territory, because it is very difficult to see how this line can be taken by the State Department about France and at the same time a policy of liqui-dating the British Empire be pursued.'[10]

These two British concerns, with the French Army and the French Empire, were closely linked to deficiencies and dangers in the American alliance. The Americans were unlikely to stay in Europe after the end of hostilities to hold down the Germans or to counter-balance the Soviet Union, and they presented an active threat to the British Empire. The restoration of France was thus in both cases a reinsurance against potential difficulties in relations with the United States, showing clearly that no final choice between the two had been made.

The position of Britain between the United States and France was made particularly difficult by a long-running conflict between Roosevelt and de Gaulle. Roosevelt maintained American recog-nition of the Vichy government, to which de Gaulle was utterly opposed, until November 1942. The first meeting between Roosevelt and de Gaulle, at Casablanca in January 1943, was a disaster. The President found someone who was immune to his famous charm and he made no serious attempt to understand how de Gaulle's mind worked. De Gaulle for his part was not in any simple sense anti-American. He recognized the crucial role of the United States in the war and gladly accepted Lease-Lend aid for the Free French in 1941. He once described Roosevelt as 'a patrician democrat whose every simple gesture is carefully studied' – which showed a better under-standing of Roosevelt than the President ever achieved of him.[11] But in all his dealings with the Americans, as with the British, he insisted on absolute independence, all the more so because his material position was so weak. This produced constant friction and exacerbated Roosevelt's hostility. Throughout 1943 Roosevelt supported General Giraud against de Gaulle in the internal French power struggle in Algiers, though without success, because Giraud was no match for de Gaulle's political skill. In May and June 1943 Roosevelt put such pressure on Churchill that he came very close to breaking with de Gaulle, but Eden and the War Cabinet prevented it. Fundamentally, Churchill did not want to choose between Roosevelt and de Gaulle, still less between the United States and France, and, through the firm and timely intervention of Eden, he was saved from doing so.

At the end of 1943 and early in 1944 relations within the British-American-French triangle approached crisis point. Rifts had appeared between Roosevelt and Churchill during 1943. In May Roosevelt tried for a meeting with Stalin (excluding Churchill) at the Bering Straits, and actually denied to Churchill that he had proposed such an idea.[12] Before the three-power conference at Teheran Roosevelt avoided any preliminary consultation with Churchill. During the conference itself he had separate meetings with Stalin and went so far as to taunt Churchill at the dinner table for Stalin's pleasure. In 1944 he evaded Churchill's pressing invitations to visit Britain, and the two statesmen did not meet that year until the Quebec Conference in September. The personal contact on which Churchill spent so much energy and ingenuity, and on which he relied so heavily, was diminishing. This came about at the very time when the disproportionate weight of the United States within the alliance was becoming increasingly obvious. When the invasion of Normandy began in June 1944 the Americans for the first time had more troops in contact with the Germans than Britain and the Commonwealth, and the disparity between the two war efforts became steadily larger thereafter.

At the same time France was re-emerging as a power, after the apparently fatal collapse of 1940. De Gaulle slowly constructed what amounted to a Provisional Government in Algiers (the French National Committee actually assumed this title on 2 June 1944, though it was not yet accepted as such by other governments). A substantial French Expeditionary Corps under General Juin entered the Italian campaign in 1943, and General de Lattre de Tassigny's *Armée B* (some 250,000 strong and armed with American equipment) was preparing to take part in landings in southern France in

1944. France was resuming its place as a political and military power on a modest but increasing scale.

The British position between France and the United States, which seemed to have been decided once and for all in 1940 in favour of the United States, was much less certain as 1944 began. The clear-cut choice which appeared to have been made was being re-opened.

During the first part of 1944 a number of strategic and political issues involving Britain, the United States and France arose, demonstrating the complexity of the situation. Let us examine three crucial questions: the bombing of French railway targets in preparation for the Normandy landings; the plan for a landing in the south of France, first code-named ANVIL and later renamed DRAGOON; and the administration of liberated areas of France, which was bound up with the recognition of de Gaulle's National Committee as the Provisional Government of France.

On 25 March 1944 General Eisenhower, the Supreme Commander for the Normandy landings, and his air commanders decided that the Allied bombing forces must ensure the disruption of enemy rail communications in north-western Europe to hinder the movement of German reinforcements to the invasion area. On the 29th the Chief of the Air Staff, Air Marshal Portal, reported on this to the Prime Minister, adding that very heavy civilian casualties would be unavoidable. Churchill was alarmed, fearing that such casualties would arouse deep resentment and cause an irreparable breach between the French people and Britain. On 3 April he took the matter to the War Cabinet, which agreed that the bombing would cause such anger in France as to outweigh its military advantages and insisted that the attacks should be limited in their scope while the question was reviewed. On 5 April Lord Cherwell, Churchill's principal scientific confidant and adviser, gave his view that the bombing plan was unlikely to achieve its objectives, even if the air forces dropped 50,000 tons of bombs and inflicted casualties amounting to 40,000 dead and 120,000 injured, which Cherwell thought probable. These terrible figures, from a trusted source, alarmed Churchill still further. At his insistence the Defence Committee (a body which at that stage of the war rarely met) discussed the matter five times, and the War Cabinet three times. Evidence as to casualty figures, and projections for the future, were closely scrutinized. Eisenhower was formally consulted and gave his full backing for the bombing plan, but the War Cabinet continued to withhold its agreement. The records of

39

these intense discussions show Churchill repeatedly using the word 'slaughter' to describe the nature of the civilian casualties in France.

Finally, with the support of the War Cabinet, Churchill appealed to Roosevelt on 7 May. Estimates of casualties had by then come down to some 10,000 fatalities, but Churchill still feared the results. 'They [the casualties] may easily bring about a great revulsion in French feeling towards their approaching United States and British liberators. They may leave a legacy of hatred behind them.' And three times, repeating the word he had used in the Defence Committee meetings, Churchill referred to 'slaughter' or 'slaughters'. Roosevelt was unmoved, replying on 11 May that he was not prepared to impose restrictions on military actions thought necessary by the responsible commanders. The bombing went ahead, with marked success and with fewer casualties than even the lowest predictions, but Churchill remained dissatisfied. He insisted on receiving reports of French reactions to the bombing each day, and told Air Chief Marshal Tedder (the air commander for OVERLORD) as late as 28 May that 'You are piling up an awful load of hatred.'[13]

This was a revealing episode. Churchill's extreme anxiety arose partly from his emotional concern for the sufferings of the French people, but also from his sense of the need for good relations with France after the war, in which he was fully supported by Eden. The British debated the matter for over a month and deferred the final decision to the last possible date. Churchill appealed to Roosevelt in powerful and emotional terms, only to find that the President imposed upon him the opposite decision. Roosevelt only needed to speak once and the whole agonized discussion came to an end.

The dispute over a landing in southern France was longer and more severe. The concept of a southern landing simultaneous with that in Normandy, to act as a diversion, was agreed at an Anglo-American conference at Quebec in August 1943, and was code-named ANVIL. By March 1944 it became clear that there would not be enough landing-craft to carry out the two operations simultaneously and the question arose as to whether ANVIL should be cancelled or postponed. For four months, from April to early August 1944, the British and Americans argued over this question.

The American Chiefs of Staff, with the support of Roosevelt, were determined to carry out the southern landings, though they had to accept postponement, first to 10 July, and later to mid-August. They had powerful reasons. They wanted to bring all available forces to bear in France as soon as possible. (Strikingly, they also wished to get *French* forces into the battle in France. This was inconsistent with Roosevelt's reluctance to restore a strong France; but the American Army had manpower problems in its infantry units and was glad of reinforcements.) They wanted to use the great port of Marseilles to bring men and supplies into France. Roosevelt, who by 1944 was coming to regard the Soviet Union as the USA's most important ally, was determined to carry out the undertakings given to Stalin at Teheran about a landing in southern France.

The case was strong, but Churchill, supported for the most part by the Chiefs of Staff, offered a tenacious opposition, which he maintained until nearly a week before the landings took place. He held that the plan for a southern landing lost its *raison d'être* when it first had to be postponed, because it no longer served as a diversion for OVERLORD. He was not convinced that Marseilles was vital as a port, and as late as June was considering the possibility of seizing Bordeaux. He did not accept the American strategic arguments about concentration on the French theatre, preferring instead to press on with the campaign in Italy, which would have to be closed down for some six to eight weeks in order to mount ANVIL. Behind this lay the psychological and political point that Churchill wanted to secure the prestige of a victorious campaign in Italy *under British command*. He wrote to Ismay on 6 July, 'Let us at least have a chance to launch a decisive strategic stroke with what is entirely British and under British Command. I am not going to give way about this for anybody. Alexander is to have his campaign.'[14] Another element in Churchill's thinking, of uncertain significance at the time and the subject of much controversy since, was the idea of pressing northwards in Italy and then turning eastwards towards Trieste, the Ljubljana Gap and finally Vienna. Churchill referred to this possibility in a telegram to Roosevelt on 28 June, though he was careful to mention only Trieste, keeping silent on more distant objectives. Even this touched a sensitive nerve with Roosevelt, who replied that 'for purely political considerations over here I would never survive even a slight setback in OVERLORD if it were known that fairly large forces had been diverted to the Balkans'.[15]

Churchill pursued this dispute with extreme severity. In a draft telegram for Roosevelt on 30 June 1944 he even contemplated using the threat of resignation. ('If my departure from the scene would ease matters, by tendering my resignation to the King, I would gladly make this contribution, but I fear that the demand of the public to know the reasons would do great injury to the fighting troops.') In the same draft he wrote that 'There is nothing I will not do to end this deadlock except become responsible for an absolutely perverse strategy.' He later thought better of the words 'absolutely perverse', but still referred to the decision for ANVIL in a telegram of 1 July as 'the first major strategic and political error for which we two have to be responsible'. If Roosevelt still pressed on, Churchill would have to 'enter a solemn protest', though the British would then do their best to make a success of whatever was undertaken.[16] In private he continued to fume. He wrote to Ismay: 'I hope you realize that an intense impression must be made upon the Americans that we have been ill-treated and are furious. Do not let any smoothings or smirchings cover up this fact. After a little, we shall get together again; but if we take everything lying down, there will be no end to what will be put upon us. The Arnold, King, Marshall combination is one of the stupidest strategic teams ever seen. They are good fellows, and there is no need to tell them this.'[17] As late as 4 August he tried to persuade Roosevelt to switch the landings from Provence to St Nazaire or southern Brittany, an extraordinary improvisation which he did not give up until 8 August, a week before the invasion actually began.[18]

Churchill did not let go of the issue even then. He requested Ismay to let him have weekly figures for landings of material at various French ports from 1 October 1944 to 24 January 1945. On 18 December he observed that 'Marseilles is very good', and that the efficiency of this route might be important if forces had to be moved quickly from Italy to France, perhaps the nearest he came to accepting that his view of the value of Marseilles might have been mistaken.[19] At the height of the dispute he was unwilling to yield any ground whatsoever. General Brooke observed that on 30 June-1 July Churchill 'looked like wanting to fight the President', and had to be restrained by the Chiefs of Staff.[20] In the event Churchill stopped short of a complete breach, but it is important to recall how near he came to 'wanting to fight the President'.

In the background to these strategic issues lay the question of the administration of the French territories which would be liberated by the Allied invasions. This had been under discussion since the middle of 1943 without any agreement being reached between the Americans, the British and the Free French. The Americans, because of Roosevelt's obstinate opposition to de Gaulle, refused to deal with the Committee of National Liberation, on the ground that this would amount to recognizing the Committee (and thus de Gaulle) as the government of France. They preferred to set up a form of military government, on the lines of the Allied Military Government of Occupied Territories (AMGOT) devised for the occupation of Italy. Eden and the Foreign Office believed that such a scheme would be certainly impractical, because the Allied forces would simply have to work with French officials of some kind, and probably dangerous, because the French people would resent being released from German military rule only to find themselves under a new military government, however friendly. De Gaulle's position was that the CNL was already the provisional government of France and that he did not require the consent of foreign powers to administer his own country. Churchill tried from time to time to arrange a meeting between Roosevelt and de Gaulle at which this problem might be resolved, but without success. He also pointed out that de Gaulle controlled considerable forces, which were placed at the disposal of the Allies, only to receive from the President the icy (and inaccurate) reply: 'I do not have any information that leads me to believe that de Gaulle and his Committee of National Liberation have as yet given any helpful assistance to our Allied war effort'.[21]

The question remained unresolved when de Gaulle left Algiers on 3 June, the point at which this essay began. On the 4th he met Churchill, who tried to persuade him to accept the American view on the question of administration, at least for the time being. De Gaulle refused, maintaining that the administration of French territory was a French affair. The two men exchanged the defiant words which are quoted on the opening page of this paper; and when the Allied troops went ashore on D-Day the issue remained unresolved. Churchill was still furious with de Gaulle, telling Eden that 'nothing would induce him to give way, that de Gaulle must go. F.D.R. and he would fight the world'.[22]

In Normandy events decided the issue, with some help from the men on the spot. When de Gaulle installed his *Commissaire de la République* in Bayeux General Montgomery found time to meet him and commend his work. Gradually it emerged that de Gaulle's representatives were the best men to do the sort of work which the Allied forces needed from a civilian administration; they also had useful contacts with the local Resistance. On the ground, therefore,

43

the policy which Eden and the Foreign Office had long proposed proved the only practical course of action. In the diplomatic arena Churchill, who had consistently supported Roosevelt's opposition to de Gaulle and the CNL, found himself suddenly abandoned. In July 1944 de Gaulle finally visited Washington, where he was greeted by the President and Secretary of State. 'My, I am glad to see you,' said Roosevelt and, 'Why, it's good to have you with us,' said Cordell Hull. British Embassy officials observed this surprising effusiveness and conjectured that it might foreshadow a change of policy which would leave Britain out on a limb, clinging to a position which the Americans were about to abandon.[23] This was indeed what happened, twice in the next four months.

First, Roosevelt announced at a press conference on 11 July, without consulting the British in advance, that he was ready to treat the Committee of National Liberation as the *de facto* authority for governing France. Oliver Harvey (a senior Foreign Office official) noted in his diary: 'Both P.M. and A.E. rather bitter at this sudden volte face without any warning.'[24] Then on 23–24 October Roosevelt moved ('somewhat unexpectedly', in the mild words of the official history of British foreign policy) to recognize de Gaulle's administration as the Provisional Government of France. The British were given hardly any notice and had to scramble hastily behind with their own recognition. Churchill telegraphed to Roosevelt: 'I was naturally surprised at the very sharp turn taken by the State Department,' which left the President an opening to blame officials for precipitate action. But there was no doubt that Roosevelt himself had 'bowled a fast one'.[25] On both these occasions the British were forced into doing in haste something which Eden and the Foreign Office had wanted to do for a long time, but had been held back by Roosevelt's obstinacy and Churchill's refusal to budge without the President. Harvey observed in his diary, harshly but correctly, that the British had gained 'minimum credit for what should have been a major gesture. We couldn't have been more stupid – thanks to P.M. and President.'[26]

In all these episodes Britain fared badly within the British-American-French triangle. When Churchill tried to spare French civilian casualties in the bombing of railway targets, with an eye to future relations with France, he was overruled. When he fought hard and long over ANVIL he was defeated. Yet when he steadfastly followed American wishes, in the matters of administration of liberated territories and the recognition of the CNL as the Provisional

Government, he found himself abandoned by Roosevelt's sudden changes of course. Churchill himself veered sharply from one attitude to another. On 6 June he declared fiercely that 'F.D.R. and he would fight the world', but on 30 June Brooke was having to restrain him from 'wanting to fight the President' over ANVIL. In none of these issues did Britain make progress with its policy of restoring France as a great power. In fact, by a strange paradox, it was the Americans who, by insisting on getting large French forces into action in France in the ANVIL operation, did much to strengthen France as a military power. If Churchill had succeeded in cancelling ANVIL, the position of France would have been much weaker. It was all very strange. Churchill wanted a strong France after the war, but did nothing at this stage to advance his object. Roosevelt wanted no such thing, yet acted in such a way as to restore French power.

The clear-cut British choice of America as against France, so often seen as being confirmed in 1944, did not exist. British policy had never been unanimous, in that Eden had often sought to curb Churchill's animus against de Gaulle. Amid the stresses of 1944 policy swayed this way and that. On the bombing issue Britain tried to 'choose' France, but failed. On ANVIL, the British opposed the Americans to the utmost of their ability, in a direction which would have damaged French interests if it had been followed. On recognition, Churchill followed Roosevelt doggedly, to the detriment of relations with France yet without long-term benefit to relations with the United States. There were no clear lines, but a set of blurred options and uncertain conclusions. Moreover, there was a disconcerting gap between the high aspirations of Churchill's policy, which sought *both* a close Anglo-American alliance *and* the restoration of France as a great power, and his actual achievements in the issues examined here, which were very slight.

It is true that the sheer weight of American power, and Churchill's long-term desires for a permanent Anglo-American association, pushed Britain strongly towards the United States. But British policy, as practised by both Churchill and Eden in their different ways, sought to avoid a choice between the United States and France. Britain tried to pursue an independent course, influencing the United States and France – and of course the Soviet Union, which had a crucial part to play – to the ultimate advantage of Britain. In the autumn of 1944 Churchill made three long journeys. In September he conferred with Roosevelt at Quebec. In October he travelled to

45

Moscow to meet Stalin. In November he went to Paris, and later to the French front line, to resume contact with de Gaulle. During the first two visits he made important gains for British interests. At Quebec he ensured that a large British fleet would take part in the Pacific war and that Alexander's campaign in Italy would continue. In Moscow he secured Stalin's acceptance of the 'percentages agreement', which provided for the predominance of British influence in Greece in return for Soviet control in Romania and Bulgaria. Moreover, this forthright piece of power politics was at least a partial declaration of independence from American policy, in its idealism and opposition to spheres of influence.

In France Churchill made no such specific gains, but he took the opportunity to expound the basis of his policy in a way which is well worth recalling. In a private conversation after the two statemen had visited the French front line, de Gaulle proposed a sort of 'blocking combination' between France and Britain, not to control America or the USSR but to put a brake on their actions. Churchill would not fall in with this, though he insisted that he would not allow any breach between France and Britain. He went on, in words which are worth quoting at length:

> But in politics as in strategy, it is better to persuade the stronger than to pit yourself against him. That is what I am trying to do. The Americans have immense resources. They do not always use them to the best advantage. I am trying to enlighten them, without forgetting, of course, to benefit my country. I have formed a close personal tie with Roosevelt. With him, I proceed by suggestion in order to influence matters in the right direction. At present, Russia is a great beast which has been starved for a long time. It is not possible to keep her from eating, especially since now she lies in the middle of the herd of her victims. The question is whether she can be kept from devouring all of them. I am trying to restrain Stalin, who, if he has an enormous appetite, also has a great deal of good sense. And after the meal comes the digestion period. When it is time to digest, the surfeited Russians will have their difficult problems. Then, perhaps, St Nicholas can bring back to life the poor children the ogre has put in the salting tub. Meanwhile, I attend every meeting, yield nothing for nothing, and manage to secure a few dividends.[27]

Here we are concerned, not with the remarkable prophecy of distant events in eastern Europe, but with Churchill's explanation of

46

his (and Britain's) independent role in great power politics. He surely exaggerated the extent of his influence, and yet the recent evidence of his journeys to Quebec, Moscow and Paris showed that his hopes had some substance. Looking back after more than half a century, we should certainly counter-balance the memory of Churchill's harsh words to de Gaulle on 4 June 1944, and his apparent choice of the United States as against France, with that of his calm exposition of 13 November. What Churchill hoped to do was to retain his contacts and influence with both, and with the Soviet Union as well, and to use all three to safeguard all he could for British interests. It was a more complex position than that which made such an impact on de Gaulle in June 1944. In the long run, it had little effect on Franco-British relations, because what men believe, or choose to remember, about the past is often more important than what actually happened. But historians should check the memory against the record. In 1944 Britain did not 'choose' the United States against France, but tried to balance between them. In many ways, that is what British governments have attempted ever since.*

NOTES

1. Quoted in Jean-Louis Crémieux-Brilhac, *La France Libre: De l'appel du 18 juin à la Libération* (Paris, 1996), p. 817.
2. Public Record Office, Kew (PRO), FO 954/9A, record of conversation, 4 June 1944.
3. P.M.H. Bell, *A Certain Eventuality: Britain and the Fall of France* (Farnborough, 1974), pp. 49–50; for the report itself, PRO, CAB 66/7, WP(40)168, 25 May 1940.
4. Quoted in Martin Gilbert, *Road to Victory: Winston S. Churchill, 1941–1945* (London, 1986), pp.277–8.
5. PRO, PREM 3/121/1, memorandum by Churchill, 12 June 1943.
6. Gilbert, *Road to Victory*, p.646. The remark was addressed to Nairn, the British Consul at Marrakesh, who had acted as interpreter – often a thankless task in conversations between Churchill and de Gaulle.
7. Quoted in Gilbert, *Road to Victory*, p.277.
8. Quoted in Bell, *A Certain Eventuality*, p.192.
9. John Colville, *The Fringes of Power: Downing Street Diaries,*

1939–1955 (London, 1985), p.563; Colville's diary for 23 Feb. 1945.

10. Churchill to Halifax, 11 Feb. 1943, PRO, FO 954/8B. The Foreign Office prepared a memorandum, dated 17 March 1943, listing American statements about restoring the French Empire – FO 371/36036, Z1762/77/17.

11. John Barnes and David Nicholson, eds., *The Empire at Bay: The Leo Amery Diaries, 1929–1945* (London, 1988), p.882, entry for 15 April 1943.

12. Warren F. Kimball, ed., *Churchill and Roosevelt: The Complete Correspondence* (London, 1984), vol.I, p.12.

13. For an outline of the whole bombing question, see John Ehrman, *Grand Strategy*, vol. V, *August 1943–September 1944* (London, 1956), pp.298–304. For the discussions in the War Cabinet and Defence Committee, see PRO, CAB 65/46, WM(44) 43rd, 57th, and 61st Conclusions, Confidential Annexes, and CAB 66/6, Defence Committee Meetings, 5, 13, 19, 26 April, 3 May 1944. Churchill to Roosevelt, 7 May 1944, and Roosevelt to Churchill, 11 May, Kimball, vol.III, pp.122–3, 127. For Churchill's continuing anxiety, and his note to Tedder, Gilbert, *Road to Victory*, p.784. It is worth adding that General Koenig, commander of the *Forces Françaises de l'Intérieur*, when consulted on the issue by one of Eisenhower's senior staff officers, said robustly that 'This is war, and it must be expected that people will be killed. We would take twice the anticipated loss to be rid of the Germans'. See Alfred D. Chandler, ed., *The Papers of Dwight D. Eisenhower: The War Years*, vol.III (London, 1970), p.1810, n.3.

14. PRO, PREM 3/271/9, Churchill to Ismay, 6 July 1944.

15. Churchill to Roosevelt, 28 June 1944, and Roosevelt to Churchill, 29 June, Kimball, vol.III, pp.214–9, 221–3.

16. *Ibid.*, pp.225–6, draft not sent, 30 June 1944; pp.227–9, Churchill to Roosevelt, 1 July 1944.

17. PRO, PREM 3/271/9, Churchill to Ismay, 6 July 1944. Churchill omitted the last two sentences when he published this note in his memoirs – see Winston S. Churchill, *The Second World War*, vol.VI, *Triumph and Tragedy* (London, 1954), pp.595–6.

18. The general debate on ANVIL/DRAGOON may be followed in Ehrman, *Grand Strategy*, vol. V, pp.225–258. Much of the contemporary discussion on the British side may be found in PRO, PREM 3/342/1–11.

19. PRO, PREM 3/343 for the weekly figures of cargo landed at Marseilles, and Churchill to Ismay, 18 Dec. 1944.

20. Arthur Bryant, *Triumph in the West* (London, 1959), p. 168, quoting from Brooke's 'Notes on My Life'.

21. Churchill to Roosevelt, 22 April 1944; Roosevelt to Churchill, 23 April, Kimball, vol. III, pp.108–9.

22. Eden, diary 6 June 1944, quoted in David Dutton, *Anthony Eden: A Life and Reputation* (London, 1997), p.170.
23. PRO, FO 371/41958, Z4439/1555/17, Washington Embassy to FO, Weekly Political Summary, 9 July 1944; Z4876/1555/17, Campbell to Cadogan, 10 July 1944. Cf. H.G. Nicholas, ed., *Washington Despatches, 1941–1945: Weekly Political Reports from the British Embassy* (London, 1981)p.384.
24. PRO FO 371/41958, Z4453/1555/17 for Roosevelt's statement and various FO minutes; John Harvey, ed., *The War Diaries of Oliver Harvey* (London, 1978), p.347.
25. E.L. Woodward, *British Foreign Policy in the Second World War*, vol.III (London, 1971), pp.82–85; Churchill to Roosevelt, 23 Oct. 1944, Roosevelt to Churchill, 24 Oct., Kimball, vol.III, pp.367, 369. The comment about 'bowling a fast one' is in *War Diaries of Oliver Harvey*, p.364, n.3.
26. *War Diaries of Oliver Harvey*, p.364.
27. *Complete War Memoirs of General de Gaulle*, English translation by Charles Howard (New York, 1984), p.728.

✻ ✻ ✻

✻ I am most grateful to David Dutton, who read this paper in draft and made invaluable comments upon it.

GREAT BRITAIN AND DOUGLAS MacARTHUR: War and Peace in the Pacific and Asia, 1941–1951

PETER LOWE

The subject of British attitudes towards General Douglas MacArthur and vice versa is one of deep contradiction and ambivalence. MacArthur was of Scottish descent, an aspect he liked to recall at appropriate moments when speaking to British visitors. He was, however, an all-American hero and practitioner.[1] Born in 1880, the son of an outstanding general, MacArthur's entire career was spent in military service: his experience extended from the immediate aftermath of the Indian wars in the United States to war against vast Chinese armies in Korea in 1950–1. MacArthur served in France in 1917–18 and held top military posts in the United States, including Chief of Staff, in the first half of the 1930s. When he retired from the army, he went to the Philippines to direct defence preparations. This deepened an interest in Asia which he acquired as a young man, largely through his father's role in the Philippines, following American annexation in 1898. He visited Japan with his father in 1905 and this stimulated his fascination with a militaristic society experiencing rapid modernization.[2] MacArthur had wide interests and he liked to range over past conflicts in the course of which he had an uncanny talent for comparing a past military leader, perhaps Julius Caesar or Napoleon, with Douglas MacArthur. He was a man of great ability, flawed by arrogance and vanity. He was a 'political general'.[3] He cultivated friendships with certain politicians and used these to apply pressure to advance his personal military objectives. In American politics he supported the Republican party. He disliked Franklin D. Roosevelt – the feeling was mutual – and thought the New Deal was dangerously interventionist and socialistic. He was attracted by the authority and prestige of the presidency.[4] He was spoken of as a possible presidential candidate in three elections – in 1944, 1948 and 1952.

Before the Pacific war British politicians and generals had little to do with MacArthur. Of course, he met British officers while serving in Europe in 1917–18, but thereafter he was preoccupied with his career in the United States. The Pacific war brought together MacArthur, the British Commonwealth and the British Empire in a marriage of convenience created by desperation resulting from the Japanese onslaught.[5] In March 1942 MacArthur left the Philippines by submarine and went to Australia to rebuild allied forces for counter-attacking Japan. He was greeted as a hero in an Australia traumatized by the swift expansion of the Japanese empire. The Labor Party was in office, led by John Curtin, with Herbert Evatt as Minister of External Affairs. Curtin and Evatt were highly critical of Britain for failing to provide adequate defence in the Pacific. MacArthur seemed to be the manifestation of the Almighty's response to Australian prayers. Circumstances compelled MacArthur to work closely with Australia.[6] The strategic situation was bad in 1942. The priority for the allies lay in defeating Nazi Germany and Fascist Italy. Despite this, the Pacific theatre was given priority in allocation of resources in 1942. MacArthur encouraged Australian leaders to press the case for more resources to be sent to the Pacific while he encouraged Republican contacts in Washington to act similarly. Roosevelt was very careful in his dealings with MacArthur, not least because the latter's name was mentioned as a possibility for the Republican ticket in 1944. In public MacArthur professed admiration for Roosevelt just as he proclaimed his respect for Australia. In private his views were critical, as revealed by Christopher Thorne.

The exigencies of the world crisis in 1941–3 were such that Britain was in no position to pursue an active policy in the Pacific. Britain's main contribution in Asia was to hold the borders of India and to plan, in conjunction with the United States and China, for a new offensive in Burma. Churchill was deeply shaken by the huge Japanese successes in 1941–2.[7] Curtin's criticism of Britain and his emphasis on achieving a closer relationship with the United States grated. Churchill wanted Britain to resume an active role in the Pacific as soon as practicable. In 1943 Australian leaders modified their previously uncritical attitude towards the Americans, as they appreciated the downside of too big an increase in American power, not least in the economic sphere.[8] MacArthur did not favour an increase in British involvement. He dealt with three British liaison officers between 1942 and 1945. The first was Colonel Gerald Wilkinson who had been despatched during the Philippines campaign. Apparently MacArthur liked him but he was suspicious of Wilkinson's communicating with Churchill via MI6.[9] MacArthur did not want any intelligence organizations involved unless he controlled them: this applied equally to American intelligence. MacArthur would not allow Wilkinson to join his staff because of his intelligence links.[10] Wilkinson wrote of MacArthur that he 'is shrewd, selfish, proud, remote, highly strung and vastly vain. He has imagination, self-confidence, physical courage and charm, but no humour about himself, no regard for truth, and is unaware of these defects. He mistakes his emotions and ambitions for principles.'[11]

MacArthur accepted the appointment of a more senior British officer, Lt. General Sir Herbert Lumsden, but regarded him suspiciously and referred darkly to his cronies that Lumsden was 'Churchill's spy'.[12] In discussions with Lumsden, MacArthur professed a firm belief in the importance of Britain – 'It always had been and was his firm wish to see a strong British Empire and to see the best of relations between the peoples of America and the British Empire.'[13] He stated that British forces should return to parts of the empire liberated from Japanese occupation. Churchill was most anxious that a British naval presence should return to parts of the empire liberated from Japanese occupation.[14] In 1944 it was feasible for this to occur. Roosevelt accepted Churchill's proposal to send a British fleet under Admiral Sir James Somerville. MacArthur welcomed the presence of the Royal Navy but this may not have been unconnected with the lack of enthusiasm for the arrival of the Royal Navy shown by Admiral Ernest J. King of the American navy.

Lt. General Sir Charles Gairdner was sent by the Prime Minister to liaise with MacArthur in the summer of 1945. Gairdner was positive in his assessment of MacArthur's desire to co-operate with Britain, writing in May 1945: 'In my opinion MacArthur stands head and shoulders above any other officer I have met here, in the breadth of his views, in the lucidity of his argument and in the unerring way he puts his finger on the essentials of a problem. . . . He is a sincere friend of the British Commonwealth. I think that it would pay a very good dividend to back him whenever it is possible without imperilling paramount interest.'[15]

Alternative sources demonstrate MacArthur's capacity for adjustment, according to his audience. Robert Sherwood visited him in March 1945, on a mission from Washington, and told Roosevelt that he 'was shocked by the inaccuracy of the information held by General MacArthur and his immediate entourage about the formulation of high policy in Washington. There are unmistakable evidences of an acute persecution complex at work. To hear some of the staff officers talk, one would think that the War Department, the State Department, the Joint Chiefs of Staff – and, possibly, even the White House itself – are under the domination of Communists and the British Imperialists.'[16] British leaders respected MacArthur's skill in directing operations. Field Marshal Sir Alan Brooke, Chief of the Imperial General Staff, held that MacArthur was the 'greatest general and best strategist that the war produced.'[17] Admiral Lord Louis Mountbatten, head of South-East Asia Command, wrote of the fascination of hearing MacArthur range broadly over strategy and remarked on the appreciable charm MacArthur could deploy.

On 2 September 1945 MacArthur presided over the formal ceremony to accept the surrender of Japan, held on the USS *Missouri*. MacArthur now embarked on the new challenging task of directing the allied occupation of Japan. President Harry S. Truman, who had succeeded Roosevelt in April 1945, appointed MacArthur to the post of Supreme Commander Allied Powers (SCAP). Truman's opinion of MacArthur was similar to that of Roosevelt, but he felt that MacArthur had to be appointed to head the occupation.[18] He was highly charismatic, possessed enormous experience and was widely respected. In addition, it would keep MacArthur out of the United States. However, he was not noted for expertise in dealing with major political-administrative matters. The gamble in appointing him succeeded. MacArthur became a man with a mission and this zeal communicated itself to others within the SCAP administration.[19] MacArthur was determined to eradicate militarism, change the constitution and secure a full democracy with a constitutional monarchy, to tame the excesses of Japanese capitalism, encourage trade unions up to a point, emancipate women and reform education. MacArthur, improbably when viewed in the American domestic context, became a deeply committed advocate of reform. He was criticized by some American businessmen and officials for going too far and sponsoring radicalism of a destabilizing character.[20] Mistakes were made and the original programme of sweeping reform was too ambitious, but in the main the occupation was successful. It assumed a more conservative nature from 1947–8, when the 'reverse course' took effect, and liberal reform was diminished and greater intervention occurred from Washington. The emphasis was now placed on incorporating Japan fully into the western scheme of stability and defence against communism.

Britain's position with reference to the occupation was ambiguous.[21] Full agreement was expressed with the aim of changing Japan into a peaceful society, although doubts were voiced as to the feasibility of certain aspects of American policy. In 1945 British politicians and civil servants assumed that the *allied* occupation would include significant British participation. Historically, Britain had played a prominent part in East Asian affairs since the opening-up of China in the 1830s. The Anglo-Japanese alliance (1902–23) constituted a fundamental feature of the foreign policies of Britain and Japan in the first quarter of the twentieth century. While the new Labour government of Clement Attlee was determined to implement a drastic reform programme at home, it had no intention of abandoning British interests in East Asia. Ernest Bevin, the Foreign Secretary, conveyed tenacity and dedication in restoring Britain's position worldwide.[22] To their chagrin the British discovered in 1945–6 that their contribution to the functioning of the occupation would be relegated to the periphery. The Truman administration regarded Japan as lying squarely within the American sphere of interest and there was no wish for active British participation. Roger Buckley has written that 'General MacArthur was neither an Anglophobe nor an Anglophile'.[23] This is correct. MacArthur was not critical of Britain, as were many American army officers who believed that British policy was unduly influenced by sordid colonial ambitions. Basically, MacArthur wanted the freedom to direct the occupation with minimal interference from any government, including the American government. In essence he enjoyed this freedom in the first phase of the occupation.

The principal British diplomatic representative in Japan, heading the British liaison mission, was Sir Alvary Gascoigne.[24] Gascoigne served for most of the occupation (1946–51). He proved an ideal appointment in terms of securing MacArthur's respect and goodwill. This was probably assisted by Gascoigne's military background. He had served in the 6th Dragoons and Coldstream Guards during the Great War and had a distinguished record. Then he joined the

Foreign Office, serving in Japan, Tangier and Hungary, before returning to Japan in July 1946. Gascoigne showed shrewdness and good judgement in his dealings with MacArthur. The vital ingredient was that Gascoigne combined being a patient listener – an indispensable quality for anyone wishing to attain a positive relationship with MacArthur – with the ability to state British views clearly and effectively. MacArthur met Gascoigne frequently and this would not have occurred had the General not deemed their meetings to be worthwhile and cordial. In addition, MacArthur sometimes needed British support in modifying initiatives coming from Washington.

Early in 1948 Gascoigne reported developing friction between MacArthur and Washington, plus speculation that MacArthur might declare his candidacy for the Republican presidential nomination.[26] MacArthur's past encouragement for trade unions, modified in 1946–7, and his enthusiasm for breaking up the *zaibatsu* (large family-dominated financial combines) alienated those American businessmen supporting the 'Japan Lobby', that is those in Washington and New York wishing to see an end to reform in Japan and the building of a new relationship as the Cold War tightened its icy grip. MacArthur told Gascoigne that big business in the United States was endeavouring to undermine him. British officials reacted by supporting MacArthur. He was considered to be performing well and no one possessing the same qualities could be discerned. Esler Dening, a prominent official, observed that 'the prospect of indefinite American occupation without General MacArthur hardly bears contemplation'.[27] On constitutional matters the British supported MacArthur's reforms but regretted that he had prevented a British national from acting as tutor to Crown Prince Akihito.[28] British officials were sceptical as to the degree of genuine change in Japan and feared that conservative nationalism would revive within a decade of the end of the occupation. This could promote anti-democratic forces in the country. Communism was vocal and enjoyed support in some trade unions and among left-wing intellectuals, but the nature of Japanese society indicated that the country was more likely to move right than left.

On occasions the discussions between MacArthur and Gascoigne were less amicable. This applied to British protests over the National Public Service Law in August–September 1948. Gascoigne reported: 'My interview with the Supreme Commander was the most painful one which I have yet had with him. . . . The mere mention by me of

National Public Service draft legislation and of our opinion thereon caused him to shout at me without stopping for one and three-quarter hours.'[29] MacArthur was annoyed because British criticism coincided with Russian censure and the Truman administration was now intervening. Gascoigne assured him that Britain had no intention of co-operating with the Soviet Union. One murky area, harder for the British to penetrate, concerned covert rearmament. MacArthur implemented demilitarization in Japan after 1945. The famous Article 9 of the new constitution, adopted in 1946, forbade the maintenance of armed forces. MacArthur liked to speak of Japan becoming the 'Switzerland' of East Asia and the Pacific. However, General Charles Willoughby, head of G-2 (intelligence) within the occupation, worked actively to recruit former army and navy officers.[30] The military adviser to the British mission, Brigadier A.K. Ferguson, reported that different sections of SCAP diverged over the defence of Japan.[31] Air bases were strengthened, notably in extending runways to accommodate B-36 bombers. Storage facilities for ammunition were improved. Underground oil storage facilities were being restored. Ferguson commented that these developments were defensive, but the Soviet Union could construe them as aggressive. Willoughby went further in preparing for a future military role for Japan as the Chinese Communists triumphed in the civil war in 1949. He permitted Japanese army officers to go to Taiwan to assist Chiang Kai-shek's régime defend the island against invasion.[32] Willoughby's political sympathies were markedly right wing and racist. It is likely that they went further than MacArthur wanted in fostering covert rearmament. Once the Korean War began in June 1950 policy changed with the creation of the National Police Reserve and with covert assistance rendered to United Nations forces by Japanese naval units.

In 1949–50 Gascoigne and officials in London criticized American policy for becoming too liberal or soft. The United States was influenced by the growth of the Cold War and it was realized that the future compliance of Japan to American strategy must be secured. Gascoigne felt that the United States was moving too rapidly towards an excessively generous approach. Part of the problem was that the occupation had continued for too long. Britain argued for an early peace treaty in 1947.[33] This was an area where MacArthur and the British were in agreement. MacArthur told Washington that lengthy military occupations were undesirable and that this was his

57

deduction from studying history. The Truman administration did not regard the conclusion of a peace treaty as a priority down to 1950, largely because of disagreements between the State Department and the Pentagon: the former was inclined towards an early treaty but the latter was not. The joint chiefs of staff argued that, given global uncertainties, it was important that American bases were retained in Japan without the difficulties that might occur when Japan regained sovereignty. Concluding a viable, balanced treaty was a complex task.[34] Britain, Australia and New Zealand did not wish to encourage faster economic growth and a possible revival of militarism. Australia and New Zealand required an American guarantee of their defence as the price they would insist on for acquiescing in a liberal peace treaty. Japan would be punished in the treaty through forfeiting formally its colonial empire. The ultimate treaty would require ratification by the American Senate, so that it had to be acceptable to the large majority of senators, which would mean that issues relating to China would have to be handled skilfully. MacArthur was not deeply involved with the treaty. Truman appointed the Republican politician, John Foster Dulles, to handle negotiations: Dulles discharged this task most capably. By then MacArthur was deeply involved in dealing with the Korean War and by the time the peace treaty was signed, in September 1951, MacArthur had involuntarily departed from East Asia following his final row with Truman. British relations with MacArthur in Japan were, on the whole, positive. Attlee, Bevin and the Foreign Office thought MacArthur directed the occupation efficiently and successfully. The British did think MacArthur had become too lenient in the last two years of his service in Tokyo, but here they revealed their own negative approach to Japanese recovery. As regards the future of Japan, MacArthur's guarded optimism was a more accurate guide than Britain's moderate pessimism.

On 25 June 1950 North Korea launched an offensive against South Korea. The situation in the Korean peninsula had been chronically unstable since the collapse of Japanese rule in August 1945. The United States and the Soviet Union agreed to divide Korea at the 38th parallel, supposedly a temporary measure pending unification at a future date. American-Soviet relations deteriorated rapidly in 1946–7 and two independent states emerged in 1948, the Republic of Korea (South Korea) and the Democratic People's Republic of Korea (North Korea), sponsored respectively by the United States and Russia. The régimes were led by Syngman Rhee and Kim Il Sung.

Each was a passionate nationalist, dedicated to uniting Korea on a basis of vehement anti-communism or idiosyncratic Korean socialism. North Korea was stronger militarily and economically: Kim Il Sung convinced Stalin that the best solution would be for the North to conquer the South. Kim did not believe that the United States would intervene, since American policy had vacillated and the United States had not given a definite undertaking of armed support to the South in the event of conflict occurring. Kim and Stalin committed a major blunder. President Truman and Secretary of State Acheson decided that it was imperative to prevent North Korea from liquidating the South. The United Nations Security Council condemned North Korea and a United Nations Command (UNC) was created in order to co-ordinate the armed response of the UN, under American leadership.[35] Douglas MacArthur was appointed, at the age of seventy, to command American forces and to lead the UNC, in addition to his existing responsibilities in Japan. Truman's reasoning for appointing MacArthur was much as it had been when appointing him to Japan in 1945: he was the obvious candidate with the greatest prestige. To this it has to be added that Truman wished to avoid possible criticism from right-wing Republicans, and one way of deflecting such carping was to have UN operations directed by a right-wing Republican. In favour of the appointment was that MacArthur possessed enormous experience of war and of high command. Against it was his age, his vanity and a developing rigidity in his thinking. Appointing a right-wing Republican to head the UNC was a double-edged weapon. The reverse side from Truman's view-point was that MacArthur would use the post to strengthen his own presidential ambition. It would be an exciting experiment for each man.

Britain supported the United States in maintaining that communist aggression in Korea must be opposed. However, the Attlee cabinet saw Europe as the priority and feared that American attention might be diverted to Asia; it was decided, rather reluctantly, to dispatch British troops to Korea in the second half of July 1950 to strengthen Anglo-American relations and to give substance to the commitment of the UN in Korea.[36] MacArthur's appointment was accepted as inevitable, but early on doubts grew in Britain regarding MacArthur's inclination to act independently. MacArthur visited Taiwan on 31 July and 1 August 1950 and this caused concern because it was suspected that MacArthur would do all he could to obtain a larger

American commitment to assisting Chiang Kai-shek's régime. Then MacArthur's belligerent message to the Veterans of Foreign Wars later in August, which he was compelled to withdraw on Truman's orders, accentuated suspicions. The first major problem involved crossing the 38th parallel, following the brilliantly executed landing of UNC forces at Inchon in mid-September, MacArthur's last great strategic success. The United States believed that it was necessary to move north of the 38th parallel so as to inflict decisive defeat on North Korea. MacArthur argued vehemently in favour of the advance and maintained that the only way to deal with Kim Il Sung's régime was to expel it from Korea and unify the country under Syngman Rhee's leadership. The Foreign Office accepted the reasons for proceeding north of the 38th parallel, but not for necessarily bolstering Rhee, and the Attlee cabinet agreed to co-sponsor a resolution in the UN General Assembly on 7 October 1950, authorizing the advance of UNC forces.[37]

The British chiefs of staff did not accept the reasons for going north and expressed vigorous and growing criticism. The three men concerned were Field Marshal Sir William Slim, Admiral of the Fleet Lord Fraser of North Cape and Marshal of the Royal Air Force Sir John Slessor. Each was a man of outstanding ability; the most influential in the context of Korea was Slessor. He emphasized the serious dangers in trying to occupy the whole of Korea. Slessor did not regard it as necessary and thought UNC troops should have halted at, or slightly above, the 38th parallel. The biggest danger was that China might decide to intervene and such a development would transform the Korean conflict into one that was far more dangerous. Slessor and his colleagues did not wish to see resources committed, on an increasing scale, to war in Korea, which could escalate into full-scale conflict with China.[38] Chou En-lai, the most significant Chinese leader after Mao Tse-tung, sent warnings through the Indian ambassador in Peking to the effect that China would intervene if MacArthur's forces continued to advance north. Stalin urged Mao to act in order to save Kim's régime and promised support but not direct Soviet intervention. Mao inclined in any case towards intervention, regarding American policy as denoting aggression towards China. Mao believed fervently that the West must learn that China could not, as in the past, be ignored or treated with contempt.[39]

MacArthur was bellicose and complacent in his assessment of China. Gascoigne summarized MacArthur's views on 3 October as follows:

In any case MacArthur claimed he had plenty of troops to deal adequately with the Chinese and even with the Russians if they should prove so foolish as to enter the arena at this stage. The Chinese, he said, had neither troops nor equipment nor air power to take him on. . . .

If the Chinese came in, MacArthur would immediately unleash his air forces against towns in Manchuria and North China including Peking.[40]

MacArthur discounted the contingency of Chinese intervention when he met Truman for a conference at Wake Island in the western Pacific two weeks later.

The egregious errors made in assessing China's intentions and capacity for inflicting grave military reverses on the UNC naturally focus in part on intelligence and why it proved deficient. MacArthur relied heavily on his veteran intelligence chief, Willoughby. He distrusted the CIA, essentially because it was controlled by Washington and he regarded all those working in the Washington bureaucracy with suspicion. Willoughby thought of the Chinese as inferior racially and erred seriously in estimating the numbers of Chinese who entered Korea in the second half of October.[41] MacArthur thought they numbered at most 90,000, whereas the real figure was approximately 250,000. The British Chiefs of Staff had earlier dispatched Air Vice-Marshal Cecil Bouchier as liaison representative, attached to MacArthur's headquarters in Tokyo. Bouchier worked hard and established positive relations with MacArthur's staff, although he did not see MacArthur himself with any frequency. Bouchier was helpful in providing information, but he tended to echo rather uncritically the information he received.[42] The Chiefs of Staff urged the merits of creating a buffer zone. The Foreign Office agreed and Bevin endeavoured to convince the Truman administration to change policy. Truman stated at a press conference in mid-November that he did not want conflict with China. MacArthur was strongly opposed to a buffer zone and castigated the British for again resorting to the kind of appeasement they had followed at Munich in 1938.[43] MacArthur remained confident that his forces could complete the task of expelling the North Koreans and those Chinese troops present in Korea. In the last week of November 1950 MacArthur discovered his mistake as huge numbers of Chinese troops launched a ferocious onslaught on the UNC and South Korean forces. On 28 November he reported gloomily to Washington: 'All hope of localization of the Korean conflict to enemy forces composed of North Korean troops with alien token elements can now be completely abandoned. The Chinese military forces are committed in North Korea in great and ever increasing strength . . . We face an entirely new war.'[44]

The Korean conflict now moved into its most dangerous and unpredictable stage. The United States might decide to use atomic weapons against China, perhaps concluding that it would be preferable to evacuate Korea. All-out war between the United States and China could occur and this might escalate into a third world war. However, MacArthur implemented the longest military retreat in American history and at a speed which puzzled the British Chiefs of Staff. In late December and the first half of January 1951 it proved impossible to obtain accurate information on MacArthur's intentions. On 9 January Field Marshal Slim told his colleagues:

> It appeared to him to be possible that General MacArthur now intended to withdraw from Korea and, having done so, to attack China by sea and air, making use of Chinese Nationalists to attack China on land. According to the latest United States estimates, the disparity between China and the United Nations forces in Korea was comparatively small and with the United Nations' overwhelming superiority of fire power and complete air supremacy it should by normal military standards be perfectly possible to hold a bridgehead. It seemed, however, that the United States troops had no longer the will to fight and were so intent on evacuation that even if General MacArthur were now definitely ordered to hold a bridgehead it seemed doubtful whether he would, in fact, be able to do so.[45]

The cabinet decided to send Slessor to Washington in the middle of January for candid discussions with the American joint chiefs. Slessor handled his important mission with courage and conviction. Commonwealth prime ministers had met in London earlier in January and Slessor was able to emphasize their deep anxiety. The principal causes for alarm were that the United States might involve the UN in full-scale war with China and that MacArthur's extraordinarily negative military campaign was difficult to fathom. Slessor spoke bluntly on the essence of the problem with MacArthur, as perceived by British leaders and public opinion: 'There was also a feeling in England that General MacArthur, whom we all recognized as being a great soldier, was nevertheless inclined to be too political and too independent of Washington control.'[46] General Omar Bradley, chairman of the joint chiefs, defended MacArthur but recognized that strains in Anglo-American relations were appreciable. MacArthur was irate at criticism of his command published in the British press. General Courtney Whitney, a leading member of MacArthur's 'court', told Bouchier on 12 January that British journalists were ignorant or pro-communist. MacArthur regarded British criticism as an attack on his integrity; Anglo-American relations could suffer in consequence. Whitney thought that MacArthur might be mollified by the issuing of a formal statement in London confirming confidence in him. This report was considered by the British chiefs and the Foreign Office who decided that silence was the best policy.[47]

The desperate military situation began to improve in the second half of January as the new head of the Eighth Army, General Ridgway, took steps to strengthen morale and to instil determination to resist into his troops. MacArthur's authority was undermined seriously by the events of the preceding two months, but his capacity for generating controversy showed no sign of diminishing. He was embittered by his experiences and by the reluctance of the Truman administration to respond more strongly to Chinese intervention. Truman and Acheson secured passage of a resolution in the UN General Assembly on 1 February, condemning China formally for aggression and establishing arrangements for enforcing economic sanctions against China. Britain supported the resolution unenthusiastically because of difficulties that would arise involving Hong Kong and Britain's recognition of the communist government in China. (Britain extended recognition in January 1950, but the United States persisted in recognizing Chiang Kai-shek's régime.)[48] MacArthur wanted to see far more drastic measures enforced, including bombing in Manchuria and use of atomic weapons in Korea and against China. The Foreign Office and the Chiefs of Staff aimed, between January and April 1951, to secure greater control over MacArthur through making more direct representations in Washington. In essence the approach adopted was to emphasize the undesirability of having two American leaders expressing diverging opinions in a delicate and dangerous situation. The aims and purposes of American policy required careful and precise definition. This was a constitutional dilemma and could only be clarified by the President.

Matters came to a head in March and April. Once the UNC succeeded in stabilizing the military position, following a counterattack, so the danger of UNC forces being expelled from Korea was avoided. Attention focused on the next step. Truman and Acheson wished to open talks with the enemy so as to explore the possibility of obtaining an armistice. MacArthur destroyed this intended initiative by issuing his own public statement, professing willingness to meet the enemy commander-in-chief, but reiterating faith in military success.[49] Discontent with MacArthur grew in Britain, in all parties and in the media. The new Foreign Secretary, Herbert Morrison, wished to make a mark swiftly so as to enhance his appeal within the Labour party as a possible successor to Attlee. General agreement existed within the government that MacArthur's power must be curbed. Pierson Dixon of the Foreign Office recommended that MacArthur should be given explicit instructions to fulfil the aims of the UN 'and so limit his military plans and if possible restrict his public trespassing into the realms of policy'.[50] Morrison urged Truman to make a firm statement. Sir Oliver Franks, the Ambassador in Washington, told Dean Rusk of the State Department that Whitehall and Westminster were preoccupied with 'MacArthuritis'.[51]

The final statements of defiance from MacArthur occurred on 5 April. The Republican minority leader in the House of Representatives, Joseph W. Martin, revealed the texts of letters exchanged with MacArthur in March.[52] MacArthur criticized his own government's policy for weakness and excessive concentration on Europe to the detriment of Asia. Also on 5 April the London *Daily Telegraph* published a remarkably outspoken interview with the General in which he blamed politicians for not properly defining aims in Korea.[53] The latter were craven and reluctant to deal robustly with China. What was needed was a tough combination of a stringent economic blockade of China and precision bombing to destroy railways. MacArthur lavished praise on the participation of British and Commonwealth forces. Morrison was preparing renewed representations in Washington when the news arrived that President Truman had removed General of the Army Douglas MacArthur from all offices held, on the ground that he was not in agreement with the policies of the United States government.

This momentous decision was seen as the best outcome by most in Britain – politicians, civil servants, defence chiefs and public opinion. Balanced statements were made in the House of Commons by

Herbert Morrison and Winston Churchill. They underlined the importance of adhering to established constitutional procedures while regretting that MacArthur's distinguished career should end in this way. Morrison stated: 'He was a great servant of the Allies during the war in the Pacific and he has proved himself a brilliant soldier. He has displayed qualities of the highest order in his conduct of the occupation in Japan. These are achievements which will be remembered long after the immediate controversy has been forgotten.'[54]

While there was widespread approval of Truman's bold action, there was apprehension that MacArthur could stimulate difficulty for Britain on his return to the United States. Republican politicians seized on the controversy to assail Truman and Acheson while depicting MacArthur as the personification of heroic American values. A joint Senate hearing was scheduled for May 1951 to investigate the reasons for his removal.[55] MacArthur and his supporters attacked Britain for encouraging the allegedly defeatist inclinations of the Truman administration while furthering its own economic interests through trading with China via Hong Kong. However, interest in the Senate hearings fell after MacArthur gave evidence at the start. While there was much respect and affection for MacArthur among the American people, there was no strong support for him becoming the Republican presidential candidate in 1952. The General gradually subsided as a public figure, thus fulfilling reluctantly his dramatically delivered address to Congress when he said that he was an old soldier who would 'fade away'.[56]

Therefore, the British experience in dealing with MacArthur was variable. He was perceived as an outstanding commander who had restored allied morale in the Pacific theatre. The firm consensus was that he had performed most ably in directing the occupation of Japan; the latter proved more successful than might have been anticipated, notwithstanding some British reservations regarding a future revival of nationalism in Japan. Where MacArthur and Britain diverged irrevocably was over the Korean War. There was a real fear that MacArthur could involve the UN in all-out war against China, which Britain held must be avoided. Of course, MacArthur was only part of the considerable and continuing friction within the Anglo-American relationship during the Korean conflict. Britain was a declining power while American might was growing. MacArthur's significance for Britain was that he accentuated British anxiety in that he symbolized the desire of right-wing American politicians and

much of American public opinion to take on 'Red China' and eliminate this threat. The reasoning was simplistic and highly dangerous.
MacArthur's dismissal did not eradicate this contingency but it
rendered it less likely.

NOTES

1. The best and most comprehensive biography of MacArthur is by D.
Clayton James, *The Years of MacArthur* 3 vols. (Boston: Houghton Mifflin,
1970–85). See also Michael Schaller, *Douglas MacArthur: the Far Eastern
General* (Oxford University Press, 1989) for a readable, concise account.
Despite a number of defects contained therein, it is worth consulting
MacArthur's *Reminiscences*, paperback edition (Greenwich, Conn: Fawcett
Publications, 1964). The latter was completed when MacArthur was elderly
and in declining health. It is rather short and includes some errors. It is,
however, revealing on the personality, particularly in MacArthur's citation
in footnotes of numerous tributes he received from distinguished world
leaders and heads of state.
2. MacArthur, *Reminiscences*, pp.37–40.
3. Michael Schaller, 'General Douglas MacArthur and the Politics of the
Pacific War', in Günter Bischof and Robert L. Dupont (eds), *The Pacific
War Revisited* (Baton Rouge and London: Louisiana State University Press,
1997), pp. 17–40.
4. See Clayton James, *Years of MacArthur* II, pp. 403–40, for a discussion
of MacArthur's involvement in the Republican party's selection of a presidential candidate in 1944.
5. For an admirable examination of Anglo-American relations during the
war in Asia and the Pacific, see Christopher Thorne, *Allies of a Kind: the
United States, Britain and the War against Japan, 1941–1945* (London:
Hamish Hamilton, 1978).
6. Thorne, 'MacArthur, Australia and the British', *Australian Outlook*
(April and August 1975).
7. See Peter Lowe, 'Winston Churchill and Japan, 1914–1942' in J.W.M.
Chapman (ed.), *Proceedings of the British Association for Japanese Studies*
vol. VI, part 1 (Sheffield: Centre for Japanese Studies, 1981), pp.39–47,
236–7. See also Ong Chit Chung, *Operation Matador: Britain's War Plans
against the Japanese, 1918–1941* (Singapore: Times Academic Press, 1997).
8. Thorne, *Allies of a Kind*, pp.364–5, 479–80.

9. Ibid, p.261.
10. Ibid.
11. Cited ibid, p.370, footnote.
12. Ibid, p.367.
13. Ibid, pp.483–4.
14. Ibid, p.649.
15. Ibid, pp.649–50.
16. Clayton James, *Years of MacArthur*, II, p.717.
17. Thorne, *Allies of a Kind*, p.649, footnote.
18. Roger Buckley, 'A Particularly Vital Issue? Harry Truman and Japan, 1945–1952', in T.G. Fraser and Peter Lowe (eds.), *Conflict and Amity in East Asia: Essays in Honour of Ian Nish* (London: Macmillan, 1992), pp.110–24.
19. The sense of mission is captured to some extent in the relevant chapter of MacArthur's *Reminiscences*, pp.308–71, although it is over-concise and ignores the final years of the occupation.
20. H.B. Schonberger, *Aftermath of War: Americans and the Remaking of Japan, 1945–1952*, (London: Kent State University Press, 1989), pp.134–60, and R.B. Finn, *Winners in Peace: MacArthur, Yoshida and Postwar Japan* (Oxford: University of California Press, 1992), pp.161–2.
21. For a lucid discussion of the British approach towards the establishment of the occupation, see Roger Buckley, *Occupation Diplomacy: Britain, the United States and Japan, 1945–52* (Cambridge University Press, 1982), pp.1–105.
22. See Alan Bullock, *The Life and Times of Ernest Bevin, Foreign Secretary, 1945–1951* (London: Heinemann, 1983) for a judicious assessment of the personality and approach of Bevin.
23. Buckley, *Occupation Diplomacy*, p.32.
24. Peter Lowe, 'Sir Alvary Gascoigne in Japan, 1946–1951', in Ian Nish (ed.), *Britain and Japan: Biographical Portraits* (Folkestone: Japan Library, 1994), pp.279–94, 340–2.
25. Ibid, pp.281–2.
26. Ibid, p.282.
27. Minute by Esler Dening, 29 January 1948, FO 371/69885/1368, Public Record Office [PRO], Kew.
28. 'Trend of Events in Japan from July 1946 to February 1951,' despatch from Gascoigne to Bevin, 6 February 1951, FO 371/92521/5.
29. Tokyo to Foreign Office, 1 September 1948, FO 371/69823/1211. The National Public Service Law entailed much controversy in 1947–8 over MacArthur's determination to curtail strike action by public service employees. Protests were made by the British and Australian governments and criticism was expressed within the United States. MacArthur believed that combative trends within public sector trade unions

rendered action essential in order to curb communist influence.

30. See John Welfield, *An Empire in Eclipse: Japan in the Postwar American Alliance System* (London: Athlone Press, 1988) and Reinhard Drifte, *The Security Factor in Japan's Foreign Policy, 1945–1952* (Ripe, East Sussex: Saltire Press, 1983).

31. Report by Ferguson, 22 May 1948, FO 371/69887/662.

32. Tokyo to Foreign Office, 17 September 1949, FO 371/75770/1015 and CIA memorandum by Hillenkoetter, 21 November 1949, sanitized copy, CIA memorandum, 1949, Harry S. Truman Papers, PSF, Truman Library, Independence, Missouri.

33. Buckley, *Occupation Diplomacy*, pp.142–58.

34. See Peter Lowe, *Containing the Cold War in East Asia: British Policies towards Japan, China and Korea, 1948–53* (Manchester University Press, 1997), pp.28–79.

35. For the antecedents of the Korean conflict, see Peter Lowe, *The Origins of the Korean War*, second edition (London: Longman, 1997). For two valuable surveys of the Korean War as a whole, see Callum MacDonald, *Korea: the War before Vietnam* (London: Macmillan, 1986) and William Stueck, *The Korean War: an International History* (Princeton, N.J: Princeton University Press, 1995). For a stimulating, incisive analysis of Korean history, see Bruce Cumings, *Korea's Place in the Sun: a Modern History* (London: Norton, 1997).

36. Lowe, *Containing the Cold War*, pp.190–4.

37. Ibid, pp.198–204.

38. Chiefs of Staff minutes, confidential annex, 3 October 1950, COS(50)160, Defe 4/36 and memorandum by Slessor, 'Policy Following on Enemy Defeat in S. Korea. Note by the Chief of the Air Staff,' 14 September 1950, Defe 4/36, PRO, Kew.

39. For discussion of Chinese policy towards Korea, see Chen Jian, *China's Road to the Korean War: the Making of the Sino-American Confrontation* (New York: Columbia University Press, 1994) and Shu Guang Zhang, *Mao's Military Romanticism: China and the Korean War* (Lawrence, Kansas: University Press of Kansas, 1995).

40. Tokyo to Foreign Office, 3 October 1950, FO 371/84099/373/G.

41. *Foreign Relations of the United States [FRUS] 1950*, VII, pp.948–60, sanitized record of Wake Island meeting between Truman and MacArthur, 15 October 1950. For a declassified account, see memorandum of conversations, folder, October 1950, box 65, Acheson Papers, Truman Library. See also Clayton James, *Years of MacArthur*, III, pp.500–17.

42. See, for example, Bouchier to Chiefs of Staff, 27 October 1950, FO 371/84070/267/G, in which Bouchier reported that there was no evidence that Chinese troops had crossed into Korea just as the first definite confirmation of Chinese military involvement arrived.

43. *FRUS 1950*, VII, p.1109, MacArthur to joint Chiefs of Staff, 9 November 1950.

44. Ibid, pp.1237–8, MacArthur to joint Chiefs of Staff, 28 November 1950.

45. Chiefs of Staff minutes, 9 January 1951, COS 8(51)5, Defe 4/39.

46. Minutes of meeting held in the Pentagon, 15 January 1951, COS (51)34, Defe 5/27.

47. Tokyo to Foreign Office, 12 January 1951, with minute by R.H. Scott, 16 January 1951, FO 371/92721/1.

48. Lowe, *Containing the Cold War*, pp.227–9.

49. *FRUS 1951*, VII, part 1, 263–4, 265–6, for the texts of draft statement by Truman, 21 March, and MacArthur's statement, 24 March 1951. For MacArthur's approach to developments in late March and early April, see Clayton James, *Years of MacArthur* III, pp.584–99.

50. Minute by Dixon, 28 March 1951, FO 371/92812/2.

51. *FRUS 1951*, VII, part 1, pp.296–8, memorandum by Rusk, 5 April 1951.

52. Clayton James, *Years of MacArthur*, III, pp.589–90, and MacArthur, *Reminiscences*, pp.438–52.

53. *Daily Telegraph*, 5 April 1951.

54. *Parliamentary Debates, Commons*, fifth series, 486, 1028, 11 April 1951.

55. *Hearings before the Committee of Armed Services and the Committee on Foreign Relations, United States, 82nd Congress, First Session, To Conduct an Inquiry into the Military Situation in the Far East and the Facts Surrounding the Relief of General of the Army Douglas MacArthur from His Assignment in That Area*, 5 parts (Washington, D.C: Government Printing Office, 1951).

56. Clayton James, *Years of MacArthur*, III, pp.615–16, and MacArthur, *Reminiscences*, p.453–60.

HISTORICAL REVISIONISM ABOUT THE ORIGINS OF THE WARS OF THE 20TH CENTURY

JOHN LUKACS

In the Compact Edition of the *Oxford English Dictionary* the word *revisionism* does not appear. *Revision*, says the OED, is 'the action of revising or looking over again; esp. critical or careful examination or perusal with a view of correcting or improving'. The related entries do not mention historians. *Revisionist*: 'One who advocates or supports revision' appears, interestingly, in the 1860s; it refers to people wishing to revise texts of the Bible. (In 1888 *The Times* reported the meeting of a Revisionist Congress, mostly involving texts of the New Testament.) That historians have criticized certain versions of events is of course obvious. Perhaps the first, and most eminent, example of a writer whose main impulse was to correct then accepted versions of legends was Thucydides, as he stated in his Introduction to the *History of the Peloponnesian War*. Yet there are few instances when the works of chroniclers were principally aimed at disproving other chroniclers' versions. Around 1700 in France there appeared a group of scholarly priests (especially Mabillon and Tillemont) who, for the first time, applied critical (or, as some people might say, 'scientific') methods to their examination of medieval documents and other sources. These so-called Erudites or Antiquaries were perhaps the first modern academic historians; yet soon their influence faded. Instead, the professional study of history and the appearance of professional historianship arose in Germany about 200 years ago, spreading thereafter across the world. Yet the notion of historical revisionism – that is, the necessary revision or criticism not of legends or of doubtful sources but of the accepted versions of events established by professional historians – was rare.

71

Of course arguments and quarrels among academic historians were never absent. But somehow the nineteenth-century view, according to which the Cathedral of Historical Knowledge was being built brick by brick, by certified professional historians – leading, for example, to an account of the Battle of Waterloo not only acceptable to British and French and Dutch and Prussian historians but also one that would be *definite* and *final* – did not recognize, as we do, that *all* history is 'revisionism' of one kind or another. Those French historians, for instance, who were divided among themselves about the virtues and the vices of the French Revolution or of Napoleon evidently belonged to opposite ideological and idealogical camps; but few of their works were seen as 'revisionist' in the 20th century usage of that term. To what extent – or, rather, when and how – 're-visionism' is justified or unjustified is, of course, a philosophical question, to which this essay is not addressed, except perhaps indirectly, and in a few sentences at its conclusion. Its scope is restricted: (1) to revisionism among historians; (2) among German, British and American ones; (3) about the origins of the wars of the 20th century.

The term *revisionism* is of German origin. It was first applied to those German Socialists who, around 1875, chose to mitigate the doctrine of the inevitability of a proletarian revolution. This Marxist usage does not concern us. But the present use of historical 'revisionism' has a German origin too. It arose after 1919, reacting to the punitive and condemnatory treaty imposed on Germany and on its First World War allies. The wish to revise these treaties, to change the then drawn frontiers of Europe, was a powerful impulse, potentially leading to Hitler and to another war. However, the aim of German historical revisionism was not directed at injustices of geography; it was directed at injustices of the record – that is, at the unjust condemnation of Germany as having been uniquely responsible for the war, stated in the Treaty of Versailles. The Germans had every reason to combat that. As early as 1919 the new republican German government began to publish documents to prove that the guilt for the outbreak of the war in 1914 was not Germany's alone. More extensive and scholarly documentation was published in a series of volumes a few years later. Germans felt so strongly about this that in 1923 a German amateur historian, Alfred von Wegerer, began issuing a scholarly journal, *Die Kriegsschuldfrage* – the War Guilt Question.

Seventy-five years after 1914 matters concerning the origins of First World War are still occasionally debated by historians: but 'revisionism' or 'revisionist' are no longer applied to them. In any event, the origins of the First World War were more complicated than those of the Second World War. No Hitler, no Second World War – more precisely, no Second World War in 1939: this is hardly arguable. Yet argued it is, sometimes subtly, sometimes less subtly, by some German historians. In this essay, which is neither a research article nor a bibliographical essay, I cannot list most, let alone all of them: my purpose is to point out certain historiographical tendencies. I must also omit works of special pleading, as for instance those by survivors of the Third Reich's hierarchy (the memoirs of Ribbentrop's widow for one) or ideologically inspired defenders of Hitler (such as David Irving). However, during the last thirty years we may find works by serious German historians (examples: Dietrich Aigner, Oswald Hauser, Andreas Hillgruber, Ernst Nolte, Rainer Zitelmann) who, without explicitly defending Hitler, state that Polish intransigence and British hostility contributed, if not led, to the outbreak of the war in 1939. Their purpose accords with the purposes of those German historians whose writings led to the Historians' Quarrel in 1986–87: to qualify or to reduce the German responsibility for the horrors of the Second World War. That is an understandable and, in some instances, justifiable impulse; still the arguments of some of these 'conservative' or 'nationalist' historians have been, more than often, questionable. They include three, occasionally connected, theses. One is that the crimes of the Third Reich were not unique, when considering those of the Soviet Union – perhaps arguable, except when a respected German historian such as Klaus Hildebrand claims that there was no such thing as National Socialism, only Hitlerism. The other, connected argument, especially pursued by Ernst Nolte, is that Russian Bolshevism had not only preceded German National Socialism but that the latter was really a reaction to the former. The third, argued by the late Andreas Hillgruber but also by others, is that after 1939 Britain was as intent to destroy Germany as was Russia – an argument then leading to the more widespread and popular German two-war theory, according to which the war of the Third Reich against the Western Powers, especially against Britain and the United States, was perhaps avoidable and regrettable, while by fighting Soviet Russia Germany acted as a bulwark of European and Western civilization; and this Germany's Anglo-American enemies, blinded by their hatred as they were, regrettably failed to understand. In the 1990s then came another wave of revisionism – in this case involving not the origins of the war in 1939 but the German-Russian war in 1941. Depending on newly found Soviet documents whose provenance and value is often very questionable, some German and Austrian writers (Ernst Topitsch) argue that Hitler's attack on the Soviet Union in June 1941 was a preventive move, since Stalin had been making ready to invade Germany around that time or shortly thereafter – an interpretation which found a few scattered supporters even in the United States and also elsewhere, despite its lack of serious substance.

Few British historians concentrated on the origins of the First World War (a recent exception is Niall Ferguson), many more to those of the Second. It is interesting that the slow but massive reversal of British opinion about Germany after 1920 had few consequences among historians. Some time in the early 1930s there developed what was at least a tacit consensus among the British people and many of their politicians that the Germans had been wrongly humiliated by the Versailles Treaty. This recognition contributed considerably to the so-called policy of Appeasement, the elements of which were complex, and the discussion of which does not belong in this essay. The willingness to give the New Germany some benefit of the doubt existed among historians too, but it was seldom expressed in their books. In any event the revolution of British public opinion and senti-ment in March 1939 brought about a deep change. After that, an inclination to actually favour National Socialist Germany hardly existed at all, except perhaps in the case of Arthur Bryant who finally thought it politic to trim his sails, to say the least, in May 1940. Nor was there any substantial change in the consensus about the origins of the Second World War until decades later. There were British writers critical of the Nuremberg Trials, but they were not historians. The only considerable exception was General J.F.C. Fuller who in his trenchant military history of the Second World War excoriated much of British strategy. (One must also consider that General Fuller had expressed his sympathies with the Third Reich as late as September 1939 and that he was at times close to the group around Sir Oswald Mosley.) In his *The Origins of the Second World War* (1961) A.J.P. Taylor, without wishing to rehabilitate Hitler, argued that Hitler was not very different from other ambitious German statesmen of the past; that, in sum, Hitler was more of a short-term opportunist and less of a long-range ideologue than it was assumed. On occasion Taylor presented his evidence on the sudden development of some of Hitler's decisions convincingly, at other times with considerable legerdemain. His principal error may have been his statement that 'Only Danzig prevented co-operation between Germany and Poland' – entirely contrary to Hitler's own statements, according to which Poland had to accept a new status as becoming a junior ally of Germany, without an independent foreign policy of its own. A change then came about ten years ago – the first crack in the national consensus according to which Churchill in the summer of 1940 was 'the saviour of Britain' (as even A. J. P. Taylor put it in one of the biographical footnotes of his *English History 1914–1945*). None of this British 'revisionism' related directly to the origins of the war in 1939, but rather to Churchill's policy in 1940–41, rejecting any possibility of an armistice with the Third Reich, with the ultimate result of the collapse of the British Empire. Maurice Cowling wrote that 'the belief that Churchill had understood Hitler . . . was not true'; others wrote that in 1940 Churchill was 'Micawber', waiting for something to turn up. Such were the interpretations of 1940 by the Cambridge historians David Reynolds and Sheila Lawlor. John Charmley went much further, questioning not only Churchill's character but also his policy to fight Hitler at any cost, including the loss of Empire, suggesting at least that not to acquiesce in Hitler's domination of Europe may have been a mistake. The main shortcoming of such arguments can be summed up by saying that with Hitler in 1940 or 1941 no Peace of Amiens (the short-lived arrangement between Britain and Bonaparte in 1802–3) would have been possible, and that the determination of the British people and of their politicians to maintain the Empire had grown faint long before the Second World War broke out in 1939.

At the beginning of this essay I wrote that *revisionism* does not figure in the first four volumes of the Oxford English Dictionary; but is included in the 1987 edition of its *Supplement*, where, rather significantly, it is stated prominently among other sub-entries: 'mostly U.S., a movement to revise the accepted versions of American history, esp. those relating to foreign affairs since the war of 1939–45'. This attribution or, rather, connection of 'revisionism' to its American concept and usage is both significant and correct, since in no country other than the United States were the successive waves of revisionism so influential in moulding public opinion and even national politics at large. The only exception to the OED statement to consider is its last clause: for revisionism, in the United States, meaning the very usage of the term, preceded 1945. Consequently, to a necessarily brief survey of the four waves of American revisionism, insofar as they relate to the origin of 20th century wars, I must now turn.

Of these four waves of revisionism the first was the longest and strongest. It began as an intellectual and academic (and sometimes also a political and ethnic) reaction against the extreme propagandistic condemnation of Germany in 1917–1919. It was a reaction by liberals and radicals against superpatriotism, not very different from (and often allied with) their opposition to American conformism to the post-war Red Scare, to the Ku Klux Klan, to the propaganda of the American Legion of the 1920s. As early as 1920, for example, *The Nation* attacked the dangers of French, not of German, militarism. In September 1921 this journal posed the question: 'Who has contributed more to the myth of a guilty nation plotting the war against a peaceful Europe than the so-called historians who occupy distinguished chairs in our universities?' They were 'willing tools' of 'professional propaganda'. The young and later distinguished Sidney Bradshaw Fay (not a typical revisionist, I must add) had already published three successive articles in the *American Historical Review* ('New Light on the Origins of the World War'), a result of his reading of the then recently published German, Austrian and Russian documents. Within five years this first wave of revisionism swelled into a tide. Revisionists now included respected members of the historical profession: the prominent Charles A. Beard, the University of Chicago historian Ferdinand Schevill, who wrote in 1926 that 'there are today among reputable historians only revisionists'. In the same year *The Genesis of the World War*, by the sociologist turned historian Harry Elmer Barnes, disdainful of France and Britain, while very favourable to Germany, was published by the reputable house of Knopf. The revisionist cause was supported by many amateur historians, also by celebrated literary figures such as Albert J. Nock and H. L. Mencken, and by the editors of some of the most prominent literary weeklies and monthly magazines of the United States.

By 1929–30 the revisionist tide was further swelled by the predictable confluence of another historical argument, about 1917 and not 1914. The time had come to revise not only the thesis of German war guilt but the story of the American involvement in the war. The first such substantial book was published in 1929 by C. Hartley

Grattan, a onetime student of Barnes. By the early 1930s article after article, book after book, was attacking American intervention in the First World War. The most serious work was Walter Millis's *The Road to War*, published in 1935. The most determined book by a professional historian was Charles Callan Tansill's *America Goes to War* in 1938. By that time their arguments had filtered down from academia and from intellectual periodicals through the reading public to the broad lowlands of popular sentiment. *The Road to War* was a bestseller, with sixty thousand copies in print by 1936. A few months later Gallup reported that 70 per cent of Americans thought it had been wrong to enter the First World War. Meanwhile Hitler, Mussolini and the Japanese were rising in power.

In 1938 and 1939 another current in the revisionist tide came to the surface. Many revisionists were now worried about what they saw as an ominous change in Franklin Roosevelt's foreign policy. (In 1932 Roosevelt's foreign policy was generally isolationist, and as late as 1935 he went so far as to suggest his acceptance of certain revisionist theses.) In September 1939 Beard published a powerful small book against American intervention in Europe, *Giddy Minds and Foreign Quarrels*. Yet by 1940 the revisionist camp was badly split. Many of the liberals were coming around to support Britain against Hitler. Others were not. In 1940 Beard came out with another book, *A Foreign Policy for America*. Eleven years later Senator Robert A. Taft published a book with a virtually identical title; yet already in 1940 it was evident that the formerly radical and Jeffersonian Democrat Beard and the conservative Republican Taft were seeing eye to eye. But before the next year was out the news of Pearl Harbor roared over them both.

Revisionism was submerged but not sunk. After 1945 came the second wave of American revisionism, attacking Roosevelt for having manoeuvred the United States into war; indeed, for having contributed surreptitiously and wilfully to the catastrophe at Pearl Harbor. Many of the historians were the same ones as before, the two principal professionals among them Beard (*American Foreign Policy in the Making, 1932–1940* and *President Roosevelt and the Coming of the War*) and Tansill (*Back Door to War*). There were, and are still, many others, but this second wave of revisionism received relatively little attention, many of the revisionist books being now printed by minor publishers. Yet the effect of this kind of revisionism was wider than the publishing record might indicate. The majority of the so-called 'conservative' movement that began to coalesce in the early 1950s was composed of former isolationists and revisionists. A principal element of the Republican surge after 1948 was a reaction against Roosevelt's foreign policy, including such different figures as Joseph R. McCarthy, John Foster Dulles, and the young William F. Buckley, Jr. It was part of the emergence of the New Right in American politics. Still, Hitler and Tojo had few public defenders, and this second wave of revisionism failed to swell into an oceanic current.

The third, and much larger, wave of revisionism came not from the New Right but from the New Left. These were the historians who during the fretful 1960s attempted to rewrite the origins of the Cold War with Russia, arguing and claiming that American foreign policy and aggressiveness were at least as responsible if not more for the coming of the Cold War as was the Soviet Union. The principal ones (again, there were many others) of these New Left historians were D. F. Fleming (*The Cold War and Its Origins*), William Applenan Williams (*The Tragedy of American Diplomacy*), Gar Alperovitz (*Atomic Diplomacy*), David Horowitz (*The Free World Colossus*), Gabriel Kolko (*The Politics of War*), Diane Shaver Clemens (*Yalta*), and Lloyd C. Gardner (*Architects of Illusion*), all of these books issued between 1959 and 1970 by most reputable university presses and trade houses. Unlike the revisionists of the 1920s and 1940s these authors had little opposition from most of their historian colleagues: for such was the, generally Leftist, intellectual tendency of the American 1960s. These authors were praised and portions of their works were anthologized in college readers and textbooks. Whereas the revisionists of the 1920s and 1930s had their greatest effect among general readers, most of the consumers of this third wave of revisionist prose were college students. When Robert Maddox, in his precise and serious *The New Left and the Origins of the Cold War* (1973), pointed out many of the dishonesties of the documentation and the inadequacies of scholarship in these books, he was treated with tut-tutting and fence-sitting by most academic reviewers, so many Vicars of Bray. However, as with so many fads and fashions of the 1960s, the tide of Cold War revisionism, though temporarily overwhelming, did not endure for very long.

By the 1990s we may detect the rise of the fourth wave of revisionism, coming again from the so-called Right rather than from the Left. We have now seen some of its evidences in Germany and in Britain. During the Reagan years in the United States there appeared a tendency to question not only the evident problems of the American welfare state but the establishment of its tenets by Roosevelt and the New Deal; and new indictments (and I fear not always well-warranted and judicious ones) of American foreign policy before and during the Second World War are also beginning to appear. In sum, there is reason to believe that this newest wave of revisionism, already apparent in Germany and Britain (and of course also in Russia), will spill over to the American side of the Atlantic too.

What revisionist historians claim, or at least emphatically suggest, is that their scholarship is better and their intellectual independence stronger than that of their opponents. Yet this has seldom been true. On the contrary, few of the revisionists have been immune to the ideological tendencies of their times. In 1917 Beard was an extreme interventionist. The United States 'should help eliminate Prussianism from the earth.' Germany represents 'the black night of military barbarism . . . the most merciless military despotism the world has ever seen'. By 1926 he was a Germanophile, influenced not only by the revelations in the German diplomatic documents but by German philosophies of history. Beard was not an opportunist, and even in the 1930s he insisted that he was not really an isolationist; rather, he was struggling with that seemingly concrete but, alas, often malleable concept of national interest. (In 1932 Beard received a twenty-five-thousand-dollar grant – a very large sum then – from the Social Science Research Council for the precise definition of 'national interest'. The result was one of his few unreadable books.) At that time he was a fervent supporter of Franklin Roosevelt, but soon he turned even more fervently against him.

The case of Barnes is even more telling. His first revisionist articles appeared in 1924, arguing for a division in the responsibilities for the outbreak of First World War. By 1926 he was going further: France and Russia were responsible. Thereafter he became more and more extreme and violent. He was invited to lecture in Hitler's Germany, as was Tansill. In 1940 Barnes volunteered to promote the circulation of official German propaganda volumes. After the war he became an admirer of Hitler: 'a man whose only fault was that he was too soft, generous and honourable'. The Allies had inflicted worse brutalities on the Germans than 'the alleged exterminations in the gas chambers'. This, of course, was the extreme case of a once talented but embittered man, driven to such statements by what he called *The Historical Blackout*, one of his later pamphlets. Everything was grist to his mill, including the most dubious 'sources' and 'evidences'. The same was true of Tansill, who in 1938 wrote in his introduction to *America Goes to War*: 'Crusading zeal is hardly the proper spirit for an impartial historian'. Yet Tansill was the prototype of a zealous crusader, in both of his big revisionist works about the two world wars. Eventually he became a member of the John Birch Society, an extremist group that even included President Eisenhower among unwitting helpers of an international Communist conspiracy.

Revisionists, especially in the United States and Germany, have often been obsessed with the idea of a conspiracy against them. During the German Historians' Quarrel the respected Hillgruber called his opponents 'character assassins'. Barnes called the anti-revisionists the '*Smearbund*'. He even thought that there was a conspiracy among booksellers not to reorder his *Genesis*. The famous American literary critic Mencken liked Barnes. In June 1940, when the German armies had marched forward into Holland, Belgium and France, Mencken wrote to Barnes that 'Roosevelt will be in the war in two weeks, and . . . his first act will be to forbid every form of free speech'. Mencken, like Barnes and other revisionists, was bitterly against a war with Hitler's Reich, whilst after the war he thought that the United States should go to war against 'the Russian barbarians'. That inconsistency, if that was what it was, was typical of the inclinations of almost all the post-Second World War revisionists. The opposite was true of the Cold War revisionists of the 1960s, who accused the United States of having provoked the Cold War with Russia, while almost all of them approved the American involvement in the Second World War against Germany. They, too, did little else but project backward their then widespread and fashionable dislike of the Vietnam War to events that had happened twenty or more years earlier, manipulating that record for their own purposes. In the 1970s most of them turned to other topics, and at least one of them (Horowitz) became a neo-conservative publicist.

There is, however, more involved here than a few historians adjusting their ideas to a prevalent climate of opinion. In some instances their writings affected national politics, through a momentum that was slowly gaining ground. In 1929 the writings of the revisionists had an influence on those members of Congress, mostly Western populists – George W. Norris, Gerald P. Nye, William E. Borah, for example – who had opposed the First World War and the Versailles treaty. By 1934 the isolationist and revisionist tide ran so strong that a Congressional committee, presided over by

Nye, found it politic to investigate the doings of bankers and munition makers and other villainous promoters of the American entrance into the war seventeen years before. (One of the Nye Committee's five counsels was an ambitious young lawyer, Alger Hiss.) In 1935 Congress passed the first Neutrality Act, a definite reaction against the memories of First World War. It was extended in 1937. By that time Senator Homer Bone of Washington could report 'a fact known even to schoolchildren in this country: Everyone has come to recognize that the Great War was utter social insanity, and we had no business in it at all.'

This illustrates a significant phenomenon to which few, if any, historians have yet devoted attention. It is the time-lag in the movement of ideas, the slowness of the momentum with which ideas move and then appear on the surface at the wrong time, giving the lie to Victor Hugo's famous saw about Ideas Whose Time Has Come. The high tide of revisionism (in the United States; and in England of pro-German sentiments) occurred in the mid-Thirties when the German danger was rising anew – and not, say, in 1919 or 1929, when there had been cogent reasons to mitigate a mistreatment of Germany. The high tide of Second World War revisionism occurred in 1954 and 1955, when the reputations of Franklin Roosevelt and of Yalta were at a low ebb. The high tide of the revisionism about the origins of the Cold War came around 1965, when American-Russian relations were actually improving.

Of course it takes time for historians to complete their researches and produce their books; but there is an agitated tone in many revisionist works that stands in odd contrast with the slow momentum of their eventual effects. One reason for this is the often weak and tergiversating reaction of the revisionists' historian opponents. In the beginning the seemingly radical performance of the former is often ignored, but then, gradually, the revisionists' ideas may be adopted by respectable historians when it seems politic for them to do so, or when they feel safely convinced by their acceptability. Thus, for example, Tansill's radical and Germanophile *America Goes to War* was praised by some of the most prominent American literary monthlies and by such eminent historians as Allan Nevins and Henry Steele Commager. Tansill traced, 'in magisterial style, the missteps which carried the United States along the road to war. It is an impressive performance, conducted with skill, learning, and wit, illuminating the present as well as the past.' This was written by Commager as late as 1938, the most ominous and successful year in Hitler's career along the road to another world war. The title of Beard's trenchant 1939 *Giddy Minds and Foreign Quarrels* is not really appropriate. So many of his colleagues' minds were not at all giddy; they were alarmingly slow. Even more disheartening was the reaction of many historians to the New Left revisionists of the 1960s, when the scholarship of those books was wanting. As Maddox wrote, 'Reviewers who have been known to pounce with scarcely disguised glee on some poor wretch who incorrectly transcribed a middle initial or date of birth have shown a most extraordinary reluctance to expose even the most obvious New Left fictions,' including false statements of fact to which tens of thousands of students were subsequently exposed in American colleges and universities. Finally, when it comes to the newest wave of revisionism, lamentably few historians have taken the trouble to track down and point out the selective methodology and occasionally sloppy scholarship in works such as Charmley's treatment of Churchill.

In science it is the rule that counts; in history, often the exceptions. And there have been exceptions to the shortcomings of scholars involved with revisionism. Millis, who, as we saw earlier, was the author of the most successful revisionist book in 1935, a few years later found himself appalled by the use people were making of his work, which, after all, had dealt with 1917, with the past and not with the then present. By 1938 Millis stood for resistance against Hitler and other dictators. '1939 is not 1914', he wrote in November 1939, when Roosevelt had to struggle against a senseless Neutrality Act. Maddox, whose study of the New Left revisionists was ignored or criticized by other historians, refused to make common cause with the New Right; he remained unimpressed by the selective argumentation of Leftist and Rightist, of Marxist and anti-Communist, of neo-liberal and neo-conservative historians alike, because of his personal integrity, the essence of human integrity being its resistance to temptations, perhaps especially to intellectual ones.

Such temptations are the bane of historians, and not only of those who are in pursuit of attractive intellectual novelty. This does not mean a defence of 'orthodox' history, because there is no such thing. Historians should be aware of the inevitably revisionist nature of their thinking and work. But the revision of history must not be an ephemeral monopoly of ideologues or opportunists who are ever ready to twist or even falsify evidences of the past in order to exemplify current ideas – and their own adjustments to them.

WAR AND 'ETHNIC CLEANSING': THE CASE OF THE 'WARTHEGAU'

IAN KERSHAW

The term 'ethnic cleansing' was not known at the time of the Nazi invasion of Poland on 1 September 1939. But what took place there-after in those parts of pre-war western Poland which were now ruthlessly annexed to the German Reich is suitably described by this phrase relating to modern-day racist-nationalist brutality. In the early 1940s a different word, but with analogous meaning, was in regular parlance in the occupied parts of Poland: 'Germanization'. Another dreadful component of the Nazi vocabulary, carried into Poland by the new masters, was 'ethnic struggle' (*Volkstumskampf*). What both terms signified was the attempt, commencing without delay, to remove large sections of the 'unwanted' population – Poles as well as Jews – from the areas incorporated into the Reich, in order to make room for a large influx of ethnic Germans from other parts of eastern Europe, such as the Baltic, Wohlhynia, Galicia and Bessarabia. The links between these plans – improvised, executed with great chaos as well as extreme brutality, and feeding ever greater radicalization – and the emergence of genocidal policy towards the Jews have become increasingly plain in the light of recent research.[1] Over time, the intention was that the population of the incorporated territories would be German, with all Jews removed and remaining Poles constituting no more than a class of illiterate and undertrodden helots. The vast numerical dominance of ethnic Poles in these regions meant that this could only be a long-term project. But that the aim was real enough was shown by the 'General Plan East' of 1941, which envisaged the deportation over a period of 25–30 years of 31 million Slavs – one reckoning estimated the figure at more like 46–51 million – eastwards, beyond the Urals, the Poles to western Siberia.[2] Meanwhile, the Nazi leadership was anxious to make a start by

83

wiping out the Polish intelligentsia, speaking already in early September 1939 of an 'ethnic extermination' (*Volkstums-Ausrottung*) and a 'political cleansing of the ground' (*politische Flurbereinigung*).[3]

The occupied territories of former Poland provided an area of racial experimentation with no holds barred for the Nazi rulers. The brevity of the war with Poland – over in little more than three weeks – left the German masters in total control, with not the slightest constraint on their inhumanity towards the conquered people in an area where Polish-German antipathies had already been aroused before the First World War and had become far more acute thereafter. In no part of occupied western Europe, in the wake of the German military triumphs of 1940, did conditions begin to compare with what transpired in former Poland. And for the Jewish minority, disliked by most of the Poles and in Nazi eyes the lowest form of existence amid a ruthlessly subjugated population, the horror was on a barely imaginable scale. Though the 'Polish question' would take longer to solve, it was presumed that a solution to the 'Jewish question' could rapidly be found.[4] It was no accident that the first extermination camp to begin operations was situated in the largest of the annexed territories of western Poland, the so-called 'Warthegau' (named after the River Warthe, which runs through the area). The Nazi leadership of the region provides a graphic illustration of the ways in which the escalation of barbarity could take place so rapidly, and with so little direction from above, other than the green light to proceed with all haste with whatever measures were felt necessary to comply with the objectives laid down in Berlin for maximum 'Germanization' in the shortest possible time.

For twenty years historiography on the Third Reich has been dominated by debate about the primacy of ideology (the 'intentionalist' position which derived Nazi policy from Hitler's ideological aims) or the dominance of the functional motor of radicalization (the 'structuralist' emphasis on internal pressures from within an ever more chaotic, competitive system). Analysis of the initiatives for 'ethnic cleansing' indicates the potential for transcending this division in interpretations. Hitler's role in directing policy in Poland was largely confined to laying down 'guidelines for action'[5], framed by his 'visionary' goals for German expansion and racial purification. Within these 'guidelines for action', Himmler and Heydrich, at the head of the Reich Security Main Office in Berlin, stipulated broad policy objectives. There was seldom any need to refer these directly

84

to Hitler. His intervention was normally only sought when his ideological 'guidelines' prompted an impasse and clashes between his underlings. He was even then not usually capable of or interested in resolving the dispute, whose very non-resolution, as a rule, both magnified the problem and led to further radicalization in the attempt to solve it. The policy objectives of the Reich Security Main Office for resettlement and population displacements were invariably so wide-ranging but at the same time so hastily put together, with little attention to potential logistical or planning difficulties, that they opened up massive scope for the most brutal initiatives from below, while offering little chance of coordination. The result was again, predictably, to intensify conflicts and disputes among the Nazi leadership in Poland, leading invariably to a further spur to finding radical solutions. Meanwhile, at every level of the rapacious occupying forces of repression and administration – both the police and the bureaucracy rapidly swelled in numbers – utter ruthlessness in dealings with the subjugated population was overtly encouraged and a determining role in shaping policy taken by the provincial leadership of party and police. The inevitable result was a dialectic of spiralling radicalization from below to meet ideological imperatives from above.

Neither the 'intentionalist' nor the 'structuralist' interpretations adequately encapsulate this process. The 'primacy of ideology' can scarcely be gainsaid. But this should not be seen as a clear set of specific 'intentions' laid down by Hitler. His 'programmatic' ideas were couched only in broad, long-term, 'visionary' goals. Without the 'primacy of ideology', it is difficult to see why bureaucratic confusion and chaos should produce war and genocide. But ideology is in itself insufficient explanation of the radicalization of the Nazi régime. This also needed initiatives from below, freed from all constraint on inhumanity and bureaucratic channeling. In a 'system' (if it can be called such) which derived its dynamism from empowering the scope for initiative, coupled with all-out 'Darwinian' competition, linked to the attainment of coordination, intense clashes in shaping of policy were inescapable – and inevitably drove forward an intensified radicalization that demanded a solution to self-created problems. The example of the Warthegau reveals this in sharp focus.

The 'Warthegau' had been established in October 1939 as one of three tracts of western Poland – the others were West Prussia and part of Upper Silesia – annexed to the Reich. Though its core was the former Prussian province of Posen, the boundaries of the Reichsgau Wartheland (as the 'Warthegau' was officially known), when laid down by Hitler, extended substantially farther, mainly for economic reasons, than the boundaries of 1918, incorporating a Jewish population of some 350,000 (8% of the total population), mainly in the Lodz area which had earlier been part of Congress Poland and had never been in German hands. The overwhelming proportion of the Warthegau's population, 4.2 millions (85%), comprised, however, ethnic Poles, while the German minority amounted only to 327,000 (7% of the population).[6] 'Germanization' in the sense of removal of over nine-tenths of the population was, plainly, not an option, at any rate not in the foreseeable future. Even so, there was specific talk in January 1940 in the planning office of Himmler in his new capacity as Reich Commissar for the Consolidation of Germandom (which gave him overall responsibility for population displacements and resettlement) of the deportation of 3.4 million Poles from the incorporated territories during the next few years as a 'reachable target'. The deportation of the entire Jewish population of the incorporated territories, reckoned at 560,000 persons, had already been envisaged for winter 1940–1.[7] By this time Himmler was speaking of the need to 'make room' for 200,000 ethnic Germans who had already been transferred to the incorporated territories, many of them from the Baltic, pointing out that he had had to defer the influx of almost 300,000 further ethnic Germans, mainly from Bessarabia and Bukovina.[8]

The question of population transfers, involving the forced deportation of Poles and Jews under conditions of horrific brutality, in line with directives laid down in Berlin, was an immediate issue facing the new rulers of the Warthegau. The two key figures, working in the closest cooperation, were the Reich Governor (and at the same time Gauleiter of the Nazi Party) Arthur Greiser, and the Higher SS and Police Leader Wilhelm Koppe, who had ultimate responsibility, as Himmler's lieutenant in the region, for deportation matters. Both were to excel in ruthlessness and in forcing the pace of radicalization through their own initiatives.

Wilhelm Koppe had been born in Hildesheim in 1896, served with distinction on the western front during the war, and had then run a food and tobacco firm in Harburg. By 1930, married with two children, he had joined the Nazi Party, led an SA stormtroop in 1931, and the following year joined the SS, where he rapidly rose through the leadership ranks. As SS leader in Danzig for some months in 1934–5, he came into direct contact with Greiser, a prominent political figure in the city. By the late 1930s he had also served as head of the Gestapo in Saxony and 'Inspector of the Security Police and the SD' [Security Service] in Leipzig. At the end of September 1939 Koppe was recommended to Himmler to take over the newly created post of Higher SS and Police Leader of the new district 'Warthe', serving at the same time as the SS chief's representative in his new capacity as Reich Commissar for the Consolidation of Germandom. Koppe's style of working, it was said at his post-war trial, was 'unbureaucratic and unconventional'. A witness at the trial remarked that 'he ruled through the telephone'. It was claimed that 'he constantly developed new plans, at times reaching into the fanastic', though was pedantically concerned at the same time with small matters of detail.[9]

Arthur Greiser was born a year later than Koppe, in 1897, in Schroda in the Posen province, the region he would later rule with an iron fist. He, too, served with distinction in the war. Embittered by the loss of his homeland to Poland following the defeat and struggling financially to provide for his wife and young children, extreme German nationalism and strong anti-Polish feelings came easily to him. He found his way by 1929, via the Freikorps, the racist-nationalist Deutsch-Soziale Partei, and the Stahlhelm, to the Nazi Party and SA in Danzig. Hitler, thought Greiser, offered the best hope of tackling the 'ethnic question' (*Volkstumsfrage*) and restoring his homeland to Germany. Within two years of joining the party, Greiser had become deputy to the rabble-rousing Gauleiter of Danzig, Albert Forster, and by 1934 had survived a number of personal scandals – earlier membership of a freemasons' lodge, financial corruption related to a gambling casino, and a messy divorce – to become President of the Danzig Senate. Arrogant and egotistic, with a high opinion of his own importance, Greiser was unctuous towards his superiors, bullying towards those below him. Compared with the vulgar Forster, he could, however, appear accommodating, or so the High Commissioner in Danzig, Carl J. Burckhardt, thought. In another characterization, Burckhardt's judgement was better. Greiser, he remarked, would do anything to gain Hitler's favour: 'a wish expressed by Hitler counted for more than a command'.[10] Greiser felt in the 1930s that he did not enjoy this favour. But following the German attack on Poland, perhaps backed by Himmler who appears to have thought well of him since the mid-1930s, Greiser was offered both state and party leadership in his home province of Posen (soon to become the 'Warthegau'), and in the immediate aftermath of the invasion he discussed directly and privately with Hitler his mandate to 'germanize' the Warthegau.[11]

Greiser evidently saw himself as Hitler's direct instrument in the mission to 'cleanse' the Warthegau in a rigorous 'ethnic struggle' and turn it into the 'model Gau' of the 'new order'. He made it plain to all and sundry that he enjoyed the highest standing with the Führer, and was acting under his personally transmitted plenipotentiary powers, for which, according to one of his contemporaries, 'his gratitude knew no bounds'.[12] It was a classic case of 'working towards the Führer',[13] to turn Hitler's 'guidelines for action' into practical, realizable policy.[14]

The initial phase of the 'ethnic cleansing' policy in the Warthegau was carried out under the illusion that the grandiose plans for population displacement and resettlement, which had been so swiftly put together, could easily be brought to fruition. Hitler had spoken at the end of September of a division of former Polish territory into three entities: 'a broad belt of germanization and colonization' (the annexed areas); a Polish zone (which turned into the 'General Government'); and a form of Jewish reserve east of the Vistula in which all Jews were to be concentrated (something which never materialized).[15] Some three weeks later, Hitler referred to the purging of the new Reich territories of 'Jews, Polacks, and rabble' to be dumped into the General Government. He spoke of a 'hard ethnic struggle' in which 'legal constraints' would not apply.[16] Though the territorial restructuring eventually took place on somewhat different lines than originally envisaged, the division between the incorporated areas (to be 'germanized') and the Polish area (the General Government) as a resort for deportees was soon established. In the rush to deport 'undesirables' from the incorporated territories to make way for incoming ethnic Germans, ideological enthusiasm went hand in hand with untrammelled brutality and administrative disorganization.

Around the time, on 12 November 1939, that Koppe ordered the initial deportations to the General Government of 200,000 Poles and 100,000 Jews to make space for an influx of Baltic Germans,[17] Greiser was publicly stating that the 'Jewish Question' was no longer a problem, and would be solved in the Warthegau in the immediate future.[18] The figures mentioned in Koppe's directive, though already

much reduced from what Himmler had had in mind less than a fortnight earlier,[19] evidently went nonetheless beyond what was
manageable, despite the draconian terror inflicted on those families
arbitrarily ripped from their homes and thrown into cattle-wagons
to be carted off to bleak futures in the south of the country. Before
the end of November the immediate target had been reduced to
80,000 Jews and Poles, to accommodate 40,000 Baltic Germans –
expulsions which were effected without delay.[20] A revised plan for
the Warthegau on 4 January 1940 indicated a new target (close to
the original one) of 200,000 Jews and 80,000 Poles. But the total
number actually deported by mid-March fell far short of this target,
amounting to 128,011 in all (of whom 87,883 had been expelled
already by 16 December 1939).[21] By this time difficulties of accommodating the deportees were already mounting in the General
Government, whose head, Hans Frank, was voicing complaints that
would culminate in a block on taking in new expellees. Even this
early, in spring 1940, severe clashes over deportation and resettlement policy were emerging. Himmler and Heydrich were pushing for
maximum speed with 'germanization'. Koppe and Greiser wanted to
prove their credentials and gain favour by meeting targets, removing
'undesirables' from their Gau, and finding space for the ethnic
Germans. Frank was keen to resist creating insoluble logistical problems for himself in the housing and feeding of untold numbers being
ejected arbitrarily into his territory. Göring, whom Frank rapidly saw
as an ally in the growing dispute, was anxious to gain forced Polish
labour for the war effort. The Wehrmacht were increasingly
concerned about scarce transport facilities being siphoned off. The
growing impasse prompted, as far as the 'Jewish Question' went, the
institutionalization of ghettos which had initially been set up as mere
transit camps. And, with regard to the majority Polish population, it
encouraged the complex process of devising regulations, finally
published only on 4 March 1941, for applying German citizenship
to specific groups within the Polish population by way of the so-
called 'German Ethnic List' (*Deutsche Volksliste*, or DVL).[22]

By the end of 1940 over quarter of a million Poles had been
deported from the Warthegau into the General Government.[23] By this
date, however, Hans Frank's opposition to further expulsions into
his domain, backed by Göring, the Reichsbahn and the Wehrmacht,
had brought the main period of deportations to a halt. As far as the
Jewish minority went, it was increasingly recognized that there was

now no prospect of attaining the goal, initially envisaged as an easy one, of making the incorporated territories 'Jew-free'. A large proportion of the original Jewish population of the Warthegau still remained, more than 160,000 of them in rapidly deteriorating conditions in the large ghetto at Lodz.[24] And a new plan produced in the Reich Security Main Office in January 1941, envisaging the 'evacuation' of 330,000 more Poles from the Warthegau in 1941, produced meagre results before being called off.[25] But expulsions did not stop altogether. By the end of 1943 some half a million uprooted and deported Poles from the Warthegau had made way for about 350,000 ethnic Germans.[26] Part of Greiser's desperate postwar defence, when on trial for his life in Warsaw, was that he had been powerless to prevent SS terror actions against the Polish population. In reality, however, Koppe could act with the full backing of the Gauleiter, who had been the fanatical supporter of the most rapid, extensive and brutal policy of deportation.

Equally close was the cooperation in the second strand of 'ethnic cleansing' in the Warthegau: the enforcement of maximum racial separation between Germans and Poles. This 'apartheid' policy highlighted the scope for variation at the regional level in interpreting broad ideological imperatives. The policy was implemented more inflexibly and fanatically in the Warthegau than in any other part of the annexed territories.

According to the decree of March 1941 establishing the 'ethnic list' (the DVL), four groups of Poles were eligible for 'germanization'. Two were entitled to German state citizenship with effect from 26 October 1939: those who had proved themselves to be of German descent through their active work in the 'ethnic struggle' (Group 1); and those who, despite passivity, had satisfactorily demonstrated their 'Germanness' (Group 2). A third group comprised persons of German descent who had developed 'connections with Polish nationality (*Polentum*)', to whom German citizenship was granted only conditionally. The fourth group were those of German descent who had actively committed themselves to Polish nationality, for example, through intermarriage. They were regarded as 'renegades' and could only be considered as applicants for German conditional citizenship.[27] Gauleiter Forster in Danzig-West Prussia – a similar procedure was followed in Upper Silesia – took a pragmatic line on the DVL. Partly to ensure that he could speedily announce that he had 'germanized' his region, he simply entered hundreds of thousands of Poles compulsorily in Group 3 of the DVL, declaring them to be German. Greiser, by contrast, held to the strictest interpretation of Himmler's guidelines, making entry to the DVL as difficult as possible. The consequence was that by January 1944 44% of the population in Danzig-West Prussia and 36% in Upper Silesia had been classed as German (in Group 3 of the DVL), whereas of the four and a half million persons in the Warthegau only 1.5% had been granted like status.[28]

Determined to follow through the ideological guidelines of racial separation to the letter, Greiser also instituted a systematic, root-and-branch attack on all facets of Polish cultural life. The Polish language was banned in schools and public places. Professors from Posen University were arrested, deported and in some cases killed, while the university itself was closed, then reopened in 1941 as a German university. Theatres, cinemas and radio stations were also 'germanized'. Collections from art galleries were confiscated, vast numbers of Polish books taken from libraries and burnt. The Catholic Church, regarded as a bulwark of Polish national feeling, was subjected to a massive onslaught. Only 6% of the churches in the Posen-Gnesen diocese remained open by 1941. Most of the clergy were imprisoned or sent to concentration camps, more than one in ten of them killed.[29]

Without any direct or specific orders from above, Greiser created a living hell for the Poles in his region, waging an assault on every facet of their economic and social life. Poles were banned from professions and from running businesses. Their farms and commercial properties were seized. They were forced to work long hours for a fraction of what was paid to Germans. They could only shop at certain times. They suffered discrimination in public transport, entry to public parks, access to children's playgrounds, and in a multiplicity of other ways. The policy of harsh discrimination was passed down the line. Local policemen were admonished not to show any leniency towards Poles and to act in accordance with the recognition that Poles were always to be regarded as enemies, not fit to be on the same level as a 'people of culture'.[30] The police in Posen saw fit to remind local government offices that Germans automatically took precedence over any Poles who happened to be awaiting attention.[31] On 22 September 1940 the Gauleiter tried by decree to enforce total 'apartheid' by threatening draconian punishment for unnecessary contact with Poles.[32] That such ordinances were necessary indicates that the strict 'apartheid' which Greiser and his underlings sought

91

was not always upheld in practice. Some ethnic Germans evidently continued to have dealings with Poles, which did not comply with Greiser's fanaticism.[33] Even so, there are few indications, especially in the first years of the occupation, that the ethnic German minority, which had itself suffered discrimination under the Poles in the interwar period and enjoyed lording it over an ethnic group that it had long seen as inferior, felt any pronounced sense of injustice or distaste for what was happening.

For the Poles, deadly retribution could strike, arbitrarily, at any moment. There was no law to protect them. They were absolutely at the mercy of their German masters. The penal system increasingly led to arbitrary court sentences, or unregulated actions by the police. Huge numbers of Poles were savagely punished for trivial offences or hauled off to concentration camps. Public hangings took place almost daily, the bodies left on the makeshift gallows to serve as a deterrent.

The chaotic barbarism, aligned to loose but vicious ideological guidelines, spawned ever new initiatives which fuelled the motor of radicalization. This is most plain in the 'Jewish question'. Desperate to be rid of the Warthegau's Jews, Greiser and Koppe found their anti-Jewish policy by mid-1941 blocked at every turn. It was at this point that the SD chief in Posen, Rolf Heinz Höppner, suggested in a memorandum, the substance of which had been discussed in Greiser's office, that serious thought should be given to killing those Jews incapable of work in the coming winter by 'some quick-working method'. 'The things sound fantastic,' Höppner wrote to Eichmann, 'but in my opinion are certainly capable of being carried out.'[34] Genocide was in the air and, as far as the Warthegau was concerned, the initiatives were emerging locally.

By mid-September, when Hitler authorized the deportation of Jews from Germany, Austria, and Bohemia to the east, Jews were already being slaughtered in their tens of thousands in the Soviet Union. With Himmler's notification that the Warthegau could expect to receive 60,000 Jews into the already grossly overcrowded Lodz ghetto, the process began which led by the first week in December to the first gassing of Jews in Chelmno. Despite strenuous objections by the ghetto administration and the head of government in the city of Lodz (now renamed Litzmannstadt), Greiser indicated his willingness to accept the Jews. By mid-October the first transports from Germany were arriving. Far from the Warthegau 'cleansing' its territory of Jews, which had been foreseen as an immediate and attainable target

92

in autumn 1939, it was now, two years later, importing Jews into the region. As the Nazi overlords of the Warthegau viewed it, further deportation possibilities were blocked; the Jews could not be housed or fed and many of them were too old, too young or too infirm to be put to work. Killing at least those incapable of work offered at least a partial solution, and one which, as we have noted, had already been contemplated in the region a few months earlier. It seems highly likely, in fact, that Greiser's readiness to accept the deported Jews had been encouraged from the Berlin end by offering him the prospect of liquidating those incapable of work. That Greiser requested – and was granted by Himmler, in agreement with Heydrich – permission to kill 100,000 Jews in his region who were incapable of work is documented.[35] The date of the request is uncertain, but probably fell in autumn 1941. At any rate within a short time of Himmler's order in September to deport Reich Jews to the Warthegau Koppe had arranged for the transfer to the region of a gassing unit previously deployed in the liquidation of mentally sick patients in East Prussia. The head of the unit, Herbert Lange, spent some time in the autumn searching out an appropriate place to set up operations to kill the Jews of the Warthegau. By November Chelmno had been chosen. Systematic gassing of the Jews from the Warthegau's ghettos began there, using two (later three) gas-vans, in the first days of December 1941. Some 150,000 Jews in all were to perish. Authorization had come from Berlin. The initiative had been taken by the regional leadership, Greiser and Koppe.

This was unquestionably the case, too, in a final piece of 'ethnic cleansing' for consideration here: the request from Greiser to Himmler in May 1942 to liquidate 35,000 Poles suffering from incurable tuberculosis. Greiser was backed in this by Koppe. Initially, both Himmler and Heydrich gave their approval. Significantly, though, Koppe was informed that final authorization would have to come from Hitler himself.[36] The need to consult Hitler was also stressed by Dr Kurt Blome, from the health office in Berlin, who had evidently been asked for his own opinion and raised a number of practical objections. The proposed 'action' was, in the event, dropped. But Greiser's own last comment to Himmler, that he felt Hitler did not need to be consulted since 'at our last discussion with regard to the Jews he told me that I could proceed with these according to my own judgement,'[37] is enlightening for the light it casts on the way vital decisions were made in the genocidal process.

The Warthegau was only one part of Poland in which such barbarous initiatives were driving Nazi inhumanity forward. But the aim to turn the province into a 'model Gau', the radicality of the attempt at 'germanization' there, the particular self-inflicted difficulties which arose in trying to 'cleanse' the region of Jews, and the closeness of the ties between the local zealots, Greiser and Koppe, and the central ideological power-house of the Reich Security Main Office under Heydrich and Himmler, provide an especially clear illustration of the ways in which Hitler's ideological inspiration was translated into genocidal action with little need for more than a green light from above.

On 22 June 1941 the German invasion of the Soviet Union marked the beginning of the 'war of annihilation' – the showdown with Bolshevism – which Hitler had envisaged since the 1920s. This was from the outset a genocidal war. In the newly conquered territories 'ethnic cleansing' plumbed depths of horror witnessed not even in the Warthegau. Grandiose schemes for the future under long-term Nazi rule give an inkling of what would have been in store in the event of a German victory. What had gone on in the Warthegau and other parts of Poland in the eighteen months or so between the conquest of the country and the invasion of the USSR had given a foretaste of what was to come, and amounted to a crucial stage in the escalation of Nazi barbarism into full-scale genocidal race-war.

NOTES

1. Most important in this respect have been Christopher Browning, 'Nazi Resettlement Policy and the Search for a Solution to the Jewish Question, 1939–1941', in his *The Path to Genocide*, Cambridge, 1992, pp.3–27, and, especially, Götz Aly, *Endlösung. Völkerverschiebung und der Mord an den europäischen Juden*, Frankfurt am Main, 1995.
2. Helmut Heiber, 'Der Generalplanost', *Vierteljahrshefte für Zeitgeschichte* (=VfZ), 6 (1958), pp.281–325, esp.pp.297–301. See also Mechtild Rössler and Sabine Schleiermacher (eds.), *Der 'Generalplan Ost'. Hauptlinien der nationalsozialistischen Planungs- und Vernichtungspolitik*, Berlin, 1993.
3. Martin Broszat, *Nationalsozialistische Polenpolitik 1939–1945*, Frankfurt am Main, 1965, p.20.

4. Glowna Komissa Badania Zbrodni Hitlerowskich w Polsce (=GK), Process Artura Greisera (=PAG) [Archive of the Central Commission for the Investigation of Hitlerite Crimes in Poland, Ministry of Justice, Warsaw, Greiser Trial], vol.27, fol.167.

5. Martin Broszat, 'Soziale Motivation und Führer-Bindung des Nationalsozialismus', *VfZ*, 18 (1970), p.405.

6. Broszat, *Polenpolitik*, p.38.

7. Aly, p.81.

8. Aly, p.85.

9. Anklageschrift gegen Wilhelm Koppe, Zentrale Stelle der Landesjustizverwaltungen (=ZSL), Ludwigsburg, Landgericht Bonn 8 Js 52/60, fols.49–54. Koppe continued to rise in Himmler's favour for his work in the Warthegau, and in January 1942 was promoted to Obergruppenführer and General of Police. He left the Warthegau in November 1943, when he was transferred as head of police to Cracow, in the General Government. Koppe survived the war, lived under a pseudonym, became a successful businessman, and when finally captured and put on trial in 1964 was deemed unfit to stand. He died in 1975.

10. Carl J. Burckhardt, *Meine Danziger Mission*, Munich, 1952, p.78.

11. Broszat, *Polenpolitik*, p.29.

12. GK, PAG, vol.36, fol.463; vol.11, fol.52; vol.13, fol.15; Burckhardt, p.79.

13. See Ian Kershaw, '"Working towards the Führer." Reflections on the Nature of the Hitler Dictatorship', in Ian Kershaw and Moshe Lewin (eds.), *Stalinism and Nazism: Dictatorships in Comparison*, Cambridge, 1997, pp.88–106.

14. At the end of the war Arthur Greiser was captured by the Americans, then handed over to the Poles. At his trial in Warsaw in 1946, he portrayed himself as no more than a scapegoat for the crimes of Hitler and Himmler. Appeals to the Polish State President (claiming, remarkably, that he had always worked for a policy of understanding with Poland and had been unaware of Hitler's plans) and even the Pope (even more extraordinary given the savagery of his assault on the Catholic Church) were to no avail. On 14 July 1946 he was publicly hanged in Poznan. For a brief biographical sketch, see Ian Kershaw, 'Arthur Greiser – Ein Motor der Endlösung', in R.Smelser, E.Syring, and R.Zitelmann (eds.), *Die braune Elite II*, Darmstadt, 1993, pp.116–27.

15. Hans-Günther Seraphim, *Das politische Tagebuch Alfred Rosenbergs 1934/35 und 1939/40*, Munich, 1964, p.99.

16. Broszat, *Polenpolitik*, p.25.

17. Instytut Zachodni, Poznan, I-441, fols. 145–9.

18. GK, PAG, vol.27, fol.167.

19. Aly, 68.

20. Institut für Zeitgeschichte, Munich, Eichmann 1460.

21. ZSL, Prozeß Koppe, fols.156, 158; Polen 179, fols.653–4.

22. Broszat, *Polenpolitik*, p.119.

23. Broszat, *Polenpolitik*, p.97.

24. See, for further detail, Ian Kershaw, 'Improvised Genocide? The Emergence of the "Final Solution" in the "Warthegau"', *Transactions of the Royal Historical Society*, 6th ser., 2 (1992), pp.57–9; and see also Aly, p.144.

25. Broszat, *Polenpolitik*, pp.97–8; Aly, pp.211–12.

26. Martin Broszat, *200 Jahre deutsche Polenpolitik*, Munich, 1963, p.227; see also Broszat, *Polenpolitik*, p.98.

27. Broszat, *Polenpolitik*, pp.119–20.

28. Broszat, *Polenpolitik*, p.125.

29. ZSL, Anklageschrift aus dem Prozeß gegen Arthur Greiser [Indictment against Greiser, German transl., from the Polish original], pp.21–6; Broszat, *Polenpolitik*, pp.143–57; Broszat, *200 Jahre*, p.230.

30. Archiwum Panstwowe Poznan, Best. Schupo Posen, 7, Dienstbefehle of Schutzpolizei Jarotschin, Nr.1, 15 Oct. 1939, Nr.5, 20 March 1940.

31. ZSL, Polen 365p, fol.609.

32. ZSL, Anklageschrift, p.38.

33. ZSL, Polen 365p, fols.472–3, 477; Polen 365h, fols.565–8, 572–3, for examples (though increasingly, it appears, from the middle of the war onwards, when the German occupiers had to reckon with the consequences of ever more likely defeat).

34. GK, PAG, vol.36, fol.567–8.

35. Berlin Document Center (=BDC), Personalakte (=PA) Arthur Greiser, Greiser to Himmler, 1 May 1942; Jüdisches Historisches Institut, Warsaw, Faschismus-Getto-Massemord, Frankfurt am Main n.d. [1961], p.278.

36. BDC, PA Greiser, Rudolf Brandt to Koppe, 14 May 1942.

37. BDC, PA Greiser, Greiser to Himmler, 21 Nov. 1942.

THE EMERGENCE OF COLONEL MIHAILOVIĆ BY RADIO

BILL DEAKIN

In early September 1941 the Royal Navy's wireless transmitter station at Rosyth in Scotland was trying to pick up and identify weak signals on YTHS, a Reuters commercial prefix for routine signals by merchant shipping. Such traffic was normally handled by the General Post Office W/T receiving station at Portishead in Somerset. There was regular contact between the two posts and Rosyth contacted its sister station in mid-September, asking it to take over the monitoring of the weak signals received on YTHS. The evidence as to dates seems to show that the first signal was picked up before 10 September 1941, when a copy of a message is recorded as having been received by SOE in London. The Mihailović files, captured by the Partisans in 1945, note the date of the first surviving radio message as 14 September 1941.

There was an air of suppressed excitement. Some W/T set in occupied Europe was seeking to make contact with the British. A chief civilian operator at Portishead, W. G. L. Parsons, set up a special group of listener-operators. Messages were *en clair* and in English and were headed 'the Yugoslav Army of the Mountains' or, at times, 'the free military W/T station of unoccupied Serbia'. The sender, however, did not understand English and, if questioned, replied 'AS.MO', meaning 'just a minute'. But there were clearly English-speakers surrounding the operator and they interrupted him from time to time with comments. Their language was so strong that Parsons felt obliged temporarily to withdraw his female staff. Portishead requested replies in coherent English. It later emerged that there were five British officers at Mihailović's headquarters who had all jumped from trains carrying prisoners of war captured on Crete through Serbia to Germany.

These early signals were forwarded on receipt by telex to the Admiralty, which passed the messages to SIS. It, together with SOE, then took over the link, which would henceforth be handled by an SIS station on Malta. On 14 September three YTHS signals, claiming to come from the 'free military W/T station of unoccupied Serbia', asked whatever British station was receiving its traffic to relay the following messages to the Yugoslav government in London:

> To Živan Knežević . . . London: Speak personally on London radio. I am listening to you every day. It is urgent. Your godfather Draga, Class 50.

> We are working every day on wavelength QRG Central European time 04.00 hours. We await your reply confirming receipt of this message in the daily bulletins in Serbian on the London radio. We listen every day to this news. We await your answer at 06.00 hours.

> I am in a place called by the name of the battalion in your fifth and fourth company. Your godfather Draga, Class 50 in Paris.

There is much confusion about the exact date of this message. Konstantin Fotić, the Yugoslav minister in Washington during the war, wrote that it was received on 13 September.[1] Knežević, the Yugoslav government's liaison officer with SOE in London, himself cited 14 September, but agreed with Fotić that it was picked up on Malta. As noted above, the first telegram in the Mihailović files in Belgrade is also dated 14 September, but marked as received in London only on 6 October! While this is the same text as delivered by King Peter and his Premier, General Dušan Simović, to Churchill on 13 October, it was clearly not the first signal. According to British sources, this composite message was dated 10 September, but transmitted between then and the 14th.

These signals were despatched in order to identify the sender to Major Knežević, but he was then absent in Cairo. Thus, according to Knežević, they were not passed by his colleagues to their superior, General Simović, until Knežević returned to England. SOE must have connived in this arrangement.

The identification of the sender in fact proved to be simple. 'Draga Class 50' was Lieutenant-Colonel Dragoslav Pavlović, who had been with Knežević in Class 50 at the École Supérieure de Guerre in Paris, while the name of the battalion mentioned in the second message was 'Suvobor', the mountain plateau in western Serbia which had been the site of an heroic battle against the Austrians in 1914 and was now the location of the Mihailović forces' headquarters.

On 25 September Knežević replied as requested in the BBC's Serbo-Croat bulletin: 'To Godfather 50. We have received all your messages and are seeking arrangements. We wish you all the very best.[2] Further signals from Pavlović followed, still in *en clair* YTHS. After a series of technical and security checks regular contact was established on 6 October. One of these checks was very personal. When at the École de Guerre, Knežević and Pavlović had shared a girl friend. A signal was sent to the latter asking the name of the young lady and the colour of her knickers. The prompt answer was 'Kathy, yellow'.[3] This seemed decisive.

Another YTHS signal on 6 October caused a stir of excitement in London 'secret circles' and formally confirmed that this link was genuine:

The Yugoslav Army exists in the country. It is commanded by Colonel Draža Mihailović. The people are eager to fight. We have not even the most necessary means for this. Up to now we are fighting only with rifles or hand grenades. The Germans are afraid. They do not know what to do. In spite of this they carry on their terrible atrocities. We have encircled Valjevo for many days already. We are pressing forward to Kragujevac and Kraljevo. The enemy, though short of aeroplanes to use against us, is still more powerful. The aerodromes at Preljina, Čačak and Požega are ready. Our headquarters are at Suvobor. On the whole of the freed territory there is not one of the enemy except as a prisoner. The morale of the Italians in Sandžak is very low. In Bosnia only the Ustaše continue to fight while the Croats flee. The Germans occupy only the Lower Morava [valley] in great strength, while the other garrisons west of there are being besieged and taken by us. We have destroyed almost all roads and railways. The Ustaše have committed terrible things against the Serbs. Not even wild beasts can be compared with them, but we have begun to extract our revenge on them. The people would be happy to see the first help arrive from the Allies. On the 9th I shall be at Požega. I can come and report. Send an aeroplane. Lieutenant-Colonel Pavlović.[4]

This message reached London two days after the first signals from Captain D. T. (Bill) Hudson's 'Bullseye' mission in Montenegro had been passed to Knežević. 'Bullseye' had been sent into occupied Yugoslavia with a vague brief to identify resistance from any quarter. Hudson was accompanied by two Yugoslav air force officers with quite different instructions. However, the receipt of the 6 October message by Portishead now made it critical that 'Bullseye' should link up with Colonel Mihailović on Suvobor and, in particular, provide him with safe codes.

According both to Knežević and to certain SOE sources in London, the existence of Mihailović and his regular army group in western Serbia was not known until 24 September, the day before Knežević's BBC message to Pavlović. But there is some evidence that Simović was also active on his own account – and well aware of the rivalries at work in his midst. After the war Simović published a selected and censored version of his memoirs in the Belgrade press. In this account he refers to the arrival in Lisbon at the beginning of August 1941 of a neutral diplomat from Belgrade who called at the Yugoslav legation in the Portuguese capital to pass on a message containing 'the first news about the establishment of a rebel core on Ravna Gora' to the Yugoslav chargé d'affaires, Slavko Kojić. The message handed over by the diplomat was sent immediately by special courier to Simović in London. The name of the commander of the uprising was mentioned by his initials, 'D.M.' Short and long wave frequencies for W/T transmissions were provided, and the report was signed 'General Staff Major Z.P.T.', whom Simović immediately recognized by his handwriting as Žarko P. Todorović. 'Because,' according to Simović, 'the report bore a much earlier date and set out arrangements for establishing links in July, all the attempts of the British secret W/T service to make contact failed . . . . My desire that we should establish direct links from London and Cairo with our rebels in the country remained unfulfilled.'[5]

This version seems to confirm that Simović knew by early August that 'D.M.' – Draža Mihailović – was in command on Ravna Gora and that Major Žarko Todorović, Mihailović's representative in Belgrade, was one of his officers. As for the 'neutral diplomat', there is a firm explanation. At his trial in 1946 Mihailović testified that 'Žarko Todorović had succeeded in making contact with the American Legation'.[6] On 12 July 1941 the counsellor of the American legation, Karl Rankin, had left Belgrade on his way back to the United States. He reached Lisbon before the end of the month, where he called on the British minister, Ronald H. Campbell, who had been minister in Belgrade when the war began. Campbell reported to London on 25 July that Rankin had told him that 'the Serbs beg him to ask that the BBC cease all propaganda and references about guerrillas in the hills of south Serbia' as such reports would bring down punitive expeditions. The guerrilla bands were in fact quite numerous, though he could give no details as to their positions or numbers, but their leaders had 'no intention of attacking the German army at present. But the Serbs did ask for full publicity about the Croat atrocities.'[7] Although Rankin did not make any reference to having had a link with the guerrillas' representatives in Belgrade, it is credible that, as a neutral diplomat, he had delivered an envelope on their behalf to the Yugoslav legation in Lisbon without informing the British. There is, however, no available British evidence to show that Simović himself approached the British intelligence agencies to ask them to establish a W/T link with Todorović in Belgrade.

Apart from this episode, Simović had another – and possibly the only – direct official link with developments in Yugoslavia as they were understood in the Middle East. He was in regular W/T contact with his minister of war, General Bogoljub Ilić, in Cairo. On the other hand, it can be assumed that the staff of the Yugoslavs' listening post in Istanbul under Jovan Djonović and Nikola Knežević (who was in charge of ciphers and communications and brother to Živan and Radoje) were already sufficiently hostile to Simović to keep back certain 'sensitive' intelligence from both him and Ilić.

On 12 September 1941 Ilić cabled to Simović a 'Report on Politico-Military Events and the Situation on the Battlefield':

The clashes of Četnik units with the occupying powers are spreading. Serbs are fighting around Rudnik, in Belgrade and its surroundings, in Montenegro and Lika, in Bosnia and Vojvodina.

According to certain reports, a limited unification of their actions has been worked out by the senior officers. In this connection the name of General Staff Colonel Dragoljub Mihailović is mentioned.[8]

This telegram is of particular significance. It proves that Ilić had no knowledge of the purpose of the 'Bullseye' mission which left Cairo for Malta by air on 8 September and landed Hudson and Majors Zaharije Ostojić and Mirko Lalatović from a submarine on the coast of Montenegro on 20 September. Otherwise, Ilić would certainly have mentioned it to his premier. The two Yugoslav air force officers, however, were certainly briefed for 'special tasks' by Brigadier Bora Mirković, the organizer of the 27 March coup d'état and another of Simović's emergent rivals in the fractious Yugoslav emigration. Ilić's signal did, however, confirm to Simović the existence and role of Colonel Mihailović, even if he already knew this from Lisbon.

On 24 September Simović received from Knežević the YTHS signals previously withheld by members of his military staff, as well as certain 'Bullseye' messages. A day or two later the BBC received a request from the Yugoslav government to broadcast the following message on its Serbo-Croat bulletin:

> To our leaders in our country. We have received your message (incomplete) on the English radio station. We listen to your long wave station every day. We have received your letter and both ciphers. Make yourselves known.

The Foreign Office agreed to the broadcast of this message, though there is no record indicating whether the diplomats were informed either of its content or of its background.[9]

Who initiated this message? 'Your letter and both ciphers' must refer to Žarko Todorović in Belgrade and to the report he sent through Lisbon. This had also referred to 'long and short waves'. 'Make yourselves known' would also imply that this message was sent under Simović's instructions and intended for Mihailović's Belgrade staff. Any signals despatched to Pavlović could more easily have gone on the YTHS link, and not over the BBC, though, of course, Knežević's 25 September reply to Pavlović *had* been sent on this latter channel. A mystery, none the less, remains.[10]

In any event, on receiving the decisive Pavlović telegram of 6 October Simović took executive action. The YTHS signal from western Serbia identifying Mihailović as the leader of the uprising moved Simović to summon a dramatic meeting of the cabinet in London on 9 October at which the King himself presided. In his memoirs Simović adds:

> In order to maintain the complete secrecy of the existence of our rebel group on Ravna Gora from enemy intelligence services,[11] and to make sure it was not discovered prematurely, I informed only the King about it. Only at the meeting of 9 October did I disclose it to the

members of the cabinet, insisting that they should keep the secret for as long as necessary.[12]

At this meeting the participants had before them the first YTHS signals and some of the 'Bullseye' messages from Montenegro. Somewhat out of character, Simović allowed himself to be pushed by the collective and frenetic excitement of the members of his cabinet to draft a formal appeal to the British government to send military supplies and to establish secure radio links with a shadowy leader just emerged on a chance W/T pick up, but identified as a respectable regular Yugoslav officer. Colonel Dragoljub Mihailović had risen to cabinet level.

The enthusiasm within the Yugoslav government-in-exile received an immediate response from Churchill and Eden. Occupied Yugoslavia offered the most tempting possibilities since the collapse of Greece for a landing in South-Eastern Europe and a potential prelude to a second front. On 13 October King Peter, accompanied by General Simović, called on the British Prime Minister, who was handed an aide-memoire. Appended to this paper were the messages received by the W/T station at Portishead, supplemented by the signals picked up later by the SIS post on Malta. This amateurish reception in an international commercial code by a General Post Office station – and its hourly study by a persistent civilian official – led to the revelation of Colonel Mihailović as the most promising leader of the resistance which had been expected in Serbia and to the build-up by British services of his noble image as the first recognizable and active resistance leader in Axis-occupied Europe.

NOTES

1. Constantin Fotitch, *The War We Lost: Yugoslavia's Tragedy and the Failure of the West* (New York: Viking, 1948), p.155.
2. Given the recognition of the putative resistance movement implied by use of the BBC, it is unclear – aside from Pavlović's request – why this

message should not have been sent over the YTHS link, which was working, albeit erratically, in both directions.

3. Knežević, *Poruka* (London), No 8.

4. YRX 05.00 GMT Message to YTHS transmitter at 03.08 GMT Portishead Radio.

5. Simović memoirs, as cited from the original by Jovan Marjanović, *Ustanak i narodnooslobodilački pokret u Srbiji 1941* (Belgrade: Institut društvenih nauka, 1963), p 194, note 324. Note that both Jovan Djonović, the royal government's delegate in the Middle East, and SOE in Cairo knew from reports by couriers reaching Istanbul of Mihailović's presence in western Serbia in July, while Simović, by his own account, had learned by early August. The Pavlović telegram giving Mihailović's name was dated 6 October. Hudson in Montenegro was told about Mihailović on 9 October. But when did SOE in London have this intelligence?

6. *The Trial of Dragoljub-Draža Mihailović* (Belgrade, 1946), p 159.

7. FO 371/30214, R7294, Lisbon telegram, 25 July 1941.

8. Quoted in Marjanović, *Ustanak*, p.198.

9. FO 371/30315, R8483/114/92. Passed to Ministry of Information by the Yugoslav government. P.J. Dixon minuted on 23 September: 'I heard later that the message would be sent *unless* we stopped it. Mr Bruce Lockhart having told me that there was no objection to this kind of message being carried in our transmissions, I accordingly took no action.'

10. It is even possible that messages from Todorović in Belgrade were being picked up *en clair* in London.

11. Presumably he feared there were Axis agents in royal Yugoslav circles.

12. Quoted in Marjanović, *Ustanak*, pp. 194–95, note 324.

TEACHING THE FREE MAN
HOW TO PRAISE
Michael Foot on SOE and
Resistance in Europe

RALPH WHITE

Michael Foot is a warrior historian, one of that generation of British scholars who served their country in the Second World War and later devoted their formidable talents to its academic study. He is in good company: the names of Sir William Deakin[1], Sir Harry Hinsley[2] and Sir Michael Howard[3] spring to mind, fellow warrior historians who between them have illuminated one of the seminal events of the twentieth century. What is fascinating about their work is the interplay of their feelings, insights and values as participants with their disciplined analysis as professional scholars. I want to explore this interplay in the case of Foot's achievements as doyen of British historians of European resistance, and to suggest that the distinctive quality of his writing, while it has several sources, lies ultimately in its fusion of moral and scholarly values.

The link between Foot's war experience and his interest in resistance is striking. An army officer throughout the war, he was a gunner major on combined operations staff, and intelligence officer to the Special Air Service (SAS) Brigade. Thus he was embroiled in the irregular and secret war against Hitler, as he explains in one of the rare but revealing moments when the authorial voice, usually so detached, permits a personal aside:

> My own war career . . . lay outside SOE, but led me sometimes to rub shoulders with it in 1942–4, and taught me a little about strategy, tactics, logistics, intelligence, planning and secrecy. I have been shot

105

at, have parachuted, have helped to plan raids, have taken part as observer in air operations and in a sea commando raid, have organized escapes, and have succeeded in hiding my military identity during German interrogations.[4]

These experiences inspired a lifelong concern with the study of resistance. This is manifest in an arresting body of published work, on which Foot's distinction as a historian is largely based.

The first, seminal, study was a detailed and original analysis of the work of SOE in one country, *SOE in France*[5]; this was complemented by his later comprehensive volume on resistance throughout occupied Europe, *Resistance*[6]. Three other directly relevant, but rather less substantial, works must be mentioned: a portrait of individual resisters, *Six Faces of Courage*[7], a study, with J.M. Langley, of the specialist British organization in promoting escape during the war, *MI9: Escape and Evasion*[8], and *SOE*, a concise overview of the organization[9]. These specialized works are buttressed by several more general studies of modern warfare, which Foot has either written or edited[10]. He is currently working on a volume on SOE activities in the Low Countries.

This extensive corpus has been supplemented over the years by a stream of individual chapters, papers, articles and reviews dealing with resistance themes. However, this is not to imply that Foot's energies have been limited to this topic. His early work on Gladstone and Liberalism, with J.L. Hammond[11], on British foreign policy[12], and his editorship, latterly with H.C.G. Matthew, of the Gladstone diaries[13], attest to the breadth of his historical interests. But these works suggest more: that Foot began his scholarly life primarily as a historian of the nineteenth century who extended his allegiance, and applied his skills, to a period through which he lived and to a war in which he participated. In this his career parallels those of other historians who have been drawn from preoccupation with earlier periods by the magnetism of the present. One thinks of Sir Lewis Namier enlarging his eighteenth century concerns to embrace the Munich era, and Lord Dacre (Hugh Trevor-Roper) expanding his seventeenth century interest to include the Third Reich. Foot shares with them the experience of being caught up in the compelling dramas of European life in the 1930s and 1940s, and of seeking to reconcile the motives of the scholar and the individual in their historical work.

What, then, makes for the character and quality of Foot's writing on resistance? Before we consider questions of scholarship and moral commitment, we must do justice to three characteristics of all his work: style, culture and a view of history. No one familiar with his books can be unaware of their literary form: of a remarkable prose style nurtured on the grammar, syntax and rhythms of the classics and the Book of Common Prayer[14], and adapted by a writer with a particular enthusiasm for the semicolon.

It was not only a sense of style that Foot absorbed from his education as a Scholar of Winchester and New College, Oxford, but a culture. Again, anyone who knows his writing will recognize the breadth of cultural reference which reinforces its stylistic form. This involves a familiarity with both the history and the literature of Britain and Europe. Readers encounter characters and sources as diverse as Caxton and Charlemagne, Hobbes and Humpty Dumpty, Malory and Manley Hopkins, Othello and Proust, Sherlock Holmes and James Bond, King Stork and King Log. Foot is a man of learning, and this becomes an important part of the message: his analysis of European resistance is both memorably recounted and finds its place in a historical and cultural context that sharpens and dignifies its significance.

Yet this framework of style and cultural reference is also a means of communication between the scholar and his audience. For Foot shares with many of his background and generation a sense of history – that is, of academic historical writing – as part of a liberal and civilized discourse between educated people. This view survives in the work of historians who seek to bring the fruits of academic research to a general audience, but contrasts, sometimes sharply, with a more prevalent idea of history as a specialist, even social scientific discipline, written in a more technical language, and communicable to a more limited and professional readership.

There is a paradox here. On the one hand Foot reaches out to his general reader with a distinctiveness of style and a wealth of reference, on the assumption that they can be shared; on the other this framework permits a degree of individuality, even idiosyncrasy, in his writing beyond the reach of his successors. Yet the paradoxes are resolved, and suspicions of cultural exclusiveness allayed, in that Foot has established a reputation as one of the most independent and invigorating of living historians.

The scholarly virtues of Foot's work are those of a professional historian dealing with a subject whose existing literature was dominated by non-academics, though this applies less to accounts of European resistance in general than to SOE[15]. Former participants offered their memoirs; other writers produced their romanticized accounts of individual resisters, particular missions and movements. Some of these works, especially those of former agents, have their evidential value, but as Foot himself remarks: 'Unfortunately, for lack of enough authentic material many of the resulting books are good thrillers, but bad history.'[16]

The point is that resistance was a secret activity, and SOE a secret organization, and the survival and accessibility of primary sources are major problems for the serious researcher. Foot was the first scholar to be allowed access to some of SOE's files from 1960 (decades before they became available to the general public). This was a result of Prime Minister Macmillan's decision to authorize a proper study of SOE's wartime record, and led eventually to the publication of *SOE in France* as a volume in the official history of the Second World War. Foot's experiences in penetrating the hitherto closed world of SOE and its sources are vividly recalled[17].

In a field so shrouded in mystery and myth the impact of a trained historian can hardly be exaggerated. The writer was able to use a variety of sources as well as SOE's archive, ranging from the more reliable agents' memoirs, diaries and secondary texts to the inimitable flashes of 'personal knowledge' and 'private information'. He also imposed a coherent structure, in which the specific activities of SOE in the field were set in two frameworks: that of the SOE's systems of recruitment, training and communication; and that of the origins, purposes, structure and development of SOE as an institution. A similarly disciplined organization distinguishes Foot's *Resistance*: the use of a wide variety of sources – though with more emphasis on secondary ones – within a structure that places the diverse activities of resistance throughout occupied Europe ('what happened') within a context that defines resistance and those who took part, describes the forms of resistance structures and techniques, and investigates the background of European politics and war from which resistance sprang.

In these ways Foot deploys his professional skills in investigating and marshalling sources and organizing his material to combat the besetting sins of so much resistance literature: the lack of authenticity and anecdotalism. Foot's great contributions, aside from his inimitable style, have been to provide accounts of SOE and European resistance that are both properly researched and set within a clear analytical framework. Yet it is possible to lose sight of these achievements as one responds to Foot's treatment of what, for him, is the heart of the matter: resisters – who they were, what they tried to do and what they achieved. For it is here that the writer's identification with his subject, and his and his fellow participants' sense of what it meant to be involved in the war, becomes palpable; it is at this point that scholarship and the moral perceptions of a generation join hands.

One can understand this sensitivity to those who resisted: for they were distinguishable. Resistance was, with the exception of the partisan forces operating behind German lines in the Soviet Union, behind Axis lines in the Balkans and among the larger maquis in the Massif Central and Alpine France, a small group, face-to-face activity. In contrast to the vast formations that dominated conventional warfare, resisters remained individuals, whether working alone or within their cells, circuits or movements. In their intelligence gathering, subversion and escape lines, resisters gave total war a human face.

This individuality was profoundly reinforced by the nature and circumstances of resistance activity itself. It was very dangerous, in that torture and death were probable consequences of capture by an enemy who was ruthlessly, and sometimes skilfully, determined to wipe out all signs of resistance in occupied Europe, and to pursue a policy of often savage reprisals within the local community. It had to be secret, both to ensure any chance of success and to maximize security, and, if properly conducted, was often an isolated and lonely experience. Finally it was the work of volunteers, men and women who were prepared, entirely of their own volition, to seek the liberation of countries which had been defeated and occupied by formidable enemy forces whose military power seemed invincible until the winter of 1942/3. These characteristics of resistance in the field have naturally attracted the non-academic writer and film maker, but they were not invented by them; the scholar has to come to terms with them too.

Foot's response is to argue that 'character, not class, made people into resisters, or collaborators, or would-be neutrals; character, not class, encouraged some of them to move from any of these roles to another, as the tides of war shifted.'[18] The evidence of the diverse composition of resistance groupings, he believes, shows that resistance was an individual, human response first; a matter of class or party or religious or secular persuasion second. The great question of who resisted is therefore answered by enumerating the qualities of character involved in resistance work: above all, for Foot, originality or unorthodoxy, whereby resisters tended 'to be out of step with their time – usually in advance of it; Pierre Bezukhovs rather than Boris Drubetskoys who trim their sails to catch every puff of social wind that may lead to their personal advancement.'[19] The training of many professional men, he implies, left them too inhibited; women, less constrained in this way, played a notable role in resistance. But other qualities were crucial: courage, strong nerves, quickness of wit, discretion, a gift of silence, resourcefulness, tenacity, patience and luck. Foot admits that not all resisters were angels, that some were in it for the money, or goods, whilst others saw resistance as adventure, almost a game. But though there were 'rascals' as well as 'heroes' in their midst, his admiration is unbounded: 'It will be clear already to readers that the author is a warm admirer of resisters, as a type of human being; in principle. He has met, and read of, too many to have a doubt that on the whole they are the salt of the earth.'[20]

It is perfectly possible for those of a different generation to share this respect for the undoubted courage and resource of many resisters. Yet Foot's personal familiarity with them and their work explains an identity which, in turn, animates his commitment to them and their cause. The fascination of his writing lies in this interplay between the coolness of the scholar and the warm involvement of the participant, an interplay which, while it may not be to everyone's taste, gives his writings much of their distinction.

This emerges graphically in his accounts of what resisters did. Because their activities were individual, dangerous and secret, Foot is able to counterpoint their formal categories – intelligence, subversion and escape – with a remarkable sense of the myriad acts of personal response in occupied Europe of which resistance was actually constituted. His writings are shot through with the exploits of resisters, detailed with an intense, Tolstoyan feeling for their particularity. So, in one sense, Foot's resistance is itself profoundly anecdotal – a compound of hundreds and thousands of essentially individual acts – as if resistance was, *par excellence*, the way in which, against the impersonal vastness of total war, individual courage and virtue were able to identify and assert themselves. Beyond this, Foot sees in resistance evidence of individuality, indeed of a surviving European humanism, to set against the conformist, collectivist tendencies of modern history and society. These tendencies were embodied in an extreme form in the Axis powers and their domination of Europe, against which the Allies were fighting and resistance was pitted.

In this struggle, what did resistance finally achieve? It is with his answer to this question that Foot nails his colours to the mast. As a military historian, he accepts that the Second World War was won principally by the formal military forces of the Allies, but he argues that resistance played a significant auxiliary role, which could have been greater had the Allies appreciated its economic and strategic value more. As a political scholar, he believes that resistance played a major part in sustaining morale in occupied countries during the war and in enabling those countries to regain their sense of identity and self respect on liberation. But, he argues, above all 'the greatest good that resistance did lay in the hearts of the people who took part in it.'[21] The fusion of scholarly and moral values could not be more explicit in the view that 'resistance's real strength in battlefield terms, in an age of armour and air warfare, was puny. But it had titanic, as it turned out invincible, strength in moral terms'.[22] Further, the unequivocal language of the political-moral argument contrasts, as will be seen, with the more nuanced terms in which the strategic-economic case is couched.

In balancing admiration for resisters' activities with realism about their results, Foot avoids optimistic or pessimistic extremes. He acknowledges the difficulty of making precise estimates of the value of the work of the many secret intelligence networks in occupied Europe, bearing in mind the existence of other sources, above all Ultra, the preference for them in orthodox service minds, and the variation in the use made of intelligence by different military commanders. Yet he is able to describe a number of intelligence coups for which resisters were responsible.[23] In contrast, the achievements of escape lines can be more easily measured and costed. Foot cites the figure of 33,517 British and American forces who returned, often with the help of local resisters, from enemy-held to Allied territory during the war, 'no negligible contribution to allied manpower'. MI9 lines alone brought back some 3,500 aircrew, at a time when it cost £5,000 to train a single fighter pilot and £23,000 to train the seven-man crew of a Lancaster bomber.[24]

Foot confirms that subversive activity occurred frequently throughout occupied Europe, especially sabotage, attacks on troops and propaganda, though less so in the case of assassination and insurrection. He concludes that 'in sheer physical factory sabotage, resistance made a sizeable but far from decisive dent in the Nazi economy'.[25] The questions, Foot notes, of deciding how large the dent was, and how bothered the Nazis were, remain open. He highlights the unresolved issues in deciding between the efficacy and economy of air bombardment and sabotage as means of attacking enemy plant, and argues that 'the use . . . made of resistance techniques since the war cannot help raising a retrospective doubt whether a lot more might not have been done with them against Hitler.'[26]

Ambushes and attacks on enemy troops were numerous throughout the war, particularly in the east by Soviet partisans, in Yugoslavia by Tito's forces, and in western Europe, especially in France in connection with D-Day and Operation Overlord. In no case does Foot suggest that these operations by themselves succeeded in liberating the countries from enemy domination; yet in each case resistance fighters played significant, sometimes substantial, roles in assisting Allied forces in their work of liberation. In the case of France, for example, he avoids any claim that resistance liberated either the country or its capital in 1944; yet he is able to detail the notable contribution made through a combination of clandestine activities, many SOE-organized and supplied, in support of Allied forces, which unquestionably facilitated their progress. These included disruption of enemy rail and telephone communications, and harassing of enemy moves by road, on a scale which palpably interfered with German efforts to support their forces in Normandy, and which later gained generous recognition from Eisenhower as Supreme Commander[27]. Again, and more generally, Foot suggests that studies of the impact of resistance activity on the German army in retreat after 1943, and in particular on the number of casualties suffered by German forces, would be illuminating.

One can find no better example of Foot's careful assessment of resistance activity than in his treatment of propaganda, and especially of the clandestine press. He stresses the importance attached by the major Allied governments to radio broadcasts in occupied Europe, and the extent of the work of the BBC, Radio Moscow, and American stations. He emphasizes the growth of the underground press throughout occupied Europe: over a thousand separate clandestine papers appeared in France alone, with contributions from leading

French writers and intellectuals. He realizes that 'work for these newspapers was just as intricate and just as dangerous as any other kind of work in resistance', and that its function of convincing the peoples of occupied Europe of the worthlessness of the Nazi cause and the possibility of Axis defeat was vital. Yet the problem remains, for Foot, that the priority attached to propaganda both by Allied governments and illustrated in the remarkable growth of the clandestine press cannot be taken as evidence of influence or impact. 'Certainly,' writes Foot 'the present writer does not believe this press was negligible, or useless; he seeks only to bring out the danger of laying too much emphasis on it.'[28]

So there is a paradox at the heart of Foot's analysis of the value of resistance. *A propos* its contribution to the military and economic side of the Allied war effort, the scholar acknowledges the difficulties in making final or unequivocal judgements, and comes to his measured conclusions as to its real but limited role – with the important proviso that more could have been made of it. *A propos* the political, psychological and moral dimension, his conclusions are more confident and emphatic. At their core is the conviction that resistance 'gave back to people in the occupied countries the self-respect that they lost in the moment of occupation'.[29] It may well have been – he concurs to a degree, with de Gaulle – 'a bluff that came off', but it nevertheless enabled individuals and countries to recover their sense of identity and self confidence. By 1945, he avers, millions of Europeans had found the courage to play some part, however slight, in resistance; they could say 'with the best of the French, *'moi, j'ai le coeur tranquille.'*[30] And the recovery of many European states post-war was sustained by knowledge of their wartime resistance and by leaders who owed their positions to their resistance records.

The greatest value of resistance was, therefore, moral and exemplary. It was expressed, not in its actual results, but in its circumstances and purposes and the qualities of those who took part in it. Ultimately, with Foot we return to the resisters themselves, and their achievement *in resisting*. He believes that what they did was in a special sense memorable, 'something that men who came later would always remember and respect'[31], for 'they kept alive ideas of dignity and originality, without which all Europe, all the world would be the poorer.'[32] He prizes above all the sense of resisters' divine bloodymindedness, and ends *Resistance* with a

113

Dutch saying, 'Only dead fishes float down the stream, live ones swim against it.'

Foot is not the only scholar to combine unconstrained admiration for what resisters stood for with a qualified view of what they achieved. Alan Milward, a historian of a different kind and generation, has locked horns with Foot in taking a far more sceptical view of the strategic and economic work of resisters.[33] Yet he too writes of resistance as 'the ultimate affirmation of every human being's right to his own individuality. The myriad acts of petty defiance do testify to the unquenchable fire of humanity. . . . Such defiance is a joyful and ineradicable testimony to the eternally renewed, anarchical spirit of mankind.'[34] So veneration for the exemplary value of resistance is not confined to one scholar or one generation, and can be, and is, shared by others. What is singular about Foot's writings is that they are imbued with a participants' sense of identity with resisters, and, more generally, by a felt knowledge, shared with many contemporaries, of what it meant to be involved in the war against Hitler. This experiential dimension can be communicated to later generations, but it cannot be relived. To the charge that historians can be too close, too involved with their subject matter, the reply is that if the scholarship is sound, and the analysis coherent, the reader has the bonus of being exposed to the *mentalité* of participants – in this case of resisters and their generation – and understanding this is an important part of understanding the whole. In Foot's case, the roles of participant and historian are splendidly fused; without any diminution of scholarship and to the benefit and interest of his readers.

This involvement fires not only his admiration for resisters, but his acute sense, as a contemporary, of both the indebtedness of his and future generations, and of the need to remember. It is hard – no, impossible – to imagine any present or future historian concluding, as Foot does, his exhaustive study of resistance in over twenty European countries with a peroration like this:

> If you who read this can say, I am not under fire; I am not under torture; I am not on the run; if I hear a noise at six in the morning, I know it is a neighbour or a milkman, not the secret police; no one in my country is arrested and held without prompt charge and trial; I can read newspapers, see and hear broadcasts, of several different views; within the laws of libel, I can say what I like about anybody;

then you owe it, in a larger degree than most historians have so far allowed, to the resistance that occupied Europe put up to Hitler.[35]

If we do owe something, and we ought to remember, then we need to know why. This, over and above the curiosity of the scholar, has led Foot to offer his accounts of SOE and European resistance, and to press on us, in memorable language, the contribution they made in the Second World War, and, especially, their exemplary worth. He convinces us that resistance had an epic quality, yet claims that 'History sometimes has to handle themes of epic, but history is not poetry.'[36] But Foot's vision of resistance, for all its scholarly virtues, is inspired by the same purpose that Auden ascribes to poetry in his magnificent elegy to W.B. Yeats. Yeats died in 1939, and the parallels between Auden's invocation of the nightmares of that year and those of the wartime occupation of Europe are compelling:

> In the nightmare of the dark
> All the dogs of Europe bark,
> And the living nations wait,
> Each sequestered in its hate;
>
> Intellectual disgrace
> Stares from every human face,
> And the seas of pity lie
> Locked and frozen in each eye.
>
> Follow, poet, follow right
> To the bottom of the night,
> With your unconstraining voice
> Still persuade us to rejoice;
>
> With the farming of a verse
> Make a vineyard of the curse,
> Sing of human unsuccess
> In a rapture of distress;
>
> In the deserts of the heart
> Let the healing fountain start,
> In the prison of his days
> Teach the free man how to praise.

For Michael Foot it is history as well as poetry that can do this.

NOTES

1. Deakin's works include *The Brutal Friendship: Mussolini, Hitler and the fall of Italian Fascism*. rev.ed. Harmondsworth: Penguin, 1966; and *The Embattled Mountain*, London: Oxford University Press, 1971.
2. Among Hinsley's studies of international history note: *Hitler's Strategy*. Cambridge: Cambridge University Press, 1951; his contribution as co-writer and editor of *British Intelligence in the Second World War*, vols. 1–4. London: HMSO, 1979–1990; and edited with Alan Stripp, *Codebreakers: The Inside Story of Bletchley Park*. Oxford: Oxford University Press, 1993.
3. Howard's books include *The Mediterranean Strategy in the Second World War*. London: Weidenfeld & Nicolson, 1968; *Grand Strategy: August 1942–September 1943*. Vol.4 of *History of the Second World War – UK Military Series*. London: HMSO, 1972; and *Strategic Deception*. vol. 5 of *British Intelligence in the Second World War*. London: HMSO, 1990.
4. *SOE. The Special Operations Executive 1940–1946*. London: BBC,1984. Author's note, p.8.
5. *SOE in France: An Account of the Work of the British Special Operations Executive in France 1940–1944*. London: HMSO, 1966 (rev.ed. 1968).
6. *Resistance: An Analysis of European Resistance to Nazism 1940–1945*. London: Eyre Methuen, 1976.
7. *Six Faces of Courage*. London: Eyre Methuen, 1978.
8. *MI9: Escape and Evasion 1939–1945* (with J.M. Langley). London: Bodley Head, 1979.
9. *SOE.op.cit.*
10. *Men in Uniform: Military Manpower in Modern Industrial Societies*. London: Weidenfeld, 1961; (ed.) *War and Society*. London: Elek, 1973; (ed.) *Holland at War against Hitler: Anglo-Dutch Relations 1940–1945*. London: Cass, 1990; (consultant ed.) *The Oxford Companion to the Second World War*. Oxford: Oxford University Press, 1995.
11. *Gladstone and Liberalism* (with J.L. Hammond). London: English Universities Press, 1952.
12. *British Foreign Policy since 1898*. London: Hutchinson, 1956.
13. *The Gladstone Diaries*. vols. I and II, 1968; vols. III and IV (with H.C.G. Matthew), 1974.
14. Foot was immersed in both the classics and the Anglican liturgy at school.
15. Relatively little historical analysis of resistance in Europe, let alone SOE, appeared in print before the 1960s: *SOE in France* was part of a wave of more scholarly writing that appeared in that decade.
16. *SOE in France*, op.cit.p.453.

116

17. Ibid. Preface pp. ix–xii; Appendix A pp.449–453.
18. *Resistance*, op.cit. p.11.
19. Ibid. p.13. The characters referred to appear in Tolstoy's *War and Peace*.
20. Ibid. p.20.
21. Hawes, S. and White, R. *Resistance in Europe: 1939–1945*. London: Allen Lane, 1975. p.219.
22. *Resistance*, op.cit.p.319.
23. See *Resistance*, ibid. pp.22–28, 305–311; and *Resistance in Europe*, op.cit. pp.205–208.
24. See *Resistance*, op.cit. pp.311–313; *MI9*, op.cit. especially Appendix 1, Statistical Summary pp.309–315.
25. *Resistance*, op.cit. p.313.
26. *Resistance in Europe*, op.cit. p.211.
27. *SOE in France*, op.cit.p.441.
28. *Resistance*, op.cit. p.60.
29. Ibid. p.319.
30. *Resistance in Europe*, op.cit. p.219.
31. *Resistance*, op.cit. p.320.
32. *Resistance in Europe*, op.cit. p.220.
33. Professor Milward has written extensively on the economic history of the Second World War in Europe including, *The German Economy at War*. London: University of London Athlone Press, 1965; *The Fascist Economy in Norway*. Oxford: Clarendon Press, 1972; *The New Order and the French Economy*. Oxford: Clarendon Press, 1970.
34. *Resistance in Europe*, op.cit. p.202.
35. *Resistance*, op.cit. p.320.
36. Ibid. Foreword p.xii.

GOOD THRILLERS, BUT
BAD HISTORY
A review of published works on the Special Operations Executive's work in France during the Second World War

MARK SEAMAN

Among the many important features of M.R.D. Foot's *SOE in France*[1] was an annotated bibliography in which he reviewed the state of the published English language literature on the Special Operations Executive's activities in France. He was clearly none too impressed with the general quality of what he had found:

> Unfortunately, for lack of enough authentic material many of the resulting books are good thrillers, but bad history. Some books by former agents have been honestly written, and their evidential value is high. . . . In other cases authors, even when they had themselves taken part in what went on, have not always found it possible to keep to the unvarnished truth. A sort of declension can be observed: from minor inaccuracies due to misinformation, or brought in to heighten the tone; through material foisted on authors by unscrupulous ex-agents of both sides protecting or inflating their own reputations; major imaginative revisions superimposed on the facts; and material printed in direct contradiction of statements made to authors by those in a position to know; down to pieces of downright fiction elaborately disguised as fact.[2]

More than thirty years on and with much of the SOE archive released by the Foreign and Commonwealth Office into the Public Record Office, it may be profitable to review these early works and gauge any advances or regressions in the quality of the literature since *SOE in France's* appearance in 1966.

The first published personal account describing SOE's activities in France during the Second World War was *Maquis* by George Millar in 1945[3]. The author had been taken prisoner while serving with the Rifle Brigade in North Africa and was subsequently imprisoned in a POW camp in Italy. A man of ingenuity and spirit, he managed to escape from a train while in transit to Germany and, after many adventures, achieved a 'home run' via France and Spain. On his return to England he was recruited into F Section of SOE and, after training, was parachuted back to France to head the CHANCELLOR circuit in Franche Comté. After the Liberation he returned to London and resolved to write an account of his adventures with the Resistance. In a later work[4] Millar described his passage into print. His commanding officer, Colonel Maurice Buckmaster, did not forbid him to write but warned that any decision over publication would ultimately rest with SOE's censorship department. He received a rather more forceful response from Vera Atkins, Buckmaster's intelligence officer,

> 'Must you write a damned book?' Vera asked finally. 'It seems rather a cheap idea, as though you did what you did to make money out of it. And I know you didn't.'[5]

Millar was not to be dissuaded and acquired an agent and a publisher. Bringing his pre-war skills as a journalist to bear he finished the draft in rapid time, completing the task in the month's leave accorded to him on his return from France. The text was submitted to SOE and, scarcely without a pause and as German flying bombs descended around him, he embarked upon a second work. At first he believed that his original typescript had 'vanished without a trace inside SOE' but 'eventually, mangled in the text and with many deletions, the thing was sent from SOE to the War Office, where it was immediately cleared for publication.'[6] In spite of paper shortage, Heinemann published 70,000 hardback copies to great public and critical success with General de Gaulle numbered amongst the book's admirers: 'This is the truth about the maquis, and the maquis is something that will become untruer, year by year for decades ahead.'[7] Millar's second book, *Horned Pigeon*[8], in which he described his time as a prisoner of war and his escape from captivity, followed soon afterwards to equal success. The record of SOE's activities in France had got off to a good start, buoyed by the quality of Millar's writing and the relatively benign attitude of Whitehall.

As the war came to an end, the stories of heroism and tragedy in France slowly began to appear in the newspapers and the work of British agents achieved even greater prominence with the award of the George Cross to several SOE personnel. On 15 February 1946 a press conference at the Air Ministry announced the gazetting the next day of the award of a George Cross to Wing Commander F.F.E. Yeo-Thomas. No mention was made of Yeo-Thomas's attachment to SOE, let alone its RF Section, but it was clear that his was a gripping story of secret work behind enemy lines and was thus reported by most of the daily newspapers. The citation barely gave a hint of a remarkable career that embraced three clandestine trips to Occupied France, capture, torture, deportation to a concentration camp in Germany, escape, recapture and ultimately the triumph of attaining the safety of the American lines shortly before VE Day. Later that year another George Cross was awarded to an SOE agent, this time a woman – Odette Sansom. Arguably her story managed to capture the popular imagination even more than that of Yeo-Thomas and it was to exert a powerful hold over the British public for generations to come. The story of a Frenchwoman, married to an Englishman, who volunteered for hazardous service in her homeland (in spite of the emotional wrench of having to leave behind her three daughters) struck an immediate chord when newspaper readers learnt of her story. This interest was fuelled rather than sated by the publication in 1949 of her story, Odette[9], with its graphic descriptions of the dreadful suffering she endured following her capture and imprisonment in a concentration camp. In the light of a later denial of access to SOE papers, there is a surprising acknowledgement that the 'War Office' made files available to the author, enabling wireless messages, training notes and operational instructions to be cited. In spite of this, at times the book reads like a novel and is imbued with a hagiographic emphasis that is on occasion all but overwhelming. It would appear not to have had the same impact upon Foot ('A popular and partially fictionalized life.')[10] as it did upon Compton Mackenzie who wrote, 'Nobody who claims to be living rather than existing in this crucial time of ours can afford not to read this book.'[11]

The following year the release of a feature film depicting Odette's wartime experiences extended the public interest in her story.

Helping to reinforce the veracity of the treatment was the participation of Buckmaster in the film who appeared at its outset to present a prologue and then portrayed himself in the drama.

In fact another female F Section agent had preceded Odette into print but the account of her wartime career, *Moondrop to Gascony*[12], while enjoying some success, achieved nothing like the acclaim attendant on that of her fellow agent. Anne-Marie Walters had parachuted into south-west France in January 1944 to act as courier for the WHEELWRIGHT circuit. Eschewing the temptation to over-glamorize the clandestine life, the book has a freshness not often to be found in the published accounts of other agents who played a more prominent role in the Resistance. Foot was sufficiently impressed to comment that it 'communicates vividly the hectic life of the maquis,' although his access to the files allowed him to identify 'some pardonable exaggerations'[13].

But in 1952 the story of one of SOE's other heavyweights, F.F.E. Yeo-Thomas, appeared in *The White Rabbit*[14], the title being the codename that the agent had used least among the many he employed during his illustrious career. The book credits Bruce Marshall as the author with the byline 'From the story told to him by Wing Commander F.F.E. Yeo-Thomas GC MC', but in truth it was an edited, not to say sanitized, version of Yeo-Thomas's own script that he had written in the hope of exorcizing his horrific memories. One of the book's reviewers recognized the sometimes intrusive presence of Marshall's personal interventions:

> 'Marshall cannot leave it alone, he cannot understand that the biographer's first duty is to get his own damn ego out of the picture.'[15]

Nevertheless the book, according to Foot 'a gruesome and mainly authentic sketch of Yeo-Thomas's career'[16], sold 50,000 copies in hardback during the first six months and remained a best seller for years, being translated into many foreign languages.

At roughly the same time as the publication of Yeo-Thomas's book, Maurice Buckmaster, the head of F Section, went into print with *Specially Employed*[17]. With becoming honesty, Buckmaster confessed in his foreword to a range of caveats regarding the text. He pleaded that the passage of time, an absence of contemporary notes, a proliferation of pseudonyms and the need to maintain secrecy regarding methods and plans might affect the book's accuracy. The reader should have been prepared for the worst but it must still have come as something of a shock to read 'I do not claim that the incidents described in these pages are completely factually accurate'.[18] Foot, perhaps believing that the less was said the better, merely commented, 'Quite so'.[19]

The same year as Buckmaster's first book (there was a second, bearing similar factual blemishes)[20], one of his most celebrated agents, Peter Churchill, went into print. As Odette's superior officer and subsequently her husband, Churchill was already a well known figure to the reading public and his book, *Of their Own Choice*[21], provided another perspective on the events surrounding both his and his wife's wartime careers. Whereas even six years after SOE's disbandment, Buckmaster had had to refer to it as 'a secret organization in the War Office', at least Churchill was able at last to concede the existence of an organization called the Special Operations Executive. Two more volumes appeared in 1954 and 1957[22], the three works receiving the plaudit from Foot, 'Readable, revealing, and reasonably accurate reports of his first mission to France, of his three later missions; and of his captivity.'[23]

Several other agents either wrote their own stories or, more frequently, had their stories ghost-written in the years leading up to the publication of *SOE in France*[24]. The quality of the books varied immensely in style, quality and accuracy. Ben Cowburn, an organizer and saboteur who made four trips to France, offered a no-frills account of his experiences with *No Cloak No Dagger*, described by Foot as 'A short clear, discreet, and vivid account'[25]. On the other hand, Christopher Burney, an agent arrested relatively soon after his arrival in France, not unnaturally concentrated upon the appalling mental and physical hardships he had to endure during his captivity in France and Germany. At the other end of the scale was Mathilde Carré's interesting but ultimately unconvincing attempt to offer an explanation for her traitorous behaviour. Jack Thomas's account of the tragic story of the Newton brothers, who like Burney managed to survive Buchenwald concentration camp, was no less gripping, but the dramatic licence taken in the narrative raised many doubts not only over the veracity of specific details but also the overall description of the agents' lives.

In addition to these published accounts of personal experiences, another series of books appeared in the early 1950s that radically altered the study of SOE's activities in France. This in particular concerned the investigations of three writers into the fate of women agents of F Section who had failed to return from captivity. The first of these was *Madeleine* by Jean Overton Fuller[26]. The author, a wartime friend of her subject, the wireless operator Noor Inayat Khan, sought to discover the full details of her heroine's endeavours. SOE had had doubts regarding Inayat Khan's temperamental suitability for clandestine work, but this complex, unworldly woman had bravely stayed in France even though London had tried to recall her following the mass arrests of other agents. Her eventual capture, attempted escape from the Gestapo headquarters, imprisonment and execution had been chronicled in the citation for her posthumous George Cross. However, Overton Fuller desired to know more and embarked upon a highly personal investigation, interviewing friends, colleagues and even former enemies in her pursuit for the truth. She admitted in her preface that she had not received much in the way of official assistance:

> The War Office were able to give hardly any information about the people she met, worked and lived with 'in the field'[27]

This may in part have accounted for the 'many trivial inaccuracies' spotted by Foot that did not, however, 'impair the dramatic force of the story'.[28] Overton Fuller's interest in SOE did not end with the publication of *Madeleine* and she embarked upon something of a one-woman crusade into some of the murkier areas of F Section's activities, particularly those involving the careers of two of SOE's most controversial figures, Henri Déricourt and John Starr. During and after the war these two agents had been the subject of extensive investigation following doubts and, moreover, specific allegations concerning their relations with the German security forces. Déricourt, ostensibly F Section's most effective air operations organizer, was accused of being a German agent and the betrayer of his SOE colleagues. Opinions were split over his guilt and his accusers and defenders in London and Paris made him one of SOE's *causes célèbres*. John Starr was an F Section agent who was arrested in July 1943 on his second trip to France. At first he behaved with conspicuous gallantry, attempting several escapes (including one with Inayat Khan) but he eventually developed a close relationship with his captors, raising doubts as to whether he had drifted on to the wrong side of collaboration. With the remains of SOE's archive then closed to researchers,

Overton Fuller relied heavily upon the oral and written testimony of those participants she could trace. Her books therefore have an immediacy and apparent clarity, but even at the time of their publication doubts were voiced regarding their reliability[29]. Thus Foot's comment about one of the books, 'several ends are left loose'[30], serves as an appropriate observation upon her other works at this time.

Dame Irene Ward, in her book on the First Aid Nursing Yeomanry[31], the volunteer unit that served as the parent body for many of SOE's women agents and personnel, continued the emphasis on the sacrifice of the women agents. She also paid tribute to the invaluable efforts of the FANYs who constituted the bulk of SOE's support staff and who carried much of the burden of the organization's wireless traffic, ciphering and clerical duties. But in many ways Ward's contribution lay less in what she wrote than with the probing questions she asked in the House of Commons on matters relating to SOE's activities in France. She found a ready ally in Elizabeth Nicholas, a journalist who, like Overton Fuller, had had a personal relationship with one of the missing agents. This desire to learn more about the fate of her friend, Diana Rowden, led her to make investigations that led to the publication of *Death Be Not Proud*[32]. Nicholas's attitude to Whitehall, in contrast to the rather more benign days of *Odette*, is revealed early in the book by her acknowledgement of the assistance she was granted in France coming as 'a welcome contrast to the shut doors I found in London.'[33] The absence of documentary sources was perhaps felt all the more acutely considering her reservations over the quality of the existing published material on SOE:

> Reading some books about, or by, those who survived, I have been astonished by the facility they reveal for retaining in the memory, over long periods of years, great slabs of detailed dialogue. This facility was even more remarkable when the dialogues in question took place between people, both dead, whom the author had never met.
>
> I do not wish to seem cantankerous. I will simply repeat that I have felt it best not to be lured into the entrancing glades of semi-fiction; I have recorded nothing in this book as having happened unless it were reported to me on first-hand evidence; conjecture, possibility, unsubstantiated theories are clearly stated as being such.[34]

The book is somewhat polemical and therefore has all the concomitant advantages of being written with a deep conviction while suffering from comparable weaknesses. The accusation that SOE callously neglected its obligations to the next-of-kin of the agents who did not return does scant justice to the remarkable work of Vera Atkins and the other SOE personnel who sought to discover the fate of their missing comrades-in-arms. That more should have been done is a very different accusation to the claim that nothing was done. There were many mitigating factors in these shortcomings, not least the alterations to F Section's constituency towards the end of the war, the actual break up of SOE and the impetus towards a return to civilian life experienced by many of its personnel. However, Foot seems to have rated the book highly: 'painful reading, as a sensitive author gradually discovers underlying horrors in secret activities. Severe strictures on F Section, some of them just.'[35]

In the meantime another semi-hagiography had appeared describing the life of the third F Section recipient of the George Cross, Violette Szabo. *Carve Her Name With Pride*[36] was very much part of the same canon as *Odette* and *Madeleine* and, like the former, was made into a successful feature film. Violette Szabo was a mother and war widow who volunteered for service as an agent, was captured on her second mission and was eventually murdered at Ravensbrück concentration camp. Her story achieved even greater pathos both on the written page and in the film by contemplation of the fate of her orphaned daughter. While conveying the bravery and sacrifice of the individual, the book added little to an understanding of SOE and its work and is simply described by Foot as a 'popular illustrated life of Violette Szabo, based partly on conversations with her parents and her friends.'[37]

Thus, in general terms, the general quality of the literature dealing with SOE's activities in France written in the fifteen years since the end of the war left much to be desired. A later writer on SOE summarized the situation:

> The late 1940s and early 1950s in England saw a succession of memoirs presenting the exploits of individual agents and the achievements of SOE in the most favourable light. The books about Odette and Violette Szabo were followed (sic) by the accounts of Maurice Buckmaster and Peter Churchill among others – upbeat, charming, ironic, modestly self-effacing, and not entirely reliable. In fact, later disclosures would prove that, if Churchill's narratives were superficial, Buckmaster's were in places actually untrue. The very least one could say about them was that they were – incomplete.[38]

126

And then came *SOE in France*. Popular interest and strong agitation by the likes of Overton Fuller, Nicholas and Ward for more information about the women agents of SOE had led to questions being asked in the House of Commons. In 1958 the Prime Minister, Harold Macmillan, authorized research to be begun into an official account of SOE. The result was that two years later M.R.D. Foot was commissioned to write a history of SOE in France. He noted in the preface to his book, 'In the turmoil of under-informed publicity that has so far appeared in English about secret operations in France, historians have been overlooked.'[39]

Now the subject enjoyed close examination by a leading historian, and by Christmas 1962 he had completed the first draft. But it was to be another three and a half years before the book was published in April 1966. Whitehall's apparent reluctance to bring the book to print was by no means the only hurdle that had to be faced.

Foot's access to veterans had been restricted by his employers. 'My access to former staff and agents of SOE was severely limited: till it had been decided that this pilot study was to appear, much importance was attached to keeping the author out of the way of interested parties.'[40]

It was inevitable that not a few of the personalities featured in his text were aghast that a major work was on the verge of publication without their having been consulted. Among the most vociferous was Buckmaster who, when he was given sight of the galley proofs, declared himself 'utterly horrified' and 'amazed by the number of mistakes'[41]. Fortunately there remained time for Foot to consider the validity of Buckmaster's thirty-five pages of comments on the text and assimilate the opinions of some thirty to forty other interested parties who were vouchsafed sight of the proofs. To a nation and, it must be said, an SOE community used to the comfortable and frequently fictionalized narratives that comprised much of the existing published literature, *SOE in France* came as a shock and immediately caused a furore. It was ironic that Foot should have been granted privileged access to the surviving SOE archive, (albeit one that no longer constituted a comprehensive coverage of SOE's activities) but had been denied access to the personal reminiscences of the veterans that formed the very cornerstone of most of the other published material.

Foot was in an exposed position. He managed to offer a balanced and authoritative counterblast to some of the more fanciful and speculative theories surrounding SOE's work in France and took a robust attitude towards the purveyors of some of the myths hoping that his book 'contradicts, directly or by implication, much that has already been printed, or circulated as gossip; other authors' credulity or inventiveness can be deplored, but cannot be helped.'[42]

But his iconoclastic approach and a belief by some that he had failed in his aim 'simply to explain what happened, without conscious bias in any direction'[43] resulted in a public dispute with some former members of SOE who did not accept that 'it seemed more important to publish as soon as possible than to make perfectionist attempts to polish and re-polish a tale that in many ways is bound to remain craggy and imperfect. I would have liked to talk to all the survivors; but owed it to them, and still more to their dead companions, to get something into print quickly to show that the dead deserve honour and that SOE's effort was not made in vain.'[44]

The argument culminated in questions being asked in the House of Commons and legal action being brought. Substantial damages were settled out of court and the book was withdrawn. A second impression of *SOE in France* appeared two years later with the contentious passages removed from the text.

The controversy surrounding the book's publication soon subsided and *SOE in France* became unquestionably one of the standard texts on SOE. It succeeded in describing how SOE conducted its affairs with the armed forces, the Foreign Office and the Free French and managed vividly to convey the drama and tragedy surrounding a vast cast of characters and organizations on both sides of the Channel.

The book has been an inspiration to subsequent writers. The glimpses of characters and events vouchsafed in *SOE in France* have led many researchers to dig for themselves into the rich loam of SOE's history. The women of F Section have remained of enduring interest. Liane Jones, one of the new generation of writers on SOE, was able to look critically at the other published works:

> the books whetted my appetite, not so much by what they told me as what they didn't. . . . Both books [*Odette* and *Carve Her Name With Pride*] were written in the decade after the war as part of a popular movement to establish gallant, pure war heroines. The pictures they painted of the two characters and their resistance work were highly coloured and dashing; they contained little reflection and very few of the insights which I sought. The stories were told in a very conven-

128

tional way, and yet the facts which they related were anything but conventional. Both books, significantly I felt, were written by men. I felt sure that if the women themselves had told their stories, I should have read something quite different.[45]

She made extensive use of interviews with surviving veterans and introduced a new perspective born of contemporary perceptions of women's role in society. A similar work but one solely concentrating on the careers of the women of the Royal Air Force who served in France appeared a year later with Beryl Escott's *Mission Improbable*[46]. The book is as much concerned with commemorating as interpreting the work of its subjects, a fact perhaps indicated by its subtitle 'A salute to the RAF women of SOE in wartime France'.[47] Both Escott and Jones were fortunate to enjoy a loosening up of Whitehall's attitude to research into SOE. From the early 1980s a succession of SOE Advisers at the Foreign and Commonwealth Office made themselves available for consultation and provided invaluable oral and written briefings from the surviving documents.

In the 1980s, a period when 'moles', cover-ups and a realization of the importance of deception in warfare seemed a staple of each day's news, the fascination with conspiracy theories did not leave SOE untouched. *All the King's Men*[48], bearing the uncompromising subtitle 'The Truth Behind SOE's Greatest Wartime Disaster', constituted a return to the Déricourt story. It sought to explain the downfall of SOE's PROSPER circuit as a cold-blooded sacrifice on the altar of Allied strategic deception. Central to the plot was an exposition of the malevolent antagonism of the Secret Intelligence Service towards SOE, but the argument relied too heavily upon conjecture and assumption. These failings did not prevent the author affirming that:

> Locking the files away rarely proves to be the end of a story. People and their recollections live on and, inevitably, an account of these events relies a great deal upon those recollections. It has been my experience that in amongst the memories of those who were there at the time lies an overwhelming determination to discover the truth.[49]

This seems more than a little at variance with a quotation from the former SOE staff officer H.N. Sporborg, ostensibly one of the author's most important sources:

129

In this world you must understand one thing: if you're going to become involved in these things, you must never, never admit anything afterwards. Anything. You have to go into it determined that, no matter what happens, you will never reveal what you have done. You must resolve to go to your grave still resolutely denying that it ever happened.'[50]

A year later Jean Overton Fuller returned yet again to the subject with *Déricourt: The Chequered Spy*[51], but to little effect. Moreover, she had already attempted yet another critical analysis of F Section's flaws with *The German Penetration of SOE*[52]. In her foreword the author stated, 'I had not meant to write more about SOE, but circumstances have conspired to bring me back to it.'[53] The circumstances simply appear to have been that the publisher asked her to write another book and she felt that she had enough research in hand to be able to offer an overview of the disasters in France and to renew her criticisms of London's control of affairs. It might have been hoped that a general book on F Section by a French historian, Marcel Ruby, would have helped add a fresh insight but *F Section, SOE*[54] proved to be a disappointment. Ruby elected to utilize only a limited number of French sources and plundered published English language works, reproducing long extracts in his text with the result that the book ultimately added little to existing knowledge. At best, its French language edition might have helped a foreign readership to understand something of SOE's work.

While a new, overall assessment of SOE's work in France awaits to be written, authors have continued to write about the careers of individual agents. Richard Heslop, an agent with a glittering career, in *Xavier*[55] concentrated on his experiences as a maquis leader, while Robert Burdett in *Watch For Me By Moonlight*[56] was at pains to castigate 'the fiction written by several ex-SOE members about their Resistance activities'[57] and his book emerged all the better for this insight. In contrast to earlier examples of the genre, more recent biographies such as *Aristide*[58] (about the celebrated agent Roger Landes) and *Bravest of the Brave*[59] (a re-examination of Yeo-Thomas's life), have benefited from a secure grounding in public and privately held documentary sources.

It will be no surprise to students of SOE's affairs in France to learn that the women agents have not been neglected. *Christine*, by Madeleine Masson[60], made more of an attempt to get under the skin

130

of the agent than other biographies and, perhaps most interestingly, suggested the impact that Christine Granville's wartime career had upon her sad, post-war life. *Jacqueline*[61] was a sound biography of Yvonne Rudellat displaying an historical depth born of decades of research and managing to achieve a respectful but balanced attitude towards its subject. In contrast, Rita Kramer's *Flames in the Field*[62], while similarly drawing upon diligent research, elected to take the route of a strongly personal investigation as had been followed by Overton Fuller and Nicholas.

Now, more than fifty years after the disbandment of SOE, its archive is, in large measure, open to researchers. It is a time when the Official Histories of SOE will be under intensive scrutiny, but there seems little doubt that, while many other works will be consigned to a category of only casual interest, *SOE in France* will stand the test of time. As M.R.D. Foot wrote in his preface:

> A single lifetime would not suffice to collect and collate all the stories of the survivors, let alone the dead. Other historians need quickly such working material as this book contains; they can use it to help their own investigations.[63]

Foot's ground-breaking work remains as indispensable as when it first appeared more than thirty years ago.

NOTES

1. M.R.D. Foot, *SOE in France*, Her Majesty's Stationery Office, London, 1966, Second impression with amendments, 1968.
2. *Ibid*, pp.453–4.
3. George Millar, *Maquis*, Heinemann, London, 1945.
4. George Millar, *The Road to Resistance*, The Bodley Head, London, 1979.
5. *Ibid*, p.401.
6. *Ibid*, p.405.
7. *Ibid*, p.406.
8. George Millar, *Horned Pigeon*, Heinemann, London, 1946.
9. Jerrard Tickell, *Odette*, Chapman and Hall, London, 1949.

10. Foot, *op. cit.*, p.463.
11. Quoted on the frontispiece of the Pan Book edition, London, 1956.
12. Anne-Marie Walters, *Moondrop to Gascony*, Macmillan, London, 1946.
13. Foot, *op. cit.*, p.463.
14. Bruce Marshall, *The White Rabbit*, Evans, London, 1952.
15. Quoted in Mark Seaman, *Bravest of the Brave*, Michael O'Mara, London, 1997, p.228.
16. Foot, *op. cit.*, p.460.
17. Maurice Buckmaster, *Specially Employed*, Batchworth, London, 1952.
18. *Ibid*, p.7.
19. Foot, *op. cit.*, p.455.
20. Maurice Buckmaster, *They Fought Alone*, Odhams, London, 1958.
21. Peter Churchill, *Of their Own Choice*, Hodder, London, 1952.
22. Peter Churchill, *The Spirit in the Cage*, Hodder, London, 1954 and *Duel of Wits*, Hodder, London, 1957.
23. Foot, *op. cit.*, p.456.
24. These included Christopher Burney, *The Dungeon Democracy*, Heinemann, London, 1945 and *Solitary Confinement*, Macmillan, London, 1961, Mathilde Carré, *I was the Cat*, Four Square, London, 1961, Ben Cowburn, *No Cloak No Dagger*, Jarrolds, London, 1960, George Langelaan, *Knights of the Floating Silk*, Hutchinson, London, 1959, Alfred and Henry Newton's story told in Jack Thomas's *No Banners*, Allen, London, 1955, Philippe de Vomécourt, *Who Lived to See the Day*, Hutchinson, London, 1961, Nancy Wake's story in Russell Braddon's *Nancy Wake*, Cassell, London, 1956, Suzanne Warenghem's story in Gordon Young's *In Trust and Treason*, Hulton, London, 1959 and Jacques Weil's story in Charles Wighton's *Pin-stripe Saboteur*, Odhams, London, 1959.
25. Foot, *Ibid*, p. 456.
26. Jean Overton Fuller, *Madeleine*, Gollancz, London, 1952.
27. *Ibid*, p. 9.
28. Foot, *op. cit.*, p.461.
29. Jean Overton Fuller, *The Starr Affair*, Gollancz, London, 1954, *Double Webs*, Putnam, London, 1958.
30. Foot, *ibid*, p.461.
31. Irene Ward *F.A.N.Y. Invicta*, Hutchinson, London, 1955.
32. Elizabeth Nicholas, *Death Be Not Proud*, Cresset Press, London, 1958.
33. *Ibid*, p. 8.
34. *Ibid*, pp.20–1.
35. Foot, *op. cit.*, p.460.
36. R.J. Minney, *Carve Her Name with Pride*, George Newnes, London, 1956.
37. Foot, *op. cit.*, p.460.

38. Rita Kramer, *Flames in the Field*, Michael Joseph, London, 1995, p.314.
39. Foot, *op. cit.*, p.ix.
40. *Ibid*, p.452.
41. *Sunday Telegraph*, 24 April 1966.
42. Foot, *op. cit.*, pp. xi–xii.
43. *Ibid*, p.ix.
44. *Ibid*, pp.452–3.
45. Liane Jones, *A Quiet Courage*, Bantam Press, London, 1990, p.7.
46. Beryl Escott, *Mission Improbable*, Patrick Stephens, London, 1991.
47. *Ibid*, p.47.
48. Robert Marshall, *All the King's Men*, Collins, London, 1988.
49. *Ibid*, p.272.
50. *Ibid*, p.278.
51. Jean Overton Fuller, *Déricourt: The Chequered Spy*, Michael Russell, Wilton, 1975.
52. Jean Overton Fuller, *The German Penetration of SOE*, William Kimber, London, 1975.
53. *Ibid*, p.7.
54. Marcel Ruby, *F Section, SOE*, Leo Cooper, London, 1988.
55. Richard Heslop, *Xavier*, Rupert Hart-Davis, London, 1970.
56. Evelyn Le Chêne, *Watch for Me by Moonlight*, Eyre Methuen, London, 1973.
57. *Ibid*, p.9.
58. David D Nicolson, *Aristide*, Leo Cooper, London, 1994.
59. Seaman, *op. cit.*
60. Madeleine Masson, *Christine*, Hamish Hamilton, London, 1975.
61. Stella King, *Jacqueline*, Arms and Armour, London, 1989.
62. Kramer, *op. cit.*
63. Foot, *op. cit.*, pp.x–xi.

RESISTANCE: THE DISCOURSE OF PERSONALITY

H.R. KEDWARD

The discourse of personality has marked all stages of the history of French Resistance. In public usage it is sometimes prevalent, sometimes muted. It captures national headlines and local ceremonials. It has its fierce defenders and fewer if voluble detractors. It is rarely exposed to serious public doubt. It denotes both individuality and heroism. A recent academic biography of Pierre Brossolette by Guillaume Piketty was admiringly reviewed in *Vingtième Siècle* by one of the most thoughtful and original resistance historians, Jean-Marie Guillon. He starts his review with the words, 'Pierre Brossolette is not one of the cohort of forgotten heroes . . . this man was not anonymous.'[1] The implication is clear; Brossolette as an individual resister stood out from other heroic individuals who are no longer remembered, or perhaps are still to be found. The discourse is alive and well.

At the same time we inhabit a world where history is regularly turned into myth. Discovering myths, inventing myths, using the concepts of mythification, recording every event or personality in terms of myth, has become an intellectual reflex. The myth of any political leader is immediately consequent on his or her death, and often precedes it. Unsurprisingly the 'myth of resistance' is current everywhere.

Myths are instrumental; they mediate the past to the present; they codify the past; they motivate the present; they define identity; they inhabit sites; they are cause and effect. Myths to the twentieth century historian are now as central as stories were to Trevelyan or Michelet. Excitingly, they are the first step of the political historian towards cultural history and towards literary theory. From the 'myth', for example, of Jean Moulin or General de Gaulle ('*Toute ma vie, je me suis fait une certaine idée de la France*') it is easy to arrive at the 'myth' of agency, closely tied to the literary debate about the so-called death of the author.

This is not the direction of this essay, though it might well have been on another occasion. It moves in the other direction, that leads back from myth into history, to more research into the personalities (resisters) and the event (resistance) itself, a journey and direction which nonetheless involves reinterpretation.

The journey in this essay begins in 1968, the year which many have seen as a watershed in the representation of resistance within France. The year was not only the year of the May *événements*, it was also the 50th anniversary of the end of the First World War. The two were interwoven in the graffiti which began to appear on the walls in the spring of 1968, most obviously the slogan, '*la guerre des moutons*' which condemned the war of 1914–18 as one in which men were 'sent to die' by military and political authority; they were 'sheep to the slaughter'. By contrast the actions of those who created the May events and those who staged the general strike were held to possess an existentialist and voluntarist quality. The slogan made this point implicitly, and thereby established a libertarian hierarchy of political causes within France; some were unacceptable because they were imposed from above, others were acceptable because they were willed from the base upwards.

Where in this hierarchy did the Resistance of 1940–1944 stand? After the war it had been exploited for political ends by both de Gaulle and the Communist Party, and the generation of *soixante-huitards* was explicitly critical of both the Gaullist and the Communist heritage. In particular in the discussions of the 1960s the public image of resistance personalities designated career-successful politicians, grounding their moral and political authority in an uncritical self-history of patriotic heroism and nationalist endeavour which had failed the post-war world. Many ex-resisters, epitomized by Georges Bidault, endorsed the imperial presence and brutality of France in the Indo-China and Algerian wars.

Ambivalence there was, however, and in a small village in the Languedoc I was witness to an astonishing public confession by a graffiti artist who at night had decorated the Monument aux Morts with a tidily-written '*guerre des moutons*' only to find in the light of morning that he had covered not the side given to the First World War, but the memorial to '*Nos martyrs de la Résistance*'. He came into the square as people assembled in the café for the evening apéritif

136

and publicly announced that he had misdirected his graffiti: he had no wish to denigrate the Resistance, only the unacceptable war of 1914–18, and he set to work at once to remove the red spray paint, amidst considerable astonishment and no shortage of heckling and debate. He was not allowed to respray the other side, nor, to my knowledge, did he return at some later date to do so. It was typical of the improvised street-event in which the serious aspirations of the *soixantehuitards* were expressed. It was typical also, I believe, of the contrast between the two wars which was made during 1968, despite the scepticism about famous resisters as career politicians. What was not in doubt was the original voluntarism of resistance, both of those who later became famous and those who remained unknown and anonymous. What 1968 did, therefore, was not to end the resistance discourse of personality, which seemed likely at one point, but to push a number of young historians into researching the scores of unknown and ordinary resisters, and it only became apparent in the series of six international conferences on resistance, staged from 1993 to 1997, just how many resistance historians, in France, in the UK, in Belgium and the Netherlands, in Italy and in the US, were all influenced personally by this *soixantehuitard* perspective.

In fact, for whatever vintage of historian, it would have been extraordinary if the early acts of resistance in the first two years of Occupation had *not* been understood as voluntary. Almost all the existing resistance histories and memoirs of the period treated it as such. And it was not only voluntary. To this was added the aura of the exceptional and the prophetic. Streets all over France had been named after individual resistance figures. Each political party had its own heroes and heroines, as Henry Rousso remarks: 'Danièle Casanova, Jean-Pierre Timbaud or Georges Politzer for the Communists; Pierre Brossolette for the Socialists; Honoré d'Estienne d'Orves adopted by the Right'.[2] And in December 1964 the ashes of Jean Moulin had been transferred to the Panthéon, an apotheosis of the Gaullist tradition which incarnated the individual act of Charles de Gaulle on 18 June 1940 and the role of his most influential envoy into France. Before 1964 Moulin had stood only marginally above other leaders in the history and collective memory of the Resistance. But with the Panthéon ceremony he became the emblematic resistance personality and hero, his hat and scarf iconic. His clandestine achievements denoted not '*la guerre des moutons*' but '*la guerre des ombres*' and his death under torture was held to be symbolic of the

137

martyrdom of France. It was a Gaullist gesture above all, but no individual resister of any political persuasion demurred.

Resistance was thus widely established as a paradigm of individual commitment, and it was this that was recast and re-invented in the existentialism and democratization of 1968, which rejected the two dominant mythic interpretations, that of the Gaullist *'nation résistante'* and that of the Communist *'parti des fusillés'*. Both were myths in the functional, mobilizing sense of creating political identities and serving post-war needs. Neither was accurate in the factual sense; the French nation had not resisted in its entirety; the Communist Party had not lost as many members to the firing squads as it initially claimed. The myths had allowed individuals to place their resistance motivations and achievements in a collective context; they allowed the collectivities of nation and party to honour their leading individuals as representative.

Essentially these myths were rejected in 1968 and in the 1970s as discourses of power and authority by those who wanted to shift the interpretation of resistance into a more nuanced and less polemical mode. There was realization through oral research that ex-resisters, Communists included, were not all imprisoned in the collective myths, and that at the grass-roots there was widespread consciousness of resistance in the first two years as a small minority phenomenon, as multifaceted, flawed and individualistic, and that this consciousness was permanently at odds, even in open conflict, with the dominant myths. This explains the wide acceptance in France given to the film by Ophuls, *Le Chagrin et la Pitié*, and to the study of Vichy by Robert Paxton, despite scattered refusals to accept the way in which they had, in Rousso's term, 'broken the mirror'.[3]

As the individuality of early resistance resurfaced in more detail in the 1970s and 1980s it took on a much more embattled and quixotic nature. Personalities became the subject of close attention; was resistance even a sign of a personality disorder? Emmanuel d'Astier de la Vigerie, one of the founders of Libération-sud, had led the way in his interview with Marcel Ophuls in 1969 for *Le Chagrin et la Pitié* when he claimed that his qualifications for early resistance lay in 'the kind of Quixotic feelings that failures can always have' and stated: 'I think you could only have joined the Resistance if you were maladjusted.'[4] Jean Cassou, the art historian and resister in the Toulouse region, had coined the perceptive, and philosophical, interpretation of the first resistance as *'un refus absurde'* and Lucie Aubrac more and more in her lectures to schools emphasized the guile and ruse which she had employed in a series of masquerades which had outwitted the Gestapo.[5]

Interviewers at the grass-roots were confronted with endless individualist stories, most of which, but not all, were endorsed by other accounts. A code and discourse of resistance as illegal, inventive, imaginative, individualistic and outrageously defiant circulated alongside the more conventional image of the prudent clandestine activist or the armed maquisard in the woods. Already, for different reasons, many of the descriptions by M.R.D. Foot of agents who were dropped into France by the British organization, the Special Operations Executive (SOE), fell into the category of the idiosyncratic and quixotic: 'SOE's work,' he wrote at the start of his classic and unrivalled study of 1966, 'was true to the tradition of English eccentricity; the sort of thing that Captain Hornblower or Mycroft Holmes in fiction, or Admiral Cochrane or Chinese Gordon in fact, would have gone in for had they been faced with a similar challenge; the sort of thing that looks odd at the time, and eminently sensible later.' His account has many short biographical sketches or comments which add colour and detail to this image of SOE's functional eccentricity. There is a coherent discourse of resistance in *SOE in France*. It is the discourse of personality. Surveying the nature of SOE agents Michael Foot writes, 'Their diversity was marked; it ranged from pimps to princesses . . . SOE employed neither supermen nor simpletons. Many agents were remarkably good; a few were remarkably bad. Some were foolhardy, some were fusspots; some, not unexpectedly, were odd, like the English captain with several daring operations to his credit, who was brave as a lion in action and drunk as a lord in between; or the Gascon major, also fearless, of whom a staff officer wrote plaintively, "I wish he would not use so much scent".'[6] Michael Foot's writing appears at times to indulge the archetype of the talented amateur, but the whole study expresses an intimate and fundamental understanding of SOE which no one has seriously disputed; these were men and women of highly distinctive personalities. It may seem amazing that this treatment of SOE has not been the object of revisionism, but everyone who thinks about it finds it hard to imagine any other way in which to encapsulate the essence of SOE, except in purely structural or functional terms, and Michael Foot is remarkably perceptive too about both structures and functions.

SOE agents, however, were specially recruited; they were chosen to be members of the special forces. They were irregulars recruited to do an irregular job. Their role was to a large extent prescribed and they were intensively trained. A certain strength of personality was high on the list of requirements. Michael Foot's discourse of personality is not out of place.

Resisters within France were different: they were not in the first instance recruited. They invented their own role. They had to create the very phenomenon of resistance out of their refusal and opposition. This difference prompted different questions about motivation, origins and strategy. Nevertheless, their personalities were in many cases seen to be no less striking than those of SOE agents; many memoirs and studies of individual resisters privilege personality over context, and some substantiate the claim made by Emmanuel d'Astier. After 1968 and *Le Chagrin et la Pitié*, refusal became a key word in the discourse of personality, and absurdity, used in the Sartrean sense, a key but contested concept. This did not indicate absurdist theatre; there was nothing of Jarry's *Ubu Roi* in the discourse, nor did it have the anti-hero dimensions of Meursault in *L'Etranger*. For reasons Camus gave later in *Lettres à un ami allemand* there was no absence of moral values in the consciousness of the resister, it was rather the element of contingency in individual revolt that accounts for the phrase '*un refus absurde*'. The statement in oral interviews, '*Il fallait faire quelque chose, n'importe quoi*' (I had to do something, no matter what) is still the most persistent way of explaining the first acts of resistance.

Naive, absurd, delinquent, rebellious: these words went into the remaking of the personality discourse of resistance, and they can still be heard. They suggest a genre of resister which became increasingly related in the 1960s and 1970s not just to contingency and to existentialist commitment, but also to the popular culture of the inter-war period when the cultural typologies of the secret agent, the private detective, the spy and the outlaw captured popular imagination largely through film. What linked these typologies together was their imagined freedom from the levelling forces of mass society presented as a dehumanizing threat by the Spanish sociologist Ortega y Gasset in *The Revolt of the Masses* in 1929, or by King Vidor in his film of 1928, *The Crowd*, or even earlier in Fritz Lang's *Metropolis* of 1926. The search, of which these different works were a part, was for a genre of individual who could not be averaged, measured or

140

restrained by the massification of society, whether social or political. The quixotic, but talented, amateur was a notable form of this genre, exemplified by Richard Hannay in Hitchcock's film of Buchan's *Thirty-Nine Steps* (1935) who embraces illegality and outlaw status in order to unmask the presence of foreign agents. Although often given a delinquent image the genre fulfilled the alter-ego of a society apparently threatened by bureaucracy and levelling to the point of automation. It plays the role in modern society that Thomas Carlyle gave to 'the eye that sees' and 'the soul that dares', and most romantic writers gave to genius and feeling, which enabled rare individuals to rise above the machine culture of the industrial revolution. The typology of the civilian resister as an unusual personality was partially shaped by the continuity of this genre from the 1930s, but even more by its spectacular revival in the 1960s, when the threat of consumerism and a one-dimensional society perceived by the New Left on the one hand, and the rampant threat of Marxist and Maoist ideologies perceived by political liberals on the other, took the place of the mass society threat of the 1920s and 1930s.

In their different and often mutually hostile ways, libertarians and liberals in the 1960s revived the genre of the unorthodox hero or heroine as the defender of freedom. Just as Richard Hannay is recognizable in many 1960s descriptions and self-portraits of SOE agents, so too the interest in resisters as unorthodox evoked the cinematic genre of hero in Hitchcock and John Ford, celebrated in the *auteur* theories of *Les Cahiers du Cinéma*. The ambivalence of the typology was also re-emphasized; many ex-maquisards, for example, began in the 1960s to express their experience of having been treated after the war both as patriotic heroes but also as unregenerate outlaws, to whom jobs or promotion were denied. It became increasingly common for individual resisters to talk about the illegal status which they had voluntarily assumed in their clandestine operations, so that resistance could not easily be interpreted as normative behaviour. This relocating of resistance in an unconventional and rebellious mould did almost as much to 'break the mirror' in *Le Chagrin et la Pitié* as the shift of emphasis towards collaboration. In this respect the words of Emmanuel d'Astier and the portrait of Denis Rake, the SOE agent who talked about his homosexual relationship with a German officer, were as integral to the revision of Occupation history as the discovery and presentation of the fascist collaborator Christian de la Mazière.

The emphasis on personality declined as research into resistance expanded and developed, and in recent years, at least since the late 1980s, its ascendancy has been reversed. The new discourse, the new codes of resistance history prioritize the context of place and of time, the context of pre-histories in the 1930s and well beyond, the context of situations arising from Vichy decisions, or from German initiatives, the context of social and political networks which operate as constraints or possibilities, the context of gender, religion and race: in short the history of resistance has become subject to the same process of contextualization that prevails in the history of revolutions, wars, syndicalist movements or any major political event. The fact that this is relatively recent might well occasion surprise. Why had historians of the Resistance not given such prominence to context before? A few, of course, had. But the discourse of personality had tended to suggest that a convincing social history of resistance was impossible: the minority and voluntaristic nature of resistance had tended to diminish the importance of context as a determinant. If only a few doctors, politicians, taxi-drivers, midwives, students, peasants, shop-keepers or whatever, resisted, what is the contextual significance of their jobs? If there **was** a significance why were not all doctors, politicians, taxi-drivers, midwives etc. in the Resistance? The very question 'Why some and not others?' took the researcher back to personality.

The fundamental change is deceptively simple; there has been a shift of conceptual awareness occasioned by the more and more frequent use of the term 'specificity'. One can research the specificity of a profession, of a village or a *quartier* within a town and reach conclusions about it as a context for resistance activity without getting involved in any generalizations about jobs, countryside, towns or regions. Discovering the specificity of certain political and social networks in the origin of resistance does not imply a wholesale politics or sociology of resistance.

The historian has similarly come to research different and relative chronologies within the resistance. Not everyone in France was affected by the same measures of victimization at the same time; what makes people angry or confident enough to resist may vary from person to person, situation to situation, place to place. Personality is one variable, but only one. Researching the others has preoccupied an increasing number of doctorates, dissertations, monographs and conference papers. The key words are specificity, context and relativity. Personality is there too, but as one of the specificities.

Specificity militates against generalization. Taking the specific Protestantism of the Cévennes, for example, it cannot be used to claim that all Protestants in the area were resisters, nor to assert that personality was irrelevant. Instead it allows a discourse of place and context to supplement or challenge the discourse of personality. Both were important at the time. In early April 1944 the flamboyant personality of two of the leaders of the Maquis Bir-Hakeim clashed with the stern prudence of the Cévenol culture. The maquis had started in South-West France; it had moved right across the south; it was mobile and daring in its exploits; it carried with it a reputation for youthful bravura which attracted recruits, but it was never rooted in a local community or structure like the majority of the Cévenol maquis. Its leaders, Jean Capel, known as Commandant Barot, and Captain Demarne, were in many ways exemplars of the talented, outrageous and heroic adventurer who has entered resistance history as the paradigm personality. Barot spoke excellent German and cavorted with German officers in order to get strategic information; he carried a false identity card as a member of the Vichy police, and would demand a respectful salute from Vichy officials. The two drove round the area in a conspicuous black Citroën, stopping and talking to Germans without caution, and the Maquis launched sudden ambushes and attacks on German patrols without consulting other maquis units. These attacks rattled the German command and undermined Vichy authority in the countryside, but their impulsive nature ran counter to the local tactics of the Cévenol maquisards. Eventually the stern and cautious particularities of the Cévenol culture forced a showdown and the Maquis Bir-Hakeim was told to leave the Cévennes. The more anonymous leaders of more anony-mous maquis groups had made the decision. Personality was forced to take second place to context. The historiography of resistance in the area has come to reflect this; we now have micro-studies of communes and localities as the optimum way into an understanding of resistance. We are still left with the question of whether Barot's conduct was symptomatic of a particular kind of personality, which arguably was a good qualification for the kind of guerrilla warfare which pitted small bands of poorly-armed maquisards against the technological strength of the German army. Those who joined the Maquis Bir-Hakeim because of its reputation for panache defi-antly defend its leaders, but it is worth noting that the successor to

Barot and Demarne, when the Maquis settled in the area near Clermont l'Hérault after heavy losses, was Captain François Rouan. Rouan was a French army officer whose political affinities were a cross between anarchism and Trotskyism; he had deserted to fight for the International Brigades in Spain, had been court-martialled, but was reintegrated as an officer and decorated for his courage, only to desert again to try and join the Free French in 1940. His personality, to judge from these basic facts, would seem to fall within the quixotic and eccentric categories, but as a resistance leader he was famed for his careful and rational approach, his insistence on preparation and his lack of flamboyance. Personality studies, if they are to enlighten the history of resistance, have to be subtle and nuanced. Rouan himself, in his explanations of why resistance thrived in certain areas and not others, pointed away from personality towards context. For him the discourse of personality minimized the enormous importance of place and local culture in the infrastructure of the Resistance.[7]

The new codes, the new discourse have anchored new categories of resistance in the evolving historiography of Occupied France. Relativity of place, job, time and person has created a relativity of definition. Jean-Marie Guillon has even gone so far as to ask whether there can be any definition of resistance outside the specific context in which it occurs.[8] A military definition of armed struggle against the Occupier only becomes widely meaningful in 1943–4. Struggle through words and information is much nearer the realities of 1940–1942. Struggle through sabotage has to be accepted. Struggle through refuge and aid given to allied airmen, Jews, resisters on the run and maquisards, defines the resistance of thousands who never thought of holding a gun or transmitting a secret code. Resistance as a state of mind which enabled people to respond to a particular crisis or opportunity, perhaps only once when the situation arose, that too has to be considered.[9] It depends entirely on the context. Every nuance of every situation calls for careful and full reconstruction before it can be placed in or outside the history of resistance. The discourse of personality has to be subject to the same contextualization.

Since the mid-1980s the privileged position of the exceptional individual resister has been dislodged surprisingly by the growth of memory studies and the analysis of commemoration. These have combined to foreground national and local sites of memory and produce new conceptual insights into the role of representation of

144

national history and culture. Pierre Nora's pioneer work, *Les Lieux de Mémoire*, has been accepted, not uncritically, as the original source of this new awareness, and it is further accepted that the fortieth and fiftieth anniversaries of events in the Second World War provided much of the content and stimulus necessary to make awareness into something approaching an academic discipline, or to be more accurate an inter-disciplinary field of study.[10] University courses in memory studies are merely one indication of this wholesale displacement of event into representation. Public memory is mythopoeic, so that memory, representation and myth form a powerful intellectual trilogy as keywords in understanding the role of the past as it is recast and exploited in an ever-changing present. It is not surprising that individual memory has largely been downgraded in this pursuit of collective and public patterns of representation. Researching the vectors of memory, as Henry Rousso persuasively demonstrated in his anatomy of the Vichy syndrome, takes us to cultural artefacts and public events.

If individual memory of resistance is sidelined it is precisely because it is individual. It cannot easily be used in memory studies as representative and therefore loses its interest as representation. It may be full of interpretations, it may well mythify an individual past, but it cannot by itself be called mythopoeic. There is even among some historians a tangible impatience with individual memory, as if it obstructs the understanding or formulation of public memory. It is in the context of high-profile war trials, of the Gestapo chief Klaus Barbie, of the Milicien Paul Touvier, and of the Vichy official Maurice Papon, that the focus on national representation of the war has almost monopolized historical discussion. In the process, and the word 'processus' has often slipped into 'procès', critical attention has been directed not only at the defendants but also at the plaintiffs. Both media and historians have wanted to question the memory of recognized resisters, in particular the two thrown onto the screen in 1997 by Claude Berri as heroine and hero, Lucie and Raymond Aubrac. The historians brought together by the newspaper *Libération* on 17 May 1997 went on to question the role of the Aubracs' personalities in resistance, to the unacceptable point of implying that a certain looseness in the details of their memoirs might indicate inadequate attention to details of organization and secrecy at the time of the Resistance. The questioners had lost touch with the fragile nature of individual memory.[11]

This scenario, played out in 1997, is set to be upstaged by an ongoing twist in the approach to resistance. It dates mainly from 1989 and the collapse of communist power. In under ten years there has been a marked growth of interest in the structures of resistance which undermined Stalinist regimes from the inside. Comparative resistance studies have begun to emerge in the place previously occupied by comparative revolutions, bringing comparisons between different models of resistance across time and place, such as the resistance of slaves to slaveowners, peasants to encroaching landlords, colonized people against imperialist rule, workers' resistance to employers, black resistance to whites in South Africa, as well as cultural resistance to Stalinist regimes in Eastern Europe. Such comparative studies thrive on the understanding of patterns and rituals of civilian and everyday resistance, emphasized by the historian Claudio Pavone as central to Italian Resistance, and analysed minutely as the protective behaviour of Malayan peasants by the anthropologist James C. Scott.[12] This comparative awareness has given a new conceptual edge to the recent shift in the historiography of French Resistance, the shift towards specificity and the foregrounding of context and place. Its most immediate effect has been the consolidation of gender-based research into resistance. The shift from gender-ignorant to gender-conscious analysis in France owes much to the feminist input from American and British researchers. Most resistance historians before the mid-1980s took pains to assert that women had been among the eminent personalities of the Resistance; Berty Albrecht, Danièle Casanova and Lucie Aubrac were names in everyone's list. There had been a major conference of women resisters in 1975, *Les femmes dans la Résistance*, initiated by the Union des Femmes Françaises and held at the Sorbonne. It was a high point in women's reclamation of their resistance past. But the impact on resistance historiography was slight, and women resisters continued to be treated either as a small number of outstanding heroines, or as an anonymous, background element in an essentially male story.

The massive shift in conceptualization, consolidated since 1989, has utilized theoretical studies of the kind of behaviour which is often shrugged away by women themselves as natural. What does 'natural' mean when used in this sense? Of course, giving shelter or food to those on the run can be called natural. But if it was so natural why were only a minority involved? This could well reinforce the

146

explanation of personality, but more pressingly there is the need to question the word 'natural', to find out how it has been constituted to eliminate the notion of choice. Men who took to the woods as maquisards never use the word 'natural' to describe their action, although it could be argued that it was an atavistic, archetypal, 'natural' male pattern of behaviour. The maquisards are right to insist on the voluntary nature of their actions. But this insistence can no longer be gender-specific. Women's actions under the Occupation are now being re-evaluated in terms of the voluntarism which has always characterized male resistance. Putting the element of choice back into behaviour seen as 'natural' by many women has become a research necessity. With it goes an attack on anonymity. Names are uncovered and revealed. Long overdue recognition is now given to ordinary women and voluntarism. So, for example, the regional newspaper *Ouest-France* in May 1998 featured Marie Ledier, a village woman of Brullemail in the Orne, who died in 1987. She was posthumously awarded the Israeli honour of '*Juste parmi les nations*' for hiding Jews in her farm continuously throughout the Occupation. One of the children hidden was André Bornstain, aged 5 in 1942 and now Alon Beeri, an Israeli citizen. His citation of Marie Ledier contained the words; 'She never asked questions. She thought it natural to take in people and children who were dispossessed.' And he concluded, 'But she risked her life to save ours.'[13] The importance of this inclusive move by authorities and historians alike cannot be overstated. But its conceptual strength has a dimension which might be missed if individual inclusion was thought to be its only achievement. Its main effect lies in a return to collective categories, driven as it is by anthropological insights. Pierre Bourdieu's concept of the 'habitus', which brings together human agency and objective social conditions in a subtle balance, is being widely used to explore the extent to which group or community resistance was both voluntaristic and determined at the same time.[14] This strengthens work on local communities who have both a collective habitus and shared habitat such as the Protestant villagers of Le Chambon-sur-Lignon who sheltered scores of Jewish children, but it also reintroduces a focus on political groupings, and a new interest in class, jobs and professions, primary schoolteachers for example. In 1997 leading historians in France finally brought out a social history of the Resistance, with chapters on the medical profession, railway workers, the middle classes, and on women, alongside chapters on

147

theory.[15] Anthropology and sociology have thus met up with the specificity and contextuality of historical research.

Is it a permanent swing away from the exceptional and if so how will it affect the discourse of personality? Francis Cammaerts, with a sensitive personality marked by being a conscientious objector at the start of the war, was far closer to grassroots resistance in the south-east of France than many other allied agents, and I like the answer which he has provided in the title of a modest documentary, made in 1995.[16] It provides a definition of resistance personalities, which incorporates many of the shifts and reappraisals over the last thirty years. The resisters featured in the documentary were, the title suggests, ordinary people. Better still, they were 'No Ordinary People'.

NOTES

1. Jean-Marie Guillon's review of Guillaume Piketty, *Pierre Brossolette, un héros de la Résistance* (Odile Jacob, 1998) is in *Vingtième Siècle*, No.59, July–Sept.1998, p.207.
2. Henry Rousso, *Le syndrome de Vichy* (Seuil, 1987) p.106.
3. Marcel Ophuls made *Le Chagrin et la Pitié* in 1969 for Productions Télévision Rencontre. It was refused a showing on state television, but was released to screening in cinemas in 1971. The television ban was lifted in 1981. Robert Paxton's *Vichy France. Old Guard and New Order* (Barrie and Jenkins, 1972) appeared in a French edition in 1973. Rousso's phrase, 'Le miroir brisé', is his title for Chapter 3 of *Le syndrome de Vichy* and covers the period 1971–1974.
4. As translated for the English edition of *The Sorrow and the Pity* (Paladin, 1975) p.118.
5. Jean Cassou, *La Mémoire courte* (Editions de Minuit, 1953) p.57. Lucie Aubrac's memoirs appeared as *Ils partiront dans l'ivresse* (Seuil, 1984) and were translated as *Outwitting the Gestapo* (University of Nebraska Press, 1993).
6. M.R.D. Foot, *SOE in France* (HMSO, 1966) pp.12, 49–50.
7. See the present author's *In Search of the Maquis* (OUP, 1993) pp.116–125, 241–4.
8. Jean-Marie Guillon, '*La Résistance au village*' in Jacqueline Sainclivier and Christian Bougeard (eds.), *La Résistance et les Français. Enjeux stratégiques et environnement social* (Presses Universitaires de Rennes, 1995) p.233.

9. The multiple shifts in definition over the last ten years were in evidence in the six conferences on '*La Résistance et les Français*' from 1993 to 1997. They are very well summarized by François Marcot in *19/20: Bulletin du Centre d'Histoire Contemporaine*, Université de Franche-Comté, Besançon, No.2, 1998, pp.9–42.

10. Pierre Nora (ed.), *Les Lieux de Mémoire*, 7 vols (Gallimard, 1984–1993). See also, Nancy Wood, 'Memory's Remains: *Les Lieux de Mémoire*' in *History and Memory*, Vol.6, No.1, 1994, pp.123–149.

11. The meeting of the Aubracs and a panel of historians was initiated by the Aubracs themselves, in order to confront the innuendo and accusation of Gérard Chauvy's *Aubrac-Lyon 1943* (Albin Michel, 1997). Klaus Barbie's claim that Raymond Aubrac was the traitor at the arrest of Jean Moulin had been repeated by Chauvy, and this was unanimously rejected by all the historians present as a complete fabrication. The meeting then unexpectedly took an inquisitorial turn. See the publication of the proceedings in *Libération*, 9 July 1997 together with reactions to the meeting by the participants.

12. Claudio Pavone, *Una Guerra Civile* (Bollati Boringhieri, 1991); James C. Scott, *Weapons of the Weak. Everyday Forms of Peasant Resistance* (Yale, 1985).

13. *Ouest-France*, 23–24 May, 1998, p.8.

14. Pierre Bourdieu, *The Logic of Practice*, trans.Richard Nice (Polity Press, 1990).

15. Antoine Prost (ed.), *La Résistance, une histoire sociale* (Editions de l'Atelier, 1997).

16. *No Ordinary People*, directed by Mike Fox for Foxy Films and Elizabeth O'Hara Boyce, produced for the BBC's 'Picture This', and shown on BBC 2 on 28 November 1995.

CHURCHILL AND INTELLIGENCE: HIS EARLY LIFE

DAVID STAFFORD

In 1932, the year before Hitler seized power, Churchill visited Blenheim (Blindheim) in Bavaria, the site of the great victory in 1704 of his illustrious ancestor John Churchill, the first Duke of Marlborough. It was a research trip, for he had embarked on writing Marlborough's biography and wanted to see the fighting terrain with his own eyes. This was totally in character, for Churchill always wanted to see things for himself. It was also a family trait. As his four-volume Marlborough biography repeatedly emphasizes, good intelligence was valued highly by the Duke. So much so, indeed, that he spent extravagantly on his secret service and generously rewarded his Chief of Intelligence, the Earl of Cadogan, with rapid promotion. Indeed, it was the Duke's heavy and unaccountable expenditures on secret service that gave the pretext for his political enemies to bring him down in 1712.

Significantly, Cadogan's role sparked an acerbic argument between Churchill and his son Randolph during the tour. The combative Randolph, who was especially turbulent round his father, dismissed the Irishman as a mere 'bell-hop' to Marlborough. Not so, responded Churchill briskly. Cadogan was 'a splendid chief of staff, chief of intelligence and Quarter-Master combined, and was always sent on in front to *see with his own eyes* [Churchill's underlining] and report . . . exactly what the position was. They each knew every inch of the game [sic] so well that action could be taken with great assurance upon these reports of high technical authority.'[1]

Thus, from the Bavarian battlefield that gave its name to the English seat of the Marlborough dynasty (and also the Second World War headquarters of M.I.5, Britain's Security Service) Churchill stressed the importance to consumers both of intelligence of high technical authority, and of seeing the evidence with one's own eyes. In that same year, too, he published his collection of essays entitled *Thoughts and Adventures*. One of them was called 'My Spy Story', and in language that could have rattled from the typewriter of a practised Hollywood scriptwriter he drew a vivid portrait of the world of secret service which he described as equal to the most fantastic inventions of romance or melodrama: 'tangle within tangle, plot and counter-plot, ruse and treachery, cross and double cross, true agent, false agent, double agent, gold and steel, the bomb, the dagger, and the firing party'.[2]

Intelligence and espionage were obviously much on Churchill's mind in 1932. Perhaps he was already aware of the crucial role it would play in the not-too-distant European future. After all, it was on this Bavarian visit that he famously failed to have lunch with Adolf Hitler – one of those intriguing meetings of history that did *not* take place – after Randolph vainly tried to arrange it through the Führer-in-waiting's crony Putzi Hanfstaegel. Churchill could sense already that the European tide was flowing towards war.

But of course it was the experience of a past war, not a future one, that enabled him to talk with authority about intelligence and espionage. For all that he is now celebrated for his leadership of Britain and its secret services between 1939–1945, he had occupied the powerful position of First Lord of the Admiralty at the outbreak of the First World War, been a Cabinet minister before that, and had fought as a serving soldier in the late Victorian army with personal experience of conflict. This is often overshadowed by his later career in discussions of his use of intelligence and it is on this early period in his life that I shall concentrate here.[3]

Churchill's experience and appreciation of the value of intelligence was built on a solid foundation. Celebrating his twenty-first birthday in 1895 tracking Spanish efforts to crush the revolt in Cuba, he noted that while the Spanish could rarely pin down the rebels, the guerrillas always knew where to find them. The reason was good and comprehensive intelligence. 'They know everything,' he observed in words that echo throughout this century's guerrilla wars, 'the position of every general, the destination of every soldier, and what their own spies fail to find out their friends in every village let them know.' His experience with the Malakand Field Force in North-West India drove the lesson further home. Here again he witnessed the importance of first-rate intelligence in fighting guerrillas, this time while accompanying a British intelligence officer, Captain Henry Stanton, on a field reconnaissance trip. Stanton's report can still be found in War Office files, and is generous in its tribute to the intelligence work of local agents. Churchill borrowed some of its conclusions, in particular the lesson that intelligence and operations should be intimately linked, with the former very firmly the servant of the latter.[4] In *The River War*, his powerful account of Kitchener's campaign in the Sudan, he singled out the importance of the work done by spies and secret agents, and from his well-publicized adventures during the Boer War drew the all-too-obvious lesson that British intelligence had been sadly lacking. Indeed, the experience provided him with material for one of his earliest interventions in the House of Commons after he entered Parliament in 1900. 'If there was one Department [of the Army] on which money could be spent with advantage,' he said during heated debates on Army reform, 'it was the Intelligence Department.'[5]

The opportunity to put this theoretical belief in the importance of intelligence to practical account finally arrived in 1909. In the midst of a national spy scare fuelled by the Anglo-German naval race and rumours of German spies at large in Britain, the Liberal Government of Herbert Asquith created the Secret Service Bureau, later to mutate into the two separate and often jealous agencies, MI5 and MI6. Churchill, now President of the Board of Trade, embraced its work with enthusiasm. Within weeks he was listening eagerly as Lieutenant-Colonel Sir John Spencer Ewart, the Director of Military Operations and Intelligence, personally explained its functions, and he instantly offered to help with commercial information his ministry might provide that could offer clues to Germany's preparations for war. Within a year he was Home Secretary, where his growing national security fears meant that he built up particularly close and confidential links with the head of the Bureau's 'home', or counter-espionage, division, Captain Vernon Kell. It was Churchill who granted the Bureau unprecedented power to carry out clandestine searches of the mails, persuaded police forces throughout the country to assist Kell in his work in compiling a registry of aliens and suspects, and led the charge for a new and more stringent Official Secrets Act. By the time he entered the Admiralty in 1911 Churchill was a companion in arms to Kell in his relentless campaign to unmask German spies in Britain. Common to both of them was the belief – in truth quite unfounded – that such agents had been infiltrated into the country to assist a German invasion. Indeed, it was at Churchill's order that in late July 1914, on the very eve of war, all known or suspected German spies in Britain still at large were rounded up and detained.[6]

By this time the safety of Britain's ultimate defence, the Grand Fleet, was being dramatically transformed by a revolutionary new source of intelligence. This was Sigint, or signals intelligence. Churchill was fascinated by it. 'Our Intelligence service,' he boasted later in his monumental history of the First World War, *The World Crisis*, 'has won and deserved world-wide fame. More than perhaps any other Power, we were successful in the war in penetrating the intentions of the enemy.'[7]

The day after war was declared he received an early afternoon visit from Admiral Sir Henry Oliver, the Director of Naval Intelligence, who was accompanied by Sir Alfred Ewing, the Director of Naval Education. One of Ewing's interests was radio telegraphy. Another, cryptography, had led him to design a cipher machine that had been seriously considered by the Admiralty only two months before. This explained his arrival with Oliver. For as soon as war broke out Oliver found his desk swamped with intercepts of German wireless messages but with no means or expertise to decipher them. He turned to Ewing for help and Ewing agreed to create an Admiralty decoding centre.

Churchill's knowledge and understanding of intercepts and their intelligence value reflected orthodox thinking. During the South African war the British had successfully broken Boer ciphers and over the next few years the War Office had carefully planned how to exploit cryptography in the next war. But the emphasis was on cable traffic, where intercepts were limited in number and restricted in value. Wireless was a new technology, and the vulnerability of messages sent over the airwaves – and hence the rich harvest of intelligence they could produce – was severely underestimated. The 1914 *Naval Annual*, for example, declared that interception posed no threat to naval wireless.

Churchill accepted this view. But events quickly revealed his error, and as with other forms of new technology he proved a quick and eager learner. On hearing Oliver's account of the intercept harvest that lay on his desk, and of Ewing's interest in cryptography, he readily agreed to their proposal. Thus was born what became known as 'Room 40', named after the room in the Admiralty Old Building that eventually became its home.[8]

Its early targets were German ciphers containing strategic intelligence. But this priority dramatically changed with the arrival of the first significant intercepts relating to a quite different source: German naval tactical traffic – operational intelligence of the highest importance that could decide the fates of the two great battle fleets that faced each other across the North Sea. Churchill rapidly understood that such high-grade intelligence needed special treatment to safeguard its secrecy. But this was only one aspect of the challenge that now faced the Admiralty. Individual intercepts themselves meant little – or worse, could be entirely misleading – unless they were properly assessed by experts familiar with the larger intelligence picture. Churchill's natural instincts resisted this conclusion. Always a 'hands-on' minister, he found the temptation to throw himself into the details of operational matters irresistible. Fortunately, he met his match in the newly appointed Director of Naval Intelligence, Captain Reginald 'Blinker' Hall. Tensions between them precipitated a decision that marks a milestone in the history of British intelligence.

Churchill, obsessed by fears of German invasion, regarded the occupied Belgian ports as dangerous staging posts and ordered that all intelligence reports from Belgium, 'as and when they arrived', should be sent directly to him. In the first week of November 1914 Hall received intelligence from an agent at Zeebrugge reporting that the Germans had rushed two or three hundred 'submarines' there. From previous reports Hall knew that this particular agent used the word to indicate any object below the sea's surface, and that what in reality he meant were mines, not submarines, of which the Germans were known to have only about two dozen. But, as dutifully instructed, he sent the raw report, exactly as received, to Churchill.

The result was an explosion. Churchill instantly rebuked Hall for giving credence to the report. Was he aware, he demanded, how many officers and men would be needed for such a huge flotilla of submarines? Was there any evidence that Germany had trained such numbers? 'The function of the Intelligence Division,' he chided, 'is not merely to collect and pass on the Munchausen tales of spies and untrustworthy agents, but carefully to sift and scrutinize the intelligence they receive, and in putting it forward to indicate the degree of probability which attaches to it.' Hall had neatly - and perhaps deliberately – hoisted Churchill on his own petard, revealing how absurd it was to provide raw undigested intelligence to a busy minister. Churchill, Hall later confessed, 'had the defects of his great

155

qualities: he was essentially a "one-man" show. It was not in his nature to allow anybody except himself to be the executive authority when any action of importance had to be taken.'

But Churchill quickly learned from experience. The day after this row with Hall he sat down and wrote out in longhand a 'Charter' for Room 40 headed 'Exclusively Secret' – a unique designation he concocted himself:

> An officer of the War Staff, preferably from the ID [Intelligence Division], should be selected to study all the decoded intercepts, not only current but past, and to compare them continually with what actually took place in order to penetrate the German mind and movements and make reports. All these intercepts are to be written in a locked book with their decodes, and all other copies are to be collected and burnt. All new messages are to be entered in the book, and the book is only to be handled under direction from COS [Chief of Staff – Oliver]. The officer selected is for the present to do no other work. I shall be obliged if Sir Alfred Ewing will associate himself continuously with this work.[10]

With this, Churchill did three things. First, he recognized the prime importance of Room 40's Sigint work and the need to give it special and top secret priority. Second, he acknowledged that intelligence needed to be interpreted by an intelligence expert if 'Munchausen tales' were not to be given credibility. Finally, by drafting the order himself, he indicated his intention to keep his close personal eye on Room 40's work. Ewing's codebreakers now focused their energies on tactical naval traffic revealing the movements of the German High Seas Fleet and enemy submarines, while Hall appointed a qualified naval officer to analyse and produce appreciations of the intercepts. This was Commander Herbert Hope, whose job was to 'extract the juice' from the raw intercepts and to provide naval expertise to Ewing's collection of cryptographers and linguists.

What was extraordinary about these 1914 arrangements was who did, and did not, receive the intercepts. In a second order – this time classified 'Most Secret' and dated 29 November 1914[11] – Churchill decreed that only one copy should be made of each intercept and it was to go, 'direct and exclusively', to Oliver as Chief of Staff, who would then pass it on to the First Sea Lord. This meant it was seen within the Admiralty by a mere handful of people. Remarkably absent from the list were any members of the Cabinet or War

Council, the supreme body created by Asquith to run the war. Outside the Admiralty the Prime Minister alone was routinely informed of Britain's great intelligence triumph – and even then he received the information only by courtesy of Churchill, who, wrote Oliver in a postwar memoir, 'would not allow anyone to know about the decyphering . . . without his permission'.[12] Security, however, was still a hazy concept, as revealed by the correspondence Asquith conducted with his confidante Venetia Stanley, often from the Cabinet Room itself. More than once he told her of 'profound secrets' he had learned from this source. He appears to have done likewise with his daughter Violet (later Violet Bonham Carter).[13]

Churchill had both seized upon a vital source of intelligence and instinctively realized its political power. He had yet to realize how complex a technical matter it would become. As the trickle of daily intercepts became a flood, his notion that one officer could handle them all had to be modified. But his determination to restrict knowledge to the smallest possible number of people in the Admiralty created a system that was over-centralized and inefficient. For one thing, Commander Hope, the intelligence analyst, at first found himself completely isolated from Room 40, and only after pleading with Fisher was he allowed to meet the producers of the reports he was expected to analyse. As for Ewing, he continued to operate independently of Hall, and while the latter personally knew about the intercepts, other members of his naval intelligence staff did not. This damaging separation of the cryptographers from intelligence was only rectified after Churchill had left the Admiralty. More harmful still, Churchill insisted that intercepts were to remain within the Admiralty, which alone would decide what intelligence should be passed to ships at sea. This proved a mistake. One episode provides an example.

Shortly after eight o' clock on the morning of Wednesday 16 December 1914 German battle cruisers loomed out of the mist off the Yorkshire coast and in indiscriminate shelling killed or injured some five hundred civilians, leaving behind an angry public demanding to know how the most powerful navy in the world had failed to prevent the attack. Churchill, who bore the brunt of the public anger, was unable to tell the whole story. 'We had to bear in silence the censures of our countrymen,' he lamented. 'We could never admit for fear of compromising our secret information where our squadrons were, or how near the German raiding cruisers had been to their destruction.'[14]

How near is revealed by the events that had begun on the previous Monday when intercepts revealed that German battle cruisers were on the move in a possible raid on the east coast. The intelligence did not reveal their destination, but it did give their time of departure and return to Germany. Churchill and his advisers decided to catch the Germans as they returned home and Admiral Jellicoe, Commander-in-Chief of the Grand Fleet, was ordered to ensure that battle and light cruisers were in place to intercept the returning German ships. He duly despatched the Second Battle Squadron to intercept them off the south-east of the Dogger Bank.

There followed a tense 36 hours. Was the intelligence correct? Was this an opportunity to strike a great naval victory by catching the Germans unawares? After alerting Prime Minister Asquith to be ready for dramatic events, Churchill waited with mounting impatience for the news. The tension broke while he was still enjoying his morning bath. The door opened and an officer came hurrying in with a naval signal. Churchill gripped it with a dripping hand. 'German battle cruisers bombarding Hartlepool,' it said. Hastily pulling on clothes over his damp body, he ran downstairs to the War Room where he found that Fisher had already arrived, and Oliver, who regularly slept in the War Room, was methodically plotting positions on the map. They showed the German battle cruisers off the Yorkshire coast. 150 miles to the east, cutting off their line of retreat, were the ships of the Second Battle Squadron. It seemed as though the trap was about to be sprung.

Yet the opportunity was missed and it soon became apparent that the Germans had escaped. North Sea mists descended and the British ships lost sight of their prey. Human error also played a part, with mistakes in signalling at a crucial moment. The episode also high-lighted deeper problems with the system for handling Room 40's intelligence. Incomplete deductions had been drawn from the initial intercept alerting the Admiralty to the raid. From the absence of any reference to battleships, Oliver had concluded that the High Seas Fleet itself was taking no part in the engagement. He was wrong. Admiral von Ingenohl, Commander of Germany's High Seas Fleet, had ordered his battle fleet out to lend support to Admiral Hipper's raiding force.

So when a subsequent intercept, in the early afternoon, revealed the presence in the North Sea of the High Seas Fleet, the War Room mistakenly jumped to the conclusion that it had just appeared and was advancing towards the British ships. Fearing an unequal encounter, they ordered them not to advance too far east. The reality was that von Ingenohl, far from advancing, had decided to retreat on *his* mistaken assumption that he was about to encounter the British Grand Fleet. The Admiralty error, compounded by a two-hour delay in transmitting a crucial intercept revealing Hipper's exact position, allowed the Germans to escape.

The Navy lamented that a golden opportunity had been lost and Churchill was dismayed. The only comfort he could draw – and it was a major one – was that the intercepts, a new and untested source, had proved reliable. As long as Room 40 continued to decipher German signals, any major enemy move into the North Sea would be detected. The Grand Fleet could now rest more secure than in the past. No longer did it have to carry out endless reconnaissance sweeps of the North Sea or to remain in a constant and anxious state of alert. That was worth a lot. 'While the priceless information lasts,' he reassured Jellicoe early in the New Year, 'we ought to rest our fleets and flotillas to the utmost.'[15] Strategically, the intercepts were showing their worth.

There remained the fear that they might dry up, and even with them the intelligence picture was never perfect. The crucial meeting in the war room on the morning of the 16th had dealt with information that, as Churchill candidly admitted, was 'obscure and uncertain'. Intelligence rarely presents a picture that is complete. But the gaps and misreadings were not helped by the rigid system Churchill had devised. Neither Room 40 itself in the shape of Ewing, nor the Intelligence Division represented by Hall or Commander Hope, were asked to comment on the intercept. Instead, the assessment was made by four people: Churchill himself, the former First Sea Lord Sir Arthur Wilson, Sir Henry Oliver, now Chief of the Naval Staff, and Admiral Fisher, the First Sea Lord.

Nor did the system permit Jellicoe and those who would have to act on the information actually to receive it. The major actors at sea remained wholly dependent on the Admiralty. As Jellicoe forcefully protested, if there were delays in Whitehall, vital intelligence was denied to the admirals. Churchill apparently took this to heart and agreed that in the event of another German raid Jellicoe would be given complete charge of the operation and that all information received by the Admiralty would be sent simultaneously to him. For whatever reason, however, this was not done, and early in 1915 there was another disappointing North Sea skirmish with the High Seas Fleet.[16]

Another product of Room 40's intelligence was highly treasured by Churchill. In January 1915 Commander Hope began to submit a daily return, based on Room 40's intercepts, of the strength and general location of the German U-Boat fleet. This contained the number of each U-Boat, the flotilla to which it belonged, a comment on its known location and any information known about its movements. In addition Hope frequently added some general comment. This intelligence did not, it should be noted, stretch to locating German submarines all, or even most, of the time. Hope's lists were compiled from intercepts of the position reports that U-Boats usually made to their home base for the first two or three days of their journey. They gave accurate information about their course and speed of advance, but once out of radio range of home base the intercepts ceased. After that, knowledge of their whereabouts came from surface sightings and sinkings. Nonetheless, Churchill minutely scrutinized these reports, making comments or asking questions. Little escaped his attention and he often suggested action. In late February 1915, for example, when Hope noted that U-33 was at Emden 'preparing for a distant undertaking', later reporting that it had gone to Wilhelmshaven where engine trouble meant it would not be ready for action until mid-March, Churchill drew Hope's attention to the first with its ominous phrase about preparing for action. 'Watch this carefully,' he instructed.[17] Even when he had no comment or query he carefully initialled Hope's reports to indicate that he had read them. This he did on 1 May when he received Hope's sheet, compiled the day before, that noted against U-20 'At sea since Apl 30: gone NW: under orders for Irish Sea'. Neither he nor Hope were to know that thirteen days later U-20 was to fire a single torpedo into the Cunard liner *Lusitania* and send it to the bottom with the loss of some 1200 lives.

Despite a voluminous literature on this perennial controversy, no credible evidence exists that Churchill deliberately plotted some conspiracy to sink the *Lusitania* and guarantee a British propaganda coup in the United States. Ironically, however, he himself thought there might have been a *German* conspiracy. Five days after the tragedy the Admiralty's Trade Division, responsible for merchant shipping, suggested that German spies or sympathizers might have penetrated Cunard's New York office and learned of the *Lusitania*'s route. The report also hinted that Captain Turner of the *Lusitania* was either utterly incompetent or, more sinister, had 'been got at by the Germans'. The impetuous and increasingly unstable Admiral Fisher endorsed the suggestion with gusto, declared that Turner had obviously been bribed, and demanded that he be arrested whatever the result of the official enquiry. Churchill grasped at the conspiracy notion and agreed that Turner should be pursued 'without check'.[18] He also embraced the suspicions that spies had been at work, ordered that security in New York should immediately be tightened up, and agreed that Room 40 intelligence should be concealed from any enquiry. This was not to cover up a conspiracy. It was to safeguard the secret that Britain was reading German ciphers. In any case, Churchill had far more pressing things on his mind than concocting some spurious conspiracy. The Dardanelles campaign was reaching its disastrous climax and he was fighting for his political survival.

Many factors far beyond intelligence explained Churchill's enthusiasm for the Dardanelles campaign, but reports in October 1914 of Turkish plans to invade Egypt, and diplomatic intercepts revealing promises to Vienna of an early entry into the war, strengthened his belligerence. After Turkey entered the war in November he seized on any evidence that would buttress his case. He was particularly fired up by a Room 40 intercept which revealed that the Turks were running dangerously low on ammunition and he instructed Hall to launch a subversive operation to stop war material passing through Roumania and Bulgaria to Turkey by recruiting Bulgarian and Roumanian agents to watch the railways and canals. 'Money should be spent freely,' he suggested, to bribe railway employees to provide intelligence about ammunition transiting the Balkans bound for Turkey. 'Not a day,' he instructed, 'should be lost in instituting this necessary service.'[19]

Another secret operation lubricated by British gold sovereigns was already underway, one of the most extraordinary episodes of the whole war. This involved George Griffin Eady and Edward Whittall, two British agents recruited by Hall whose mission was to bribe the Turks to leave the war. Using as their principal intermediary the Grand Rabbi of Turkey, their principal contact was Talaat Bey, the acting Minister of Finance and Minister of the Interior. In February 1915 news filtered back to London that certain Turks were willing to talk peace, intelligence that further spurred Churchill's enthusiasm for the Dardanelles scheme. By early March things had progressed to the point where the Turks had agreed to meet Eady and Whittall and soon they were on their way to the Turkish town of Dedeagach and a meeting with Talaat.

At this point Hall briefed Churchill more fully on the operation and for the first time revealed the huge sum of money – some £4 million – involved. Churchill was taken aback. 'Who authorized this?' he demanded. 'The Cabinet surely knows nothing about it?' Hall replied that he had done it on his own initiative. 'I imagine they'd be glad enough to pay,' he added. Flabbergasted, Churchill turned to Fisher: 'Do you hear what this man has done? He's told his people they can go up to four million to buy a peaceful passage! On his own!' Then, before he could say more, Fisher interrupted, and, referring to the impending naval assault on the Dardanelles, insisted, 'No, no. I'm going through tomorrow or as soon as the preparations can be completed.' With Churchill still recovering from Hall's confession, Fisher ordered Hall immediately to break off all negotiations. 'There was nothing to be done,' recorded the Director of Naval Intelligence sadly, 'but obey orders.'[20] In reality, cancellation of the bribery scheme made little difference. Eady and Whittall were unable to promise Talaat the one thing vital to his political (not to mention physical) survival: that Constantinople would remain in Turkish hands after the war was over. Behind the scenes, the city had already been promised to the Russians. After twenty-four hours Talaat broke off negotiations and Eady and Whittal returned to Salonika.

This did not stop Churchill clinging to the hope that divisions amongst the Turks might lead to a Turkish collapse or withdrawal from the war. Only a week before the Gallipoli landings, he seized hungrily on information from an agent on Corfu suggesting that Enver Pasha, the most pro-German minister in the Turkish Government, was seriously isolated and that Talaat Bey still remained open to an early peace. Success at the Dardanelles, argued Churchill, would tear open the rift and spark revolution and peace in Constantinople. Maurice Hankey, the assistant secretary to the Cabinet and legendary Whitehall 'man of secrets', who was fully briefed on the background, dined with Churchill at Admiralty House and found him 'extremely optimistic.' Three days later a Russian secret agent in Constantinople repeated the story about Turkish ammunition shortages and Sazonov, the Russian Foreign Minister, passed it on to Grey, who informed Churchill. Immediately he sent it to Admiral de Robeck, commander of the British naval force at the Dardanelles, suggesting that he incite the Turkish forts to fire as much as possible. But de Robeck firmly resisted this Churchillian prod.

Half the globe distant from the Dardanelles another naval engagement threw revealing light on the intelligence war. On a sunlit Sunday morning in Cumberland Bay in the virtually deserted Juan Fernandez Islands, four hundred miles off the coast of Chile, the German light cruiser *Dresden* blew herself up to avoid capture by British ships that had caught her unawares at anchor. It was the final chapter in a saga that had begun late the previous year.

In November 1914 the German Far Eastern Fleet commanded by Admiral Graf von Spee inflicted a resounding defeat on British ships off Coronel. Shortly afterwards the humiliation was avenged at the Battle of the Falklands when von Spee went down with his flagship and his warships were sunk. Only one escaped, the *Dresden*. For the next three months she eluded her pursuers off the coast of Chile. Finally she was forced by lack of coal into Cumberland Bay. Here, as her captain signalled by radio using the German merchant navy code, he planned to meet up with a collier organized by the German Naval Attaché in Chile. In contrast to Royal Navy ships in the North Sea, those based in the South Atlantic had been provided with details of the German merchant vessel cypher. As a result the *Glasgow*, the principal pursuer of the *Dresden*, was able to intercept and decipher her captain's message, surprise her at anchor in Cumberland Bay and open fire. After retaliating with a couple of rounds 'for the honour of the flag', the *Dresden* blew herself up.

The sinking of the *Dresden* again revealed how Churchill regarded the intercepts as almost private property. Having heard from the *Glasgow* of her lucky intercept, Churchill responded by ordering an immediate attack. Learning of this from 'Blinker' Hall, Maurice Hankey, assistant secretary to the Cabinet, immediately sounded the alarm. Cumberland Bay was in Chilean waters and Chile was a neutral power. Churchill's order had serious political implications. Hankey informed Asquith, who was completely in the dark about the whole affair. The next day the Prime Minister hastily convened a meeting with both Churchill and the Foreign Secretary, Sir Edward Grey. What transpired may be guessed from events that followed.

163

Asquith emerged from the encounter looking heated and, nine days later, ignoring the niceties of international law and under direction from the Admiralty, the *Glasgow* opened fire and precipitated the *Dresden's* self-destruction.[21]

There is an intriguing footnote to this story. After the initial salvoes Captain Ludecke of the *Dresden* raised the white flag and sent a Lieutenant by pinnace to protest that his ship had already been officially interned by Chile. But this was *ruse de guerre* while Ludecke prepared to scuttle the ship. The Lieutenant who boarded the *Glasgow* under the flag of truce, a taciturn fair-haired officer and Ludecke's most trusted *aide*, was named Wilhelm Canaris. A World War later, now an Admiral, he was to head the German *Abwehr* as one of the major players in the intelligence war.

In the years up to his departure from the Admiralty at age 40, Churchill had confronted most of the major intelligence issues that were to appear again during the Second World War. So far as signals intelligence was concerned, these involved its distribution, assessment, security, operational use and its strengths and limitations. He had made mistakes and learned lessons, as had the Admiralty: its Operational Intelligence Centre during the Second World War was to handle affairs much better. Churchill, however, never lost his appetite for the raw material itself, as his now legendary insistence on seeing his 'golden eggs' (Ultra) demonstrates.

He also revealed himself as a ready user of other weapons in Britain's intelligence armoury. Horrified though he was by the sums involved, he was perfectly ready to subvert the Turkish Government through bribery, and more than willing to spend money employing secret agents in the Balkans if it could help. As Prime Minister twenty-five years later, he was to spend up to $13 million in bribes administered by the Secret Intelligence Service to ensure that General Franco's Spain kept out of the war.[22] And although the opportunity had not arisen during his months at the Admiralty, his prewar experiences of imperial frontier wars against rebels had impressed him with the subversive potential of guerrilla movements behind enemy lines. From here sprang the impulse that led him in 1940 to create the Special Operations Executive (SOE) to 'set Europe ablaze' by promoting sabotage, subversion and guerrilla war behind enemy lines. It was a strategy he also promoted vigorously against the Bolsheviks after the October Revolution.

Churchill also emerged from his early contacts with MI5 as particularly susceptible to spy fever. Kell's reports about German spies, while factually correct, were presented as evidence of a larger German invasion plan, which was untrue. Churchill accepted Kell's assessments, frequently conjured up the nightmare image of a German descent on the British Isles and was a willing participant in the great round-up of aliens in 1914–1915. After the fact, he accepted that spymania had frequently got out of hand, but nonetheless excused it on the grounds that it 'constituted on the whole an important additional element of security'.[23] This was also his position in 1940 during the invasion fear that gripped Britain after the fall of France, when thousands of enemy aliens were again interned and many deported overseas – sometimes with tragic results. Now Prime Minister, Churchill was in the vanguard – so long as invasion loomed. As soon as it diminished, he permitted the release of most internees, and by the time victory came he was deploring the threat to individual liberties posed by an overly zealous MI5.[24]

Churchill's use of intelligence in this early phase of his long political career not surprisingly reveals the flaws familiar in other facets of his life: impatience, impetuosity, obsessive over-enthusiasm. Yet it also displays boldness, imagination and originality. Above all, he rapidly learned the impressive power that control of intelligence could confer on those prepared to use it. It was not simply the power over enemies that impressed him. Its political influence had also become obvious. He was almost certainly aware, for example, that 'Blinker' Hall had played a part in his downfall. At the height of the crisis over the Dardanelles, Fisher impetuously abandoned his post as First Sea Lord. Deeply shocked by his behaviour, and believing he was no longer fit to hold office, senior Admiralty officials asked Hall to raise the matter with Asquith. Instead, he consulted Lord Reading, the Lord Chief Justice, telling him of the repeated friction between Churchill and Fisher and of his blunt opinion that the latter was no longer fit to hold his post. 'If either of them is to leave the Admiralty,' Reading finally asked, 'which of them is it to be?' It was the crucial question for which Hall had been waiting. 'Regretfully,' he replied, after a pregnant pause, 'I have to say both.'[25] While powerful political currents against Churchill were also at work, there is little doubt that Hall's intervention helped seal Churchill's fate. One obvious lesson he drew was that no future intelligence chief should be permitted such unbridled power, and that if ever *he* became prime minister intelligence and its producers would be firmly subordinate to his commands. Moreover, as leader of the nation at war, he should be careful to ensure that in discussing intelligence matters with his advisers he should play on a level playing field, hence his insistence that he should see as much as possible of the raw product of Ultra. Far from being simply an example of his obsession with detail, it was a hard-headed and calculated reminder that he was not an automatic pushover for advice that his intelligence experts might deliver.

Churchill stood head and shoulders above his political contemporaries in grasping the importance of intelligence and harnessing it to his cause. Secret service, with all its melodrama, trickery, deception, plot and counter-plot, certainly appealed to the schoolboy romantic within him. Yet far more important were the measurable and pragmatic benefits it brought him as politician, statesman and war leader. Secret intelligence was power that gave him leverage over political colleagues, military advisers and allies, as well as strategic and tactical advantage over enemies, while subversion and special operations offered valuable alternatives to conventional military and political force. All this he learned very early in his life and his enthusiastic nurturing and promotion of British intelligence during the Second World War grew from roots that took hold long before the First and were grounded in vivid personal experience. As soldier and journalist he witnessed how vital good intelligence was to the conquered and conqueror alike, and how conventional military forces could be vulnerable to the calculated strategems of the weak and the occupied. For the rest of his political career Churchill was to see in the secret service an essential tool of statecraft.

NOTES

1. Churchill to Duke of Marlborough, 25 September 1932, in *Winston S. Churchill*, by Martin Gilbert, Vol 5 Companion [henceforward *CV*], Part 2, 477–8. For Churchill's views on Marlborough's secret service, see this author's 'Marlborough's Secret Service' presented to the symposium on 'Winston Churchill's Life of Marlborough', Blenheim Palace, May 1998; to be published by the Churchill Center, Washington D.C.

2. Winston S. Churchill, 'My Spy Story', in *Thoughts and Adventures* (London 1932), pp 71–2.

3. For a more extended treatment, see David Stafford, *Churchill and Secret Service* (London, John Murray, 1997). M.R.D. Foot provided an overview of similar territory in his Address to the Toronto Churchill Society for the Advancement of Parliamentary Democracy in 1988 entitled 'Churchill and the Secret Services'. See also Christopher Andrew, 'Churchill and Intelligence', in *Intelligence and National Security*, Vol 3, No 1, July 1988, and David Jablonsky, *Churchill, the Great Game, and Total War* (London, Frank Cass, 1991).

4. WO 106/290, Public Record Office, Kew; Churchill, *The Malakand Field Force*, 276–7.

5. David Stafford, *Churchill and Secret Service* (London 1997), pp 26–7.

6. Nicholas Hiley, 'The Failure of British Espionage against Germany 1907–1914', *Historical Journal*, Vol 26, No 4, 1983, 867–89.

7. Churchill, *The World Crisis 1911–1914*, pp 461–2.

8. Patrick Beesly, *Room 40: British Naval Intelligence 1914–18*, passim; for Oliver, see William James, *A Great Seaman*, and for Ewing, A. Ewing, *The Man of Room 40*; also R.V. Jones, 'Alfred Ewing and Room 40', in *Notes and Records of the Royal Society of London*, Vol 34, 1979–80, pp 65–90.

9. 'Lord Fisher and Mr Churchill,' Hall Papers, Churchill College, Cambridge, p 1.

10. Beesly, *Room 40*, p 16.

11. *CV* III Pt 1, p 281.

12. 'Recollections of Rear-Admiral R.D. Oliver,' OLV 12, Vol 2, pp 102–3, National Maritime Museum, Greenwich.

13. See e.g. Asquith to Venetia Stanley 21 December 1914, in Gilbert, *CV*, Vol 111, Part 1, 322; and Violet Bonham Carter, *Winston Churchill As I Knew Him*, (London 1965) 347.

14. *The World Crisis 1911–1914*, p 478.

15. Churchill to Jellicoe, 4 Jan 1915 (Draft: all references to 'priceless infn' deleted before despatch). *CV*, III, Pt 1 pp 368–9.

16. Patrick Beesly, *Room 40*, (London 1982), pp 57–61.

17. 'Captain H.W. Hope's Notes on Fleet Movements and Submarine Reports (with remarks by the First Lord) 1914–1916,' in ADM 137/4168, Public Record Office, Kew.

18. Churchill 14 May 1915, ADM 137/1058.

19. *The World Crisis 1915*, Appendix III, p 547.

20. 'Lord Fisher and Mr Churchill' p 4. For Eady and Whittal, see G.R.G. Allen, 'A Ghost from Gallipoli,' *Journal of the Royal United Services Institute*, May 1963, pp 137–8; Roskill, *Hankey: Man of Secrets* pp 158–161; Gilbert, *Churchill*, loc. cit, pp 470–471.

21. Roskill, *Hankey*, p 160. For the *Dresden* affair, see Beesly, *Room 40*, pp 72–9; Geoffrey Bennett, *Coronel and the Falklands* pp 173–6; Heinz Hohne, *Canaris* p 30.
22. Stafford, *Churchill and Secret Service*, 202–3.
23. Churchill, 'My Spy Story,' loc cit, p 71.
24. Stafford, *Churchill and Secret Service*, 257–8.
25. 'Lord Fisher and Mr Churchill,' Hall papers 3/5. Also Beesly, *Room 40*, p 137 and Gilbert *Churchill* Vol III pt 1 pp 585–6.

SOME RAF PICK-UPS FOR FRENCH INTELLIGENCE

HUGH VERITY

Much has been published about air operations for the Special Operations Executive (SOE) but little about those for the Secret Intelligence Service (SIS). However, the first three clandestine landings in occupied France by moonlight during the Second World War were for agents reporting to SIS. Throughout the war at least one hundred pickups were completed for SIS compared with about eighty for SOE.[1]

At the outbreak of the war SIS seems to have had little representation in countries that were overrun by Germany in the summer of 1940. However, a number of autonomous intelligence networks soon developed and made contact with SIS. They were short of wireless sets, training and air transport. These were things that SIS was able and anxious to supply, or extract from the Air Ministry, in exchange for use of the intelligence produced. In the Lysander Flight of No 161 Special Duties Squadron RAF pilots were lucky enough to meet a number of secret agents that they landed or picked up (although without knowing their names or jobs) and their escorting officers. This essay will tell some anecdotes about them remembered through two gauze curtains: the secrecy of those days and the misty memory of old age.

Felix

SIS started to put its own agents into France as early as 1940. Philip Schneidau (*Felix*) was the passenger picked up on two of the first three Lysander landings in occupied territory – in October 1940 and May 1941. He had been born in France of British parents and had married a French girl. In 1940 he was a sergeant interpreter in the RAF until the fall of France when he was commissioned as a Pilot Officer by SIS to be parachuted into France. He naturally went to see

169

his wife Simone at their home near Fontainebleau. Their young son Peter had to be briefed on how to react to any nasty German who asked, 'When did you last see your father?'

In September 1940 the Air Ministry had established a very small special duties flight to drop parachutists and to pick them up. Its commander, Flight Lieutenant W.J. Farley, and Philip had together worked out how the pick-up could be done. The Lysander – a high-wing single-engined monoplane with a robust fixed undercarriage – had proved too slow and vulnerable in its original daylight role, Army Co-operation. Its short landing and take-off ability was ideal for the role envisaged by SIS.

The rear cockpit had to be stripped of the gun mounting and air gunner's seat and provided with a wooden bench facing the tail. Wide enough (just) for two people, it was hinged so that luggage could be stowed under it. To enable passengers to climb in and out a narrow ladder was permanently fixed to the outside of the fuselage. To double the radius of action a torpedo-shaped extra fuel tank was mounted between the wheels.

There was no navigation aid suitable to add to the pilot's front cockpit. While over the Channel he could get radio bearings by voice transmission but over France he had only dead reckoning and map reading to navigate by with a compass, a clock and an airspeed indicator. On the Lysander's arrival over the field, agent and pilot would identify themselves by exchanging pre-arranged Morse letters flashed by torch and the aircraft's signalling lamp. The agent would then run round three torches that he had fixed on short sticks switching them on – unless he had a helper who could do those at the far end of the 150-yard-long triangular flare-path.

At about 0115 on 20 October 1940 all this had worked as planned. Farley landed on the right of the first torch, slowed down between the other two torches, taxied back to the first torch and stopped facing into wind, ready for take-off. Philip ran round collecting the torches and climbed in. After his take-off, Farley had problems. A bullet from a German sentry wrecked the compass, which was between his knees. His radio set would not work. It was soaked with rain because he had removed the rear canopy to make it easier for Philip to climb in. After map-reading by moonlight for a while, the weather became atrocious, with low cloud and heavy rain. Obliged to climb and wait for a clearance to let down, he finally had to crash land with dry tanks near Oban in Western Scotland. Farley and

Schneidau were briefly arrested by local police as possible spies. Thus ended the first pick-up in France of World War Two.

While in France Philip had started an intelligence network in Paris. This was financed initially by his father-in-law Paul Shiffmacher. Matthilde Carré (*La Chatte*) would denounce him. He just survived the war in Buchenwald and lived until he was 93.

On Philip's second jump into France, which was in March 1941, a roaring wind blew his parachute into a tree. This knocked out two molars and caught up the wireless set which he took one and a half hours to recover. The friendly dentist who fixed his teeth told him that he had been obliged to help a German colonel by attaching his gold to the back of his front teeth before he went home on leave. As a reward the dentist had been made a member of a German officers' club, where he frequently invited Philip to dine and chat to other members.

On his second pick-up, which was on 10 May 1941, Flying Officer Schneidau's pilot was Flight Lieutenant Gordon Scotter. He had to evade German night-fighters with mounted searchlights on the way home.

Armand

By October 1941 Philip had become Flight Lieutenant Philipson on the staff of ISLD (Inter-Service Liaison Department) as SIS was now calling itself. It was in that capacity that he was at RAF Tangmere on the night of 1 October 1941 to welcome Roman Czerniawski (*Armand*) who had just been picked up near Compiègne by Squadron Leader John Nesbitt-Dufort. Captain Czerniawski had been a pilot in the pre-war Polish air force. In France in 1940 he missed the evacuation of Polish units in June and stayed behind to set up an intelligence network which he called *Inter-Allié*. He later wrote a book about it.[2] Betrayed by his assistant Matthilde Carré, who had also denounced Paul Shiffmacher, Czerniawski was arrested by the Germans. They did a deal with him that they would fake his escape and protect his associates if he would go to England as their double agent. In London General Sikorski decorated him with the Virtuti Militari, the top Polish gallantry award.

Having offered his services to British Intelligence as a double agent working for them, he was employed by the XX (20 or double-cross) Committee and eventually became a key contributor to *Fortitude South*,[3] the deception plan for Operation Overlord in 1944. In this role he was *Brutus*. By 1961 he was Wing Commander Garby-Czerniawski and happily married to an English lady who

171

had helped him with the English in his book.

I had lunch with him in the Polish Officers' club in London in the middle '70s when I was researching my book *We Landed by Moonlight* and had him to lunch with me in the Special Forces Club. Some time later I wanted to check a point with him and telephoned his home. His wife told me that he no longer lived there and that she did not know where he was.

Whippy

Armand's pilot, Squadron Leader John Nesbitt-Dufort, was known as 'Whippy' because he had once had to make a forced landing among the wild animals at Whipsnade zoo. He had taken over command of the Lysander pick-up flight at the end of September 1941 when it was part of No 138 Special Duties Squadron. His pick-up of *Armand* on 1 October was near Estrées-Saint-Denis. It was called Operation BRICK after the code name of the agent responsible for the field, Lieutenant Mitchell, a French gunner officer. Roger Mitchell's grandfather was a Scottish immigrant whose family had retained English as a second language. General de Gaulle had sent Roger into France to liaise with the Poles, pretending to be an Englishman.

Mitchell was flown to England on 7 November by Whippy, whose other passenger was Claude Lamirault (*Fitzroy*) the head of SIS's *Jade-Fitzroy* intelligence network. In his book *Mémoires Résistantes*[4] Alya Aglan says that Lamirault parachuted into France five times, but I have only found three pick-ups that took him to England. He may also have travelled by sea on operations met by Pierre Hentic (*Maho* for maritime operations and *Tréllu* for air ones).

Whippy's fourth and last pick-up was his third to be received by Mitchell. Operation BERYL on 28 January 1942 was near Issoudun in the unoccupied zone. After he landed, his passenger, André Simon, son of the founder president of the Food and Wine Society, stowed the luggage of the two passengers bound for England and climbed down the ladder. In climbed Maurice Duclos (*Saint Jacques*) and Roger Mitchell. Duclos, a pre-war convicted Cagoulard, had founded the first Free French intelligence network. According to Faligot and Kauffer,[5] he had broken a leg when he parachuted to the Dordogne in February 1941 and had been looked after by Gabriel Jeantet, a Cagoulard friend who worked for the Vichy government. (Cagoulards, literally men wearing hoods, were an extreme right-wing group.)

Whippy flew north for about an hour, hedge-hopping below low cloud in very bumpy air and heavy rain. When ice started forming on his windscreen he turned back and tried without success to find a way round or over the freezing rain. At 8500 feet he saw that the ice on the leading edge slats was about four inches thick. The Lysander was almost impossible to fly. As he would soon be low in fuel he decided that the best thing for his passengers would be a forced landing in the unoccupied zone. Some 18 kilometres east of Issoudun he found a field that, by moonlight, looked good to land on. The end of his landing run was abrupt. He had not seen a ditch, which stopped him with his tail up in the air.[6]

After trying to burn the aircraft with the little fuel that was left, pilot and passengers set off on foot, but Whippy had been flying for seven hours and was soon too tired to go on. Leaving him with Mitchell in a little shepherd's hut, Duclos walked on towards Issoudun. He arrived at the railway station hotel bar at about 0700. All the railway men were enjoying their breakfast brandy. Duclos walked round shaking hands with a Masonic handshake until he found a fellow Freemason, the stationmaster, Monsieur Combault. He was prepared to take the terrible risk of hiding and feeding Whippy for a month until the next moon period. Whippy arrived in civilian clothes provided by the Jolivet family of Grand Malleray, according to Alain Rafesthain's *La Liberté Guidait Leurs Pas*.[7]

In all the excited local activity that followed Whippy's crash a curé was arrested because he was thought to be the pilot. (Several priests had given soutanes to help evading aircrew cover their uniforms.) The charred Lysander was totally destroyed by a train after the low-loader transporting it was 'accidentally' stalled on a level crossing just as a train was approaching.

On the night of 1 March 1942, Whippy's successor, Squadron Leader Alan ('Sticky') Murphy, picked him and his passengers up in a borrowed Anson. Under a thin crust of ice the ground was soft and the Anson sank in until Whippy told the passengers to jump up and down together. It gathered flying speed so slowly that he named it 'Gormless Gertie'. This was the first twin-engined pick-up ever.

PART TWO

Rémy

Two nights earlier, Sticky Murphy had picked up Gilbert Renault Roulier, the legendary Colonel *Rémy* who had built up the Free

French intelligence organization *Confrérie Notre-Dame (CND)* which he had founded in 1940. A pre-war film producer, he would become a prolific writer of memoirs and history of the Resistance.

In *Secret Flotillas*,[8] Sir Brooks Richards tells how *Rémy* made arrangements with Captain Slocum's section of SIS for a fishing boat from the Scilly Isles to pick up his wife and children off the coast of Brittany. On the night of 26 March 1942 Flying Officer Guy Lockhart flew him back to France but overran the flarepath and was stuck in ploughed ground until seven men could push the Lysander round. After 17 minutes he could take off carrying to England Christian Pineau, a founder of *Libé-Nord*, one of the small spontaneous Resistance networks in the occupied zone, and François Faure, an assistant of Rémy's, who had been an architect before the war and, after the war, would join the D.G.E.R. (*Direction Générale des Études et Recherches* or foreign intelligence service). This was one of the pick-ups described by Pineau in *La Simple Vérité*.[9]

Pineau and Faure were only in England for a month until 27 April when Sticky landed them on Robert Delattre's field NNE of Rouen where he had picked up Rémy at the end of February. This time his passengers to Tangmere were the burly Jacques Robert and Pierre Brossolette with the white streak in his hair dyed black.

Jacques Robert had been an outstandingly determined tank commander in 1940. The Free French recruited him early in 1941. A big boisterous and very friendly visitor to Tangmere Cottage, it was said that he had to have an extra large parachute because of his weight. He did so well in the *Confrérie Notre-Dame* that the 30-year-old head of de Gaulle's secret service, André Dewavrin (*Passy*), wanted Rémy to promote him to take over running the CND. Rémy did not think Robert (*Rewez*) competent enough for such heavy responsibility. So Robert broke away from Rémy and set up his own intelligence network called *Phratrie*. By December 1942 this made an excellent impression on Major Manuel, Passy's deputy, when he inspected it on the Côte d'Azur. In Noguères' opinion[10] Robert proved the error of Rémy's judgement by building up *Phratrie* to be as valuable as the *CND* itself all over the South of France.

In his pseudonym *Rewez* Jacques Robert was awarded the OBE. His citation said *inter alia* that he was 'the founder of perhaps the most productive of the Free French organizations in military intelligence.' In 1944 Major Robert parachuted in uniform to the maquis in the Creuse, leading an allied team. His guerrilla exploits fully deserved the DSO that he was awarded. The switch from intelligence to action was possible in the BCRA (*Bureau Central de Renseignements et d'Action*). It is hard to imagine anybody transferring from the SIS to SOE during the war, although the reverse switch did occur after the war.

Lockhart

On the night of 28 May 1942 Flight Lieutenant Guy Lockhart was unsuccessful and had to return to Tangmere empty handed. He had found no welcoming letter flashed from his target field north of Châteauroux. The agent, André Simon, was already in prison. (He had quite recovered by the day in 1944 when he gave me lunch in the *Écu de France*, although, studying the wine list, he said that there was nothing there worth drinking and ordered a jug of iced water.) On that same night Flight Lieutenant John Mott became irretrievably bogged southeast of Issoudun. The *chef de terrain* (agent in charge of the ground party) Claude Lamirault was assisted by Pierre Hentic, who generously gave Mott his papers to help him on the run. Then, being caught without any papers, Pierre was accused of being the pilot and thrown into the same cell as André Simon. Mott was caught by Vichy police but eventually escaped from Italian custody. The Germans proudly exhibited his Lysander in their museum of captured enemy weapons near Paris until they were driven out of France.

In June Squadron Leader Guy Lockhart, who had been promoted twice since he was a Flying Officer in March, replaced Sticky Murphy as C.O. of the Lysander Flight. Such were the problems in the networks in France that no pick-ups were required in June or July 1942. The pilots practised their night navigation by finding and bombing railway targets.

At the end of August Guy flew to a field of the *Phalanx* intelligence network run by Christian Pineau. It was on an enormous meadow near the Saône and not far from Pont-de-Vaux. The agent *Tarn* arrived late and, according to Guy, drunk. He laid out the flarepath of three torches across a ditch that broke Guy's undercarriage. Pineau was so furious with *Tarn* that he decided that he should be executed on the spot. But he could not bring himself to carry out his decision as they walked side by side along the railway line to Macon after Guy had burned his Lysander. Instead he sent a letter to a senior policeman in Lyons who was a member of *Phalanx*, to arrange for *Tarn* to be imprisoned on a black market charge.[11] Henri Morier

(*Legrand*), who was part of the reception team at every pick-up for *Phalanx*, delivered this letter. He was totally blind but in good heart when I called on him in Lyons in 1996.

Pineau arranged for Guy, who was now calling himself 'Wing Commander Henry', to stay a couple of days with Yves Farge[12] in Lyons on his way to a maritime pick-up near Narbonne. This went seriously wrong because some coastguards interfered, but Guy succeeded in swimming out to a felucca with Polish officers who took him to Gibraltar.

Phalanx

The coastguards caught Pineau and he was imprisoned on a black market charge but he managed to escape. He was delighted to welcome to *Phalanx* Pierre Delaye (*Claude*). Delaye was an expert radio operator and a qualified *chef de terrain*, who made impeccably detailed arrangements for pick-up landings. It was he who arranged all subsequent pick-ups for *Phalanx*, until he was shot dead while transmitting. A plaque on the bridge in the middle of Loyettes commemorates him.

On 15 January 1943 it was east of Lyons and a few kilometres from Loyettes that I did my first successful Lysander pick-up. Delaye climbed up on the port undercarriage with his hair blowing in the wind from my idling propellor. He asked me if I was Lockhart. Pineau and two young trainees climbed into the back and I flew them to Tangmere. They were warmly welcomed by Major Tony Bertram who took them to his house at Bignor where his wife Barbara[13] gave them bacon and eggs and put them up for the rest of the night. Tony was a SIS escorting officer and his house was a safe house for agents leaving for the field or returning from it via RAF Tangmere.

On the night of 19 March 1943 Pineau's *Phalanx* welcomed Jean Moulin, General Delestraint and Pineau himself on a little island between the Loire and a canal near Melay, north of Roanne. Flight Lieutenant John Bridger flew the Lysander. Pineau described[14] how good it was to be greeted by Delaye and Morier. They set off in a light van through the little roads high in the Beaujolais country to Macon and then by train to Lyons. Ten minutes after John took off a German patrol drove on to the island. A woman who lived nearby, woken by the noise of the Lysander, had telephoned her German lover. In the morning the village was ordered to dig trenches across the field.

In 1990 a local association which had been started by Pierre Dru, the mayor of Melay, assembled about 2000 people including ministers, the Préfet, mayors and the late John Bridger's son, for the inauguration of a large monument commemorating that operation. Made of polished granite it records the names of the pilot and his passengers. At this ceremony Christian Pineau, then an ageing former foreign minister, spoke movingly about Jean Moulin, his fellow passenger to Melay. A few months after their return to France they were in the same prison. Pineau was ordered to shave Moulin while he lay dying from his tortures. Pineau could not quite hear the few words that Moulin struggled to whisper but heard that they were in English.

Another landing that John Bridger did with Delaye and Morier was on 15 April 1943, again near Loyettes. He picked up Pineau's 17-year-old son Claude and Henri Morier, who was on his way to be qualified as a *chef de terrain*. The third passenger was Major Robert Wackherr. He remembered meeting Pierre Brossolette that night in Tony Bertram's house near Tangmere. Brossolette had been picked up near Rouen by a double Lysander pick-up flown by Peter Vaughan-Fowler and James McCairns. Others they picked up included Colonel Passy and Yeo-Thomas. The *chef de terrain*, Jacques Courtaud (*Jacot*), wrote to me in 1984 under cover of a letter to Barbara Yeo-Thomas in which he said: '*Je suis un vieux monsieur qui a 80 ans, mais qui est encore solide*'.

Jacot

He had been an aircrew radio operator in Air France who was in Argentina at the beginning of the war. In January 1942 he left Buenos Aires for Glasgow in a Dutch ship and joined the Free French. After three months' training in England as a secret radio operator, a *chef de terrain* and a parachutist, he was dropped into northern France to meet Gilbert Roulier (*Rémy*), who made him chief of the radio operators of his *Confrérie Notre-Dame* and responsible for its air operations. He later helped *Rémy* and his family to leave Brittany by a maritime operation.

Jacot's description of operation *Liberté/Juliette* on 15 April 1943 gives an agent's eye view of a pick-up that went well – as most did by that date. He wrote: (in French):

'My third operation near Rouen was a double Lizzy, with five passengers to leave: Col Passy, Yeo-Thomas (the 'White Rabbit'), Pierre Brossolette, Captain Ryan, an American aviator, and Jargon, a radio operator. At midnight we were all there. I laid out the flarepath and had a moment of emotion when I heard an engine, but it was a false alert. At about 0115 I heard another engine noise and it really was the throbbing (*ronflement*) of a Lysander. I flashed my recognition signal and he replied. I switched on my first lamp and *Dutertre*(Roger Hérisse), who was at the base of the 'L', switched on the other two. After a normal landing the aeroplane came back along the landing strip and stopped facing into wind. Two BCRA agents stood up in the fuselage and climbed down. The pilot jumped down from the aeroplane, gave me some chocolate and cigarettes and asked for some information about the field. I hurried the departure once the third passenger, the White Rabbit, had climbed in. The Lizzy took off easily with the usual roar(*fracas*).

'Then I made the agreed signal to the second aeroplane, which was waiting. His approach and landing were impeccable. The roof slid back and Jean Cavaillès got down. Suitcases were quickly unloaded and I made the American Ryan climb in followed by Jargon, to whom I gave the mail and the luggage. I shouted O.K.! to the pilot and the second Lizzie took off in its turn with the noise of thunder.'

Jacot did not add that Yeo-Thomas (*Shelley* or *Le Lapin Blanc*) had arrived at the farmhouse near the field in a hearse with a lot of weapons covered by flowers. This was because the German army in that area had recently been reinforced.

The next pick-up for which Jacot was responsible was a fiasco. He listened to the BBC for the personal message that the operation was on that night while in his flat in Paris, but German jamming was so bad that he could not hear it, so he sent his chauffeur home. Meanwhile his deputy, *Dutertre*, and the passengers were on the field, north of Estrées-Saint-Denis, without the necessary torches and not knowing the recognition signal. Peter Vaughan-Fowler made repeated passes over the field but all he could see was newspapers being burned.

Jacot's fourth successful pick-up went well. It was one of a series of successful doubles flown that summer by Peter and Mac. Henri Morier arrived after training in England. The five passengers leaving included Madame Grenier going to join her husband, the communist *Député*. Madame Grenier was so plump that Jacot remembered how hard he had had to push her to get her up the ladder. Another was Bernard Cordier, an Air France pilot, who would be one of the two French Lysander pick-up pilots in Peter's Flight in Italy and Corsica a year later. After the war Cordier became a Trappist monk called

Frère Baudouin. In 1992 his Abbot gave him a day's leave to attend the inauguration of a monument to pick-ups near Saint-Vulbas, one of which he had done.

Less than a fortnight after his fourth pick-up Jacot was arrested by the Gestapo in Paris, imprisoned in Fresnes and taken to Buchenwald. He came back to France just two years later. An all too frequent sequel to these operations was the fate of the good people who gave hospitality to our reception committees and passengers. For example Gaston and Marie Courseaux, farmers in Gournay-sur-Aronde, who had sheltered the passengers for Jacot's last pick-up, were betrayed and arrested. They were deported to Germany and died there.

PART THREE

Most of the networks already mentioned were loyal to General de Gaulle and controlled by his BCRA, though using SIS facilities. There were, however, two other large intelligence groups: the Alliance, which was larger than the CND in occupied France[15] and chose to report directly to the British SIS; and the old pre-war intelligence and security services that the Vichy government of Marshal Pétain was allowed to maintain under the Armistice until November 1942. This was no longer allowed by the Germans after Operation Torch, the Allied landing in French North Africa, which was followed by the German occupation of the hitherto unoccupied zone in the South of France.

Marie-Madeleine

The Alliance intelligence organization was founded by Commandant Georges Loustaunau-Lacau (*Navarre*) of the *Légion Française des Combattants*, a Vichy propaganda and spy network.[16] In the spring of 1941, not wanting to be subordinate to General de Gaulle, he preferred to work directly with the British. He agreed working arrangements in Lisbon with Commander Kenneth Cohen (*Keith Crane*) of the SIS French Country Section.

In May Navarre was arrested for seditious plotting in Algiers and his chief assistant, Madame Marie-Madeleine Meric, took over the Alliance. After being allowed to escape, Navarre was arrested again in Pau in July and sentenced to two years in prison. Meric resumed command, signing her signals Poz 55 and drafting them in the masculine gender. She was smuggled to the French Embassy in Madrid in the boot of a car under diplomatic mailbags and met Cohen's representative in Lisbon. He was startled to find that Poz 55 was an attractive 32-year-old mother of two.

She decided that all the main members of the Alliance should be referred to as animals or birds. She was called *Hérisson* (Hedgehog). Her operations chief, Major Léon Faye, a pilot of the *Armée de l'Air*, was *Aigle* (Eagle). Less appropriately, the head of her air operations section *Avia* was the Lieutenant Pilot Pierre Dallas, known as *Cornac* (Mahout). The pretend Englishman 'Crawley', parachuted in to teach the *Avia* team how to receive Lysanders on pick-ups, signed my copy of Marie-Madeleine's book *L'Arche de Noé*[17] with his real name 'Arthur-Louis Gachet alias *Heron*'. The Germans too called the Alliance *die Arche Noah*.

From August 1942 to September 1943 161 squadron Lysanders did a successful pick-up for Marie-Madeleine every month except December and February. Twice in 1942 the little grass airfield at Thalamy, near Ussel, was used before the Germans obstructed it with stakes. This was where Marie-Madeleine inaugurated a fine granite stele in honour of RAF pickups in 1977 – an occasion which was rather spoilt by the local *Député*, Jacques Chirac, reading out seventeen typed pages of speech. It was Roland Creel (*Labrador*) who had helped Marie-Madeleine to organize the stele.

Léon Faye was the Alliance's most frequent Lysander passenger, before and after three visits to England. As a very experienced pilot who well knew his way around France from the air, it was painful for him to be unable to talk to the pilot when he could have been helpful if there had been any common language. Only some of the pilots could talk French and could therefore train *chefs de terrain* more easily at RAF Tempsford in between moon periods. Faye's first return to France in September 1942 was particularly alarming for him while John Bridger was hedgehopping near Lyons beneath low cloud in heavy rain. Faye knew that there were factory chimneys and wireless masts nearby. After landing near Loyettes one wheel sank in deep mud. Bridger unscrewed the fairing and brought it back in the rear cockpit, which was unoccupied because the intended passenger had decided that no pick-up could be attempted on such a foul night.

Marie-Madeleine declined invitations to come to England herself until July 1943, in spite of her arrest in November 1942. She had helped with the arrangements for General Giraud to sneak into Algeria in a submarine of the Royal Navy at the request of SIS. As an intermediary she had used Maurice MacMahon, the *Duc de*

Magenta, who was a famous aerobatics ace. She was helped to escape from prison by three Corsican police inspectors who were rewarded by an uncomfortable flight from Thalamy to Tangmere in Peter Vaughan-Fowler's Lysander. Their names were Piani, Rutali and Reverbel and this was their first flight. One of them was hauled into the rear cockpit upside down. When he landed at Thalamy Peter teased Pierre Dallas because his lights were dim and seemed to go off and on from time to time. The reason was that the *Avia* team had been on the run and had lost their torches. They had used candles.

Nigel West wrote that the Alliance was at its peak in 1943 when it had 3,000 agents and thirty wireless sets, all reporting to SIS[18]. Although the 'Noah's Ark' had serious losses in early 1944, including Dallas, the animals were still providing excellent intelligence. An example was the map fifty-five feet long giving details of all the defences of the Cotentin peninsula. Jean Sainteny (*Dragon*) brought this with him when Flight Lieutenant Murray Anderson picked him up near Angers in March 1944.

Ex-Vichy

David Stafford said that in 1942 SIS's closest links with France were with the pre-war Intelligence Service, many of whose members were serving Vichy.[19] It ran networks in the occupied and unoccupied zones.

Services transferred to Algiers and preferring General Giraud to Marshal Pétain or General de Gaulle, but happy to work with SIS or the American OSS, included Major Paul Paillole's counter-espionage network under *Travaux Ruraux* cover, the army *Service de Renseignements (SR)* under Lieutenant Colonel Rivet, who was for a time General Giraud's head of secret services, and the Air Force's *SR (Air)* under Jean Bezy.

Colonel Georges Ronin had secretly led the revolt against the occupation within the Vichy government, maintaining contact with Wing Commander Winterbotham and Lieutenant Commander Bill (Wilfred?) Dunderdale of the SIS. He transmitted information to London via Lisbon and by wireless sets brought to Vichy by diplomatic bag from Lisbon. Having transferred to Algiers, he could renew these contacts face to face in London, in December 1942, though strictly forbidden by Darlan and Giraud to meet General de Gaulle. In his preface to General Jean Bezy's book *Le SR (Air)*, Paul Paillole attributes to Ronin the honour of being the creator of the French Air Force's intelligence service and its networks in France from July 1940 until the Liberation[20]. The pick-up pilots' main contact with them was with René Gervais. McCairns picked him up near Estrées-Saint-Denis in October 1943 and he spent one month in England. His agents, including the Belgian Georges Bourguignon, kept an eye on Luftwaffe-occupied airfields for the benefit of the Royal Air Force.

Ronin's representative in London, Badré, made arrangements in 12 Caxton Street ('Dunderdale's Circus') with the operations officer, Flight Lieutenant Schneidau (*Philipson*), for André Duthilleul (*Oscar*) to be parachuted into France. After meeting Gervais at Vichy, *Oscar* laid on about one pick-up a month from July 1943 until December, when he was arrested. His successor Roger Camous continued to use the field near Estrées-Saint-Denis in 1944.

A parallel network for *Travaux Ruraux* was set up under Robert Masson (*Samson*) with young Michel Thoraval (*Parrain*) as air operations officer. Selected by Paillole and parachuted to France in January 1943, he was picked up in February by Flying Officer F.E. ('Bunny') Rymills who had trained him at Tempsford to be a *chef de terrain*. The next landing he received was John Bridger's Lysander in April. Several metres of high-tension cable were trailing from it. One tyre had burst bouncing off the other side of a valley. John tried to flatten the other tyre with his Smith and Wesson .38 but it needed the heavier revolver of Michel Thoraval's assistant, the gendarme Antoine Herrmann.[21]

Two nights later Wing Commander P.C. Pickard, Commanding Officer of No 161 Special Duties Squadron, landed a Hudson on Michel Thoraval's flarepath on the Causse-Méjean near Florac in the south of the Massif Central. This was Pick's fourth successful Hudson pick-up. The twin-engined low-wing converted passenger aircraft needed a strip 1000 metres long – twice as long as a Lysander strip – but could carry three times as many passengers and had a much longer range. Passengers had to sit on the floor. To save weight there were no seats. In his booklet *Un Parmi Tant d'Autres*,[22] Michel tells how he drove Pick along the strip that had been left when much of the area had been ploughed. They decided that the take-off should be down-wind as the wind was light and there would have been high ground to avoid if the take-off were into wind. The flarepath had to be laid again, using cars with dipped headlamps as markers instead of the usual electric torches. This could have proved dangerous if a swing to port had developed.

Michel Thoraval's next and last pick-up was in May, on the same strip. Organized by SIS through *Travaux Ruraux* it was at the request of Winston Churchill. He wanted General Georges, the former Chief of Staff of the French army, to take his part in arguments with General de Gaulle. This operation had such high priority that Group Captain 'Mouse' Fielden, Captain of the King's Flight and Officer Commanding RAF Tempsford, decided to do it himself. After taking off as dawn was breaking, Mouse explained to Thoraval that they had been very late arriving because they were lost until they saw the coast of the Mediterranean, a long way beyond the target. They had not enough fuel left to return to England.[23] They landed near Algiers and General Georges went straight to General Giraud.

By 1998 *le Docteur* Thoraval – a dentist actually – was the executive director of Colonel Paillole's old comrades' association, the *Amicale des Anciens des Services Spéciaux de la Défense Nationale (ASSDN))*

Conclusion

Having skipped lightly over some exploits of those who gathered information about the enemy in France, the reader may be wondering if all the effort and losses were justified by the results. Was not the product of Ultra enough to make all this human intelligence on the ground redundant? It should be remembered that Ultra was only available at the highest levels of command. Normal sigint (signals decrypts) could not deliver, for example, the detailed maps of the defences of the Atlantic Wall (stolen from the Todt organization) nor the locations of underground bunkers storing V-weapons. Very large numbers of detailed locations of launching sites for these had been received from intelligence networks and from an individual agent in France before the first news of them came from sigint.

A huge amount of timely intelligence was essential to victory in World War Two. It was actually produced by the complementary efforts of interdependent sources: signals intelligence, air photography and patriotic people on the ground. Of these the most useful in France (where the use of landlines reduced the quantity of sigint until the telephone systems were sabotaged on the eve of D-Day) were probably the men and women in the intelligence networks. According to Hinsley, by the spring of 1944 agents' reports from France and the Low Countries were being received at the rate of 150 a day.[24] Before the landings in June 1944 these reports provided the bulk of order of battle details on all the enemy forces, as well as targets for air photography and air attack. In the heat of the battle for Normandy, Hinsley shows how sigint took over the lead in providing up-to-date order of battle information.

The intelligence networks in France had loyalties to different leaders but they were united in wanting to work for the defeat of Nazi Germany and the liberation of France. And they all used the same air taxi service.

NOTES

1. Hugh Verity *We Landed by Moonlight – Revised* Crécy (Manchester, 1998) Appendix B.
2. R. Garby-Czerniawski *The Big Network* (George Ronald, 1961).
3. F.H. Hinsley and others *British Intelligence in the Second World War Vol Three, Part Two* (HMSO, 1988) pp 48,49.
4. Alya Aglan *Mémoires Résistantes* (du Cerf, Paris, 1994).
5. R. Faligot and R. Kauffer *Les Résistants* (Fayard, Paris, 1989) 152.
6. Hugh Verity *op cit* App C.
7. A. Rafesthain *La Liberté Guidait Leurs Pas* (Royer, France, 1993) 90,92.
8. Brooks Richards *Secret Flotillas* (HMSO 1996) 129–131.
9. C. Pineau *La Simple Vérité* (Phalanx, Paris 1983) 146–149.
10. H. Noguères *Histoire de la Résistance en France, Tome 3* (Laffont, Paris, 1972) 102.
11. C. Pineau *Op Cit* 233–237.
12. Yves Farge *Rebelles, Soldats et Citoyens* (Grasset, Paris, 1946) 10,11.
13. Barbara Bertram *French Resistance in Sussex* (Barnworks, Pulborough, 1995).
14. C. Pineau *Op Cit* 288.
15. D. Porch *French Secret Services* (Farrar, Strauss and Giroux, New York, 1995) 187.
16. D. Porch *Op Cit 195.*
17. Marie-Madeleine Fourcade *L'Arche de Noé Tome I* (Fayard 1968, Le Livre de Poche 1971).
18. Nigel West *MI6 British Secret Service Operations 1909–1945* (Weidenfeld and Nicolson 1983) 152.
19. David Stafford *Churchill and Secret Service* (John Murray 1997) 267.
20. J. Bezy *Le SR Air* (France-Empire, Paris 1979) 8.
21. M. Thoraval *Un Parmi Tant d'Autres* (ASSDN Paris, 1984) 18.
22. M. Thoraval *Op Cit* 20.
23. M. Thoraval *Op Cit* 23.
24. Hinsley *Op Cit* 28.

'SOMETHING BEAUTIFUL FOR "C"'
Malcolm Muggeridge in Lourenço Marques

E.R.D. HARRISON

The second volume of Malcolm Muggeridge's autobiography is one of the most vivid memoirs in intelligence literature.[1]

Muggeridge portrays himself as the James Bond of Lourenço Marques, drinking, loafing and philandering but nevertheless comprehensively fooling his ponderous adversaries. Overall, he claims considerable success as Secret Intelligence Service [SIS] Head of Station in Lourenço Marques. In contrast, other former SIS officers such as Lord Dacre and Graham Greene believe Muggeridge was a failure. Lord Dacre writes that Muggeridge was 'quite useless in Lourenço Marques . . . [and] recalled in some disgrace'. Graham Greene told his biographer that 'Muggeridge was not a success which made him very anti the SIS and he knows that he was a bit of a flop'.[2] Although the SIS has not yet released its records, much documentary evidence concerning Muggeridge's work in Portuguese East Africa or Mozambique is available in the files of the British Special Operations Executive [SOE], the American Office of Strategic Services [OSS] and the German Foreign Office. Although it is not yet possible to present a complete picture of Muggeridge's work for SIS, does the available evidence from the archives support Muggeridge's claims for his tour of duty in Mozambique, or was he indeed a flop?

Muggeridge complements boasting about his own achievements as a spy with belittling the value of secret intelligence. Yet the intelligence war in Portuguese East Africa did matter. During 1942 Southern Africa assumed primary strategic importance. The British Empire was fighting for its life in Egypt and supply convoys went the back way round the Cape of Good Hope to avoid running the gauntlet

185

of Axis bombers in the Mediterranean. Ships taking the route via the Cape had to carry on through the bottle-neck of the Mozambique Channel between Portuguese East Africa and Madagascar. From 1942 British and American ships using the Mozambique Channel provided an inviting quarry for German U-Boats. Allied shipping movements in the Southern Oceans thus became a prime target for Axis Intelligence. Agents in the ports of South Africa and Mozambique watched Allied shipping and reported to the German Consulate in Lourenço Marques, the capital of Mozambique.[3]

Muggeridge was to face a formidable array of antagonists. The senior German official there was the Consul-General, Paul Trompke, under whose name the intelligence reports went to Berlin. Although Muggeridge does not mention Trompke in his memoirs, for a time SOE considered him enough of a danger to plan his assassination with a car bomb. The German spy-master was Trompke's number two, Luitpold Werz. Werz had joined the German Foreign Office in 1933 and the Nazi Party the following year. From 1936 he had worked at the German Legation in Pretoria. In 1937 the Nazi Party gave him a glowing reference: 'Werz has a very good reputation. He is very hard-working and above all lives very modestly'. On the outbreak of war Werz withdrew to Lourenço Marques. He was an enthusiastic supporter of Hitler's war and played the piano in his hotel to celebrate the fall of Sebastopol.[4]

Working from the German Consulate in Lourenço Marques, Werz built up an extensive espionage system. His South African experience qualified him to control the German spying there and Lourenço Marques was an excellent base, four hundred miles from Pretoria across a frontier which was easy to cross. Instructions were passed to agents and sympathizers by couriers or by radio, and the reports which came back to the Consulate were passed by radio to the German Foreign Office, Secret Service [Abwehr] and the Reich Security Head Office. The German Consulate also forwarded shipping intelligence gathered by a network run by the *Bayer* representative in Mozambique, Justus Leidenburg.[5]

The activities of the Nazi Consular staff were supplemented by those of the energetic Italian Consul, Umberto Campini, whom SIS considered a greater danger than Werz. Campini's distinguished service in World War One had earned him the Military Cross. He joined the Italian Foreign Service in 1928 and in December 1936 was transferred to Aden, where there was little to do but watch British ships. After being granted safe conduct by the British Foreign Office, Campini arrived in Lourenço Marques in December 1941. His espionage was directed against both shipping and South African military targets. SIS reported that 'In Lourenço Marques itself Campini has built up an elaborate organization for the purposes of contacting Allied seamen with a view to eliciting information, in which organization he makes extensive use of prostitutes, dockhands, etc. . . . He also obtains shipping intelligence from his intelligence networks within South Africa in such places as Cape Town, Johannesburg and Durban. . . . He has at least one agent in Pretoria who provides him with highly secret industrial information. . . . In addition, he runs a network over the border of Portuguese East Africa which is engaged in the collection of information about South African military dispositions and movements.' Campini's reports to the Italian Foreign Office were being read by the British from early 1942 onwards, and from the end of 1942 Trompke's reports were also deciphered in an unbroken sequence. Britain was also reading Portuguese consular and diplomatic codes.[6]

Whereas the Axis diplomats in Lourenço Marques reacted to the onset of total war with aggressive espionage, their Allied counterparts regarded intelligence activity with prudish horror. The British Consul General in Lourenço Marques, C.K. Ledger, had sent home for analysis German coding material put through the door of the British Consulate in error by a German seaman, who mistook it for his own Consulate. But otherwise Ledger found counter-espionage distasteful and jibbed at installing an illegal transmitter in the Consulate. The OSS card index epitomized Ledger as 'a good man but hopelessly weak. Completely sold on the Portuguese and determined to defend their point of view. . . . Does not take any part in counter-espionage activities.'

The American Consul General, Austin Roe Preston, was also a cautious figure. Preston had arrived in Lourenço Marques as Consul in February 1942. By July he was urging that his post should be made a Consulate General. Preston won this bureaucratic battle and by May 1943 he had been confirmed as Consul General. But he had less appetite for fighting the Axis. The OSS card index summed him up as 'A man prone to perpetual worry. A slave to State Dept. precedents and prerogatives. States he is paid to "execute Dept. instructions only". Amiable but weak. Not cooperative in any way.' The South African Consul General Eugene Scallan was the only Allied Consul who took an active part in the intelligence war. Scallan's principal intelligence source was a member of the Mozambique Secret Police. Corrupting the Portuguese police was essential for intelligence operators in Lourenço Marques.[7]

The fastidious Allied consular personnel in Mozambique mostly shied away from confronting the vigorous espionage activities of their Axis counterparts. This left the way clear for a swarm of British and American intelligence officers to descend on Southern Africa in general and Mozambique in particular. The influx began with the British MI5, who offered the South African authorities assistance. As a British Dominion, the Union of South Africa was within the remit of MI5. After Nazi agents run from Mozambique successfully carried out sabotage in the Rand mining district during January 1942, MI5 sent out an officer to counter German activities organized from Portuguese East Africa. A second MI5 officer was despatched to the Union to work on port security. By late 1942 OSS was represented in the Union by Goodhue Livingstone, who was attached to the US Legation. Livingstone traded material with South African Intelligence, who provided a list of enemy agents in Mozambique.[8]

SIS was the first Anglo-American Secret Service to arrive in Mozambique itself. As foreign territory, Portuguese East Africa fell within the remit of SIS. Campini's espionage first drew SIS attention to Mozambique. As we have seen, Campini's messages were being decoded by British code-breakers. The resulting 'Black Jumbos' – the cover name for decrypts of diplomatic signals – were circulated to interested parties in Whitehall. Brigadier Stewart Menzies, the Chief of the Secret Intelligence Service, also known as 'C', considered a series of Campini signals from early 1942 important enough to be shown to Churchill. Campini had provided accurate intelligence on the British invasion of Madagascar, though this had not been passed to the Governor of the island. Menzies realized he needed a man in Lourenço Marques, and sent out Muggeridge, who arrived at the end of June 1942. Muggeridge worked under cover of the British Consulate-General. His main work was for the Iberian sub-section of Section V, the part of SIS responsible for counter-espionage. According to the official history, SIS had tasked Muggeridge to investigate Axis activities in the ports in East Africa and to obtain intelligence about Madagascar. In other words, he was given both a counter-espionage and an espionage role. By summer 1942 SIS had another officer working Madagascar from Diego Suarez and by

January 1943 SIS had decided to keep on a representative in Madagascar. Muggeridge's original espionage role was redundant. Instead he did a little spying on the Portuguese.[9]

In late 1942 Muggeridge acquired the services of Steptoe of Shanghai, who arrived in Lourenço Marques after being exchanged by the Japanese. SIS London agreed that Steptoe could stay on in Mozambique. An old SIS hand, Steptoe drew attention through a funny walk which conveyed an aura of mystery. Muggeridge recruited as his principal agent a conspicuous figure in the local German community, Baron Werner von Alvensleben, who was also employed by the German Consulate.[10] Alvensleben had joined the Nazi Party on 1 February 1932. SOE later commented that 'After a bit he began to see through the "façade" and became an anti-Nazi, and that is why he is working now with us. His view is that the Nazis are ruining Germany and, while he will fight against the Nazis, he will not fight against Germany, in other words he is not a traitor to his country.'[11]

Muggeridge was soon joined in Mozambique by an SOE representative, whose arrival was also prompted by the intercepted messages from Campini, in particular a Black Jumbo which suggested the Portuguese were facilitating Axis subversion in the Union. An SOE official noted in May 1942 that 'Selborne [the Earl of Selborne, Minister for SOE] feels that we should draw the attention of the Foreign Office to this as a reason for getting them to take a very lenient view of our activities in Portuguese East Africa when we ask them for permission to do things which might be obnoxious to the Portuguese authorities there. I must say that the whole B.J. does make our policy of appeasing the Portuguese government look pretty silly.' In the light of this evidence, the Foreign Office conceded that SOE could take action within Mozambique, 'provided the Foreign Office agrees in each instance'.[12] 'Nero' Grieve, the SOE representative on Mauritius, was transferred to Lourenço Marques in late 1942 to work against the Axis under cover of representing the firm of Grieve and Irwin, Insurance Brokers, Cairo, a genuine firm with which he was connected. Grieve's cover was scarcely helped by his huge size and shaved head. By 1943 he was assisted by Adams, who worked under cover as a public relations officer. SOE found it easy to work with Muggeridge, who misleadingly wrote in his memoirs that 'I really had . . . no clear idea of what, if anything, Nero [Grieve] was up to.' In fact they cooperated very easily.[13]

Last of the Allied Intelligence Services to arrive in Mozambique was the OSS, whose representative Huntington Harris took up his post in December 1942. Harris was a member of a prominent Chicago family with a PhD in Sociology. By June 1943 he was responsible for serving the requirements of both the Intelligence and Counter-Intelligence branches of OSS in his area. He worked under cover of the War Shipping Administration and, like Muggeridge, sat on the Shipping Advisory Committee set up in March 1943 with Ledger as Chairman in order to improve the security of British and US shipping in Lourenço Marques. Harris and Muggeridge moved into a property together on the outskirts of Lourenço Marques with a garage that had a door into the house through which agents could pass without being noticed. Although both Harris and Muggeridge were mainly concerned with counter-espionage, they also collected intelligence on the Portuguese military.[14] As Harris and Muggeridge for the most part worked together, Harris' intelligence reports probably had much material in common with those Muggeridge was sending SIS. During his first four months in Lourenço Marques, Harris sent to Washington a table of the German and Italian intelligence organizations with about a hundred photos and descriptions of individuals obtained from the files of the Portuguese Security Police. He had also submitted the complete order of battle and location of Portuguese troops in Mozambique and a description of every major airfield. He had further reported on the South African propaganda designed to provide the basis for any future move of the Union against Mozambique. Together with the British he had established two secret radio transmitters, one in Mozambique and one in Swaziland in case diplomatic cable and pouch facilities inside Mozambique were disrupted.[15]

Muggeridge not only ran agents with Harris, he also worked effectively with Grieve on a series of covert operations. Perhaps the most useful was the rescue of some South African troops who were stranded in Lourenço Marques when, in November 1942, the British troop ship SS *Nova Scotia* was torpedoed off Portuguese East Africa. British and South African business people led by Francis Spence, a British shipping agent, mixed with the South African soldiers and gave them civilian clothes to avoid their internment. Spence then approached Muggeridge to provide taxis to take the soldiers to the Swaziland border. Helped by Grieve, Muggeridge duly obliged and the soldiers escaped home. Although Jan Smuts, Prime Minister of

South Africa, was tickled to death over the affair, Ledger thought it ill-mannered of the soldiers. As Richard Ingrams points out in his biography, Muggeridge omitted Spence's role from his account of this incident in his memoirs and 'the impression is given that he himself single-handedly organized the rescue operation'. In fact a British civilian played the chief part and SOE helped as well.[16]

Britain was finally initiating more active measures in Mozambique. An Italian tanker, the *Gerusalemme*, was interned in Lourenço Marques harbour and Grieve sought to bribe the Captain to put to sea. In December 1942 Grieve reported by bag that 'I hope to get through to the Captain this week and things should then move fast'. Grieve was working through two SIS agents whom he interviewed in Muggeridge's room at the Consulate in the presence of Muggeridge and Steptoe. Although one of the SIS agents, a Polish refugee, described the Captain of the *Gerusalemme* as '*prêt à tout*', he proved very elusive. While Grieve was still waiting for his meeting with the captain SOE London received a copy of a Campini intercept stating that the Captain of the *Gerusalemme* had been approached by a British agent. London concluded that Grieve was blown and withdrew him temporarily from Mozambique.[17]

The decision on whether or not Grieve should return to Mozambique was left to the Head of SOE's South African Mission, Lieutenant-Colonel A.W. Smith. On 10 February 1943 Smith reported to London that 'full satisfactory investigation in Lourenço Marques fails to produce any evidence pointing out Grieve is connected in any way with any secret activity: indeed he seems to have escaped even normal suspicion falling inevitably on all foreigners . . . Grieve can return to locality with cover undisturbed. This is view held by Muggeridge on the spot.' Grieve returned to Lourenço Marques in March and worked closely with Muggeridge to encourage anti-Fascism in the Italian community.[18]

Muggeridge's excellent cooperation with Grieve in the field was quite at odds with the ideas of Menzies back in London. On 18 February Menzies had written to Sir Alexander Cadogan, the Permanent Under-Secretary at the Foreign Office. 'There is really nothing for SOE to do in Portuguese East Africa, since all that is needed is the collection of intelligence, which is my responsibility. . . . The goodwill and assistance of the Portuguese Government will almost certainly cease if SOE or any other British authority takes physical action behind the backs of the local Government. . . . SOE activity in Portuguese East Africa may thus actually defeat our object by endangering my intelligence organization.' While Menzies was busy damning the idea of SOE action in Mozambique, his man in Lourenço Marques was busy facilitating it.[19]

To increase the pressure on Campini SOE mounted a kidnapping operation which caused a diplomatic rumpus. This operation was the shanghai-ing from Mozambique to British territory of Alfredo Manna, the head of Campini's network for shipping espionage. Hinsley and Simkins give a bland account of this affair which ignores SOE's role. They write simply that 'British agents kidnapped Alfredo Manna', rather as if Richard Hannay and Sandy Arbuthnot suddenly popped up in Portuguese East Africa and whisked away an obnoxious Italian. In fact three British secret services were involved in a complicated and successful operation.[20]

In his memoirs Muggeridge omits the central role of SOE in this operation. The actual idea came from Ferreira, the Deputy Chief of the Lourenço Marques Police, who had long been on the SIS payroll and by Spring 1943 was taking money from SOE. He proposed that he should kidnap Manna, 'the most dangerous non-official Italian', as Smith termed him, under the guise of taking him in for questioning and then hand him over to the British at the Swaziland border. Ferreira was to get £100 and a recommendation for the MBE. Manna was familiar with the whole Italian organization in Lourenço Marques and it was expected that his interrogation would provide valuable intelligence. In March Muggeridge sounded out the MI5 representative in Pretoria about the proposed operation. The latter contacted his London HQ, who expressed interest and wished Manna's interrogation to take place in London. In May Smith visited Lourenço Marques and discussed the proposal thoroughly with Muggeridge and Grieve. Smith reported to London that 'I considered that there was a tendency to rush the job without proper preparation. It was a ticklish proposal and nothing should be done without the most careful consideration. Moreover it was Muggeridge's view that Manna could be held in Swaziland by SOE, carried by SOE through Union territory and placed by SOE on board a ship without informing either the High Commissioner, in whose charge the Colony of Swaziland is, or the Union Government. I told Muggeridge most emphatically that I would not, under any circumstances, permit SOE to be a party to a plan so ill-devised.' On his return to South Africa Smith obtained the consent of both Smuts and Lord Harlech, the High Commisioner, to the Manna operation. Although, in theory, under the terms of SOE's operations in Mozambique, the kidnapping required the sanction of the British Foreign Office, in practice it was by-passed. As the British action service, SOE had responsibility for carrying out the operation.[21]

On the night of 21 May Manna was decoyed by a 'taxi dance' girl, or prostitute, called Anna Levin to a remote parking place near the beach. There he was badly beaten up by Ferreira and several other men and kidnapped. He was driven off in his own car with two others following. Both he and his car were dumped over the border. On arrival in Swaziland Manna was hospitalized for a considerable time, during which Muggeridge popped up to interrogate him, although he had assured Smith he would not do so in view of the importance, in Smith's prim words, of 'keeping the Swaziland roads pure for some time after the operation'. Eventually Manna was moved to Durban, where Huntington Harris arrived, demanding to question him. Smith high-handedly refused Harris access to no obvious purpose, cutting him out at the moment of triumph. Instead Smith asked an MI5 officer to carry out an interrogation. MI5 vetoed this on the grounds it might alienate the Commissioner of the South African Police. Instead Manna was questioned by Adams of SOE. Manna said that he was perfectly willing to work for the British if he could only be returned to his wife and son in Lourenço Marques and he signed a statement to that effect. He claimed that he had offered his services to the Swaziland Commissioner of Police but had been turned down. But these were obvious lines for Manna to try once he was in British hands.[22]

On 25 May 1943 SOE's African Section informed Sir Charles Hambro, the Executive Director of SOE, also known as CD, that Manna's kidnapping had taken place: 'You will, I think, be pleased to know that this was done in conjunction with Muggeridge, and that Broadway [SIS] has expressed its satisfaction to us about the trans-action.' The obvious question, of course, is 'Who in Broadway?' Perhaps the head of the Iberian sub-section of Section V, Kim Philby, was able to put a gloss on the operation which appealed to his supe-riors. On 19 June 1943, having seen the preliminary report from the field, CD described it as 'an excellent SOE operation about which I am saying nothing in my normal report' and informed Selborne, who commented briefly but favourably. On 21 July Hambro read Smith's full report, which was accompanied by a memo stating that 'by agreement between us and "C" [SIS] the Foreign Office has not been told anything about this operation.'[23]

Soon after his role in supervising the Manna operation Smith was recalled to London. His successor as Head of the South African Mission was Lieutenant-Colonel L.T.S. Hawkins, who was sent out from London. Having removed a key link in Campini's organization, British Counter-Espionage now sought to do the same for Werz. After visiting Hawkins for a consultation Grieve told Muggeridge that the kidnapping of Alois Muellner [Operation Armpit] would be an acceptable operation if MI5 considered it desirable. On 4 July Muggeridge told Broadway that 'from my point of view it would be very desirable as Muellner is responsible for organizing communications between Werz and Union. It would also be practicable, especially in view of improved police contacts.' As a new Chief of Police was arriving on 15 July, Muggeridge asked for a speedy decision. Hawkins also sought to put the pressure on. In a personal telegram on 7 July to Hambro Hawkins reported that Ferreira had undertaken to carry out the whole operation in a police car assisted only by his own hand-picked police, 'provided operation takes place before July 12th as such an opportunity for job without any risk will never recur. We are giving permission to act provided we do not repeat hear from you before morning July 9.'[24]

On 8 July SOE London hurriedly consulted the Broadway Headquarters of SIS, where, on Patrick Reilly's instructions, an officer said that the matter would have to go before Menzies, and possibly the sanction of the Foreign Office would have to be obtained. The SOE officer demurred at this and said that he saw 'no necessity for the matter as arranged to be referred to the Foreign Office'. While SIS gave way on this point, they did telegraph their representative in Cape Town and asked him to get approval from Forsyth, the Head of the South African Department for External Affairs. Courtney Young of MI5 rang SOE and stated that MI5 were all in favour of the operation. Forsyth also gave his agreement. By early evening Menzies had approved the operation and SIS telegraphed Muggeridge. Lieutenant-Colonel L.F. Sheridan of SOE was nevertheless suspicious that Menzies would double-cross him, writing that 'I feel that, even though the operation be completely successful, Menzies may take the opportunity to inform the Foreign Office, emphasizing the risks run and pointing out the irresponsibility of SOE.' Nevertheless, British Intelligence had produced a decision with impressive speed. But it was all for nothing. In a quite unrelated development, Campini told the Portuguese authorities that a number of Italians due for repatriation would try to escape to South Africa. As a result, border controls were greatly tightened. Under such circumstances it was impossible to kidnap Muellner and the operation was postponed.[25]

Manna's disappearance had caused a stir in Lourenço Marques and attracted too much attention. There was a dividend in this for Allied Counter-Espionage as the operation sent an intimidating signal to other Axis agents who realized they might be next. But the affair enraged the Allied consular officials. When Hawkins discussed the Manna operation with Forsyth, 'It appeared that what had apparently upset [the Union] was the fact that too many people seemed to have some knowledge of [the kidnapping of Manna] in Lourenço Marques. I refer particularly to the South African Consul General who reported officially to Forsyth on the matter although he had no intimate knowledge of the operation.' Forsyth told Hawkins that as Muggeridge held an official position as British Vice Consul in Lourenço Marques he should not be involved in actual operations as there might be far-reaching consequences. In Lourenço Marques there was talk of an official enquiry. When this proposal was dropped, Hawkins wired Grieve that 'News very satisfactory and will set minds of Pretoria and London at rest. It was feared that official enquiry would show Muggeridge was involved and therefore the British Consul and perhaps the South African Consul would also be compromised.' Under the circumstances it was unfortunate that Muggeridge put it about that Scallan had seized Manna.[26]

Muggeridge took so many risks that he alarmed SIS. Amongst the documents he had allowed Alvensleben to see and report about to the German Consulate was a secret paper the SIS Station in Lourenço Marques had compiled of 'Intelligence required for planning purposes and for commanders of projected operations' in connection with a hypothetical Anglo-South African invasion of Portuguese East Africa. Such material could have damaged Britain's relations with Portugal and so was totally unsuitable for passing to the enemy. When German propaganda made use of the material in an Afrikaans broadcast Trompke protested bitterly to the German Foreign Office, pointing out that the British would now look for the hole in their secret service. Trompke urged that no further details should be broadcast and in particular Muggeridge should not be mentioned by name. Trompke's telegrams were being read at Bletchley Park and his desire to keep Muggeridge in place must have undermined the latter. Indeed Trompke could scarcely have discredited Muggeridge more tellingly had he meant to.[27]

The bad judgement Muggeridge showed in the material he made available to Alvensleben and the leaking of his role in the Manna affair prompted SIS to recall him. Graham Greene later said that Muggeridge was recalled 'because he was trying inefficiently to run a double-agent – Johnson? – but was giving away more important things than he got'. This was a reference to Alvensleben. But in addition to this intelligence deficit, there was also a risk that Muggeridge might sour Britain's relations with Portugal. From late June 1943 Britain was negotiating with Portugal for facilities in the Azores. Indeed the Foreign Secretary Anthony Eden proposed to the Portuguese Ambassador that he should visit Portugal in secret to help the negotiations. Muggeridge was a loose pop-gun in a key Portuguese colony at a time when Anglo-Portuguese relations were of particular importance to the Foreign Office, Menzies' key patron. Muggeridge had become an embarrassment and had to be removed. He left Lourenço Marques in July 1943 under a cloud, not, as he implied in his memoirs, because troopships could once again use the Mediterranean. Certainly the Mozambique Channel declined in importance, but the region was still important enough for SIS to replace Muggeridge. They sent out a young officer named J.H. Brown [pseudonym chosen by the author] who held the rank of Vice Consul under Ministry of Information cover. At the level of personal relations, Muggeridge was a hard act to follow. Brown soon tangled up the complex web of agents Muggeridge had bequeathed him.[28] The new SIS representative also found it difficult to pick up the threads of Muggeridge's relationships with OSS and SOE. While Muggeridge was in Lourenço Marques there were misunderstandings between OSS and SOE. Once Muggeridge left, OSS and SOE drew closer and SIS was increasingly left out.

In *My Silent War* Kim Philby incorrectly links Muggeridge's recall with SIS losing interest in Campini. In fact Campini outlasted Muggeridge in Lourenço Marques by nearly four months. After Mussolini's fall Campini refused to obey instructions from the Badoglio Government to cooperate with the Allied Consuls. After he openly sided with Mussolini's new régime, the Portuguese expelled him. Before he left he transferred his espionage operations to the

196

German Consulate. The British underestimated Campini and were convinced they could extract evidence from him to support a case for Werz' expulsion. So when his ship, the *Angola*, reached Cape Town on 4 November 1943 Campini was questioned on board the ship. But the interrogation was botched and Campini deployed a shield of righteous innocence to deflect the questions of the MI5 representative, who was preoccupied with scoring useless propaganda points. A Lieutenant Jackson asked Campini why he had thrown in his hand with Mussolini. He replied that 'even if we lose the war, we want to go in the world . . . with a high face and not with a spot of dishonour'. Campini told his interrogators that Werz had raised with him the possibility of an action by the British on Mozambique. Campini said he too felt this was possible and 'even the Portuguese sometimes felt that way,' to which Lieutenant Jackson stoutly retorted, 'What an impossible idea. We're not the Axis.' Campini's interrogation yielded nothing. The naive hope that he would spill the beans on Werz was disappointed.[29]

For all their code-breaking advantages in the intelligence war, the British and Americans had great difficulty in nailing Werz once and for all. They saw Alvensleben as the key tool for gathering evidence against him, which would persuade the Portuguese to expel the German Consul. But running Alvensleben was far from straightforward. Hawkins reported to London in December 1943 that Alvensleben 'is very nervous that Brown, through his lack of discretion, will blow him to the German Consulate'. By March 1944 matters had deteriorated further and Hawkins had to report that 'at the present moment . . . Alvensleben is only giving information to Grieve and Huntington Harris, and this only on the understanding that Brown is not informed.' Certainly Brown's inept agent-running in Mozambique puts Muggeridge's efforts in a better light.[30]

Both SOE and MI5 became so concerned about Brown's performance that they asked OSS to put pressure on the Secret Intelligence Service for his removal. On 11 February 1944 OSS Washington telegraphed Huntington Harris that they had made a strong protest to SIS concerning Brown, but that 'if SIS suspect SOE pressure to remove Brown they may do nothing. Suggest SOE keep mum unless other mistakes made by Brown.' By Spring 1944 the concerted pressure to remove Brown succeeded and he was recalled. But it proved more difficult to get rid of the tenacious Werz. He only sailed finally from Lourenço Marques in November 1944, when the war was all but over.[31]

The inability to reveal evidence from decrypts when making diplomatic protests was a severe limitation in the counter-espionage war. The strategy of counter-intelligence based on gathering evidence for diplomatic moves in Lisbon was agonizingly slow to produce results. Once the Azores bases were safely in the bag, greater success might have been achieved through more strident overtures in the Portuguese capital, or through snatching Werz's agents in the same way as Campini's agent Manna. Muggeridge's activism was missed. Certainly Muggeridge was not simply a flop in Lourenço Marques. He played a key role in some successful operations, though he would have been more at home in SOE than SIS. But the intelligence he fed the Germans was too good: 'not unimportant', as the German Foreign Office assessed it. Overall, Muggeridge had the defects of his virtues, and tended to go too far. On May 25 1943 Smith wired Hambro that 'Although Muggeridge is quick-minded and original he is quite irresponsible in action: he is unable to think out the steps of an operation and its probable results.'[32] On secret service, it seems, it is usually better to err on the side of caution.

NOTES

1. I would like to thank the Nuffield and Scouloudi Foundations and the European Studies Research Institute of Salford University for their support of my project on the Intelligence War in Southern Africa from which the evidence in this chapter is drawn. I would also like to thank the following for their assistance: Lord Dacre of Glanton, Mr Richard Ingrams, Mr Peter Simpson-Jones CBE, Dr Richard J. Aldrich, Dr Glyn Stone, and Dr Ralph White. I am greatly indebted to Mr Duncan Stuart, CMG, SOE Adviser, Foreign and Commonwealth Office, for providing me with a summary of the SOE file on 'Operation Smokescreen'. Dr T. Grupp of the Political Archive of the German Foreign Office also very kindly searched for materials. Many of the documents consulted contain symbols instead of names: I have used names in the text and retained the original symbols in the references.
2. Malcolm Muggeridge, *Chronicles of Wasted Time Vol. Two The Infernal Grove* (London 1973); Lord Dacre to the author, 5 September 1996; Norman Sherry, *The Life of Graham Greene Volume Two: 1939–1955* (London 1994) p.170.

3. Public Record Office [henceforth PRO] DO 119/1150, The Office of the High Commissioner for the United Kingdom, Cape Town [E.J. Harding] to Lord Harlech, 3 July 1942; HS 3/14, draft letter SO to Foreign Secretary 30 March 1942; *Auswaertiges Amt Bonn Politisches Archiv*, [henceforth AABPA] R101022 Fiche 2629, note of 22 November 1940.

4. Peter Simpson-Jones, *The Lighter Side of Spying* [Typescript in Imperial War Museum] p.21; US National Archives Two at College Park [henceforth US NA Two] Berlin Document Center Microfilm Partei-Korrespondence (sic) A3340-PK-TO45 Frame 1350 Gauleitung Muenchen-Oberbayern der NSDAP 23 June 1937; Richard Ingrams, *Muggeridge. The Biography* (London 1996) p.127.

5. Albrecht Charisius and Julius Mader, *Nicht länger geheim. Entwicklung. System und Arbeitsweise des imperialistischen deutschen Geheimdienstes* (3rd edition Berlin 1978) p.669.

6. Materials on Campini's early career kindly provided by Professor Paola Carruci of the Archivo Centrale Dello Stato, letter of 23 January 1998; US NA Two RG226 E92 B603 F25 Campini, Umberto; PRO DO 119/1151 Harding to Harlech 31 December 1942; FO 371/34646 *UMBERTO CAMPINI*; P.W. Filby, 'Floradora and a Unique Break into One-Time Pad Cyphers', *Intelligence and National Security* 10/3 July 1995 p.413; F.H. Hinsley and C.A.G. Simkins, *British Intelligence in the Second World War Volume Four Security and Counter-Intelligence* (London 1990) p.207; PRO HW 14/35, *Portuguese Section. Duplication of code-books* April 1942.

7. PRO HS 3/16 *Report on Visit by W/S to P.E.A.* 11 May 1943; DO 119/1150, E.J. Harding to Harlech, 3 July 1942; HS 3/15 AD4/1003 to CD 29 June 1943; US NA Two R59 123 P 922/404, 421 and 427, RG 226 E92 B603 F25 Preston; Bradley F. Smith, *The Shadow Warriors. OSS and the Origins of the CIA* (London 1983) p.202.

8. Hinsley, *Security and Counter-Intelligence* pp.154–55; US NA Two RG226 E134 B293 F1677 Coordinator of Information to Stone, 21 November 1942, B175 F1109 Stone to Coordinator of Information, 8 December 1942.

9. PRO HW 1/533, Foreign Ministry Rome to Italian Consulate, Lourenço Marques no. 58 of 27 April 1942; HW1/548, Campini Lourenço Marques to Foreign Ministry Rome no. 109c of 1 May 1942 and 112c of 2 May to Rome and Lisbon; HW1/555 Campini Lourenço Marques to Foreign Ministry Rome no. 113c of 2 May 1942; HW1/553, Campini Lourenço Marques to Foreign Ministry Rome no. 117c of 4 May 1942; Malcolm Muggeridge, *Like It Was. A Selection from the Diaries of Malcolm Muggeridge* (London 1981) p.186; idem, *Infernal Grove* p.150; Ingrams, *Muggeridge* pp.122–4; Hinsley and Simkins, *Security and Counter-Intelligence* p.155.

10. Muggeridge, *Infernal Grove* pp. 170–174; Hinsley and Simkins, *Security*

and Counter-Intelligence p.155; Richard J. Aldrich, 'Britain's Secret Intelligence in Asia During the Second World War' in *Modern Asian Studies* 32/1 (1998) p.185.

11. Bundesarchiv Lichterfelde NSDAP Mitgliedsausweis Werner von Alvensleben; PRO HS 3/24 Ref:D/130 DZ1 to AD4 5 November 1943.

12. PRO HS 3/14 internal memo 16 May 1942, AD/S to AD 22, May 1942, Peter Loxley, Foreign Office to CD, 14 June 1942, ADW/206/600 to A.C.S.S., 20 June 1942, CD/2380 to Loxley, 24 June 1942.

13. Letter from SOE Adviser, 23 July 1998; PRO HS 3/20, Progress Report No. 3; HS 3/16, Report on visit by W/S to Portuguese East Africa, 11 May 1943; Muggeridge, *Infernal Grove* p.174.

14. US NA Two RG226 E314 B292 F1674, OSS to Ebert, 22 June 1943; RG59 862.20253Q/4, Preston to Secretary of State, 18 June 1943; Muggeridge, *Infernal Grove* ibid.

15. US NA Two RG226 E134 B286 F1635, Africa Section, S.I. to Director, O.S.S., 11 May 1943.

16. Ingrams, *Muggeridge* p.128; PRO HS 3/16 DZ9 to DZ4, 20 December 1942.

17. PRO HS 3/16, L/B to W., 28 October 1942; W. to AD/P, 28 October 1942; CT to Navycharge Durban, 4 November 1942; CT from Durban no. 1007, 5 November 1942; CT to Durban no. 0775, 5 November 1942; DZ9 to DZ4, 21 December 1942; WB to WS, 28 December 1942; CT from Durban no. 1138, 5 January 1943.

18. PRO HS 3/13, LFS/444 Lt.-Col. L.F. Sheridan to Anthony Lincoln, Colonial Office, 26 January 1943; HS 3/14, CD/3985 *Directive from CD to WS*, 16 December 1942; HS 3/16, CT from Durban no. 1183, 10 February 1943; *Report on Visit by W/S to PEA* 11 May 1943.

19. PRO ADM 199/2493, C/2318 to Sir Alexander Cadogan, 18 February 1943.

20. Hinsley and Simkins, *Security and Counter-Intelligence* p.207; Letter from SOE Adviser, 30 July 1998.

21. Hinsley and Simkins, *Security and Counter-Intelligence* p.207; Letter from SOE Adviser, 30 July 1998; PRO HS 3/16 *Report on Visit by W/S to PEA* 11 May 1943.

22. US NA Two RG 226 E92 B603 F25 Levi, Anna; Letter from SOE Adviser, 30 July 1998.

23. PRO HS 3/14, AD4/876 to CD 25 May 1943; Letter from SOE Adviser, 30 July 1998.

24. PRO HS 3/18, CXG 946 Lourenço Marques 4 July 1943, CT from Cape Town no. 448, 12 July 1943.

25. Ibid., Africa Section note of 8 July 1943, AD4 to VCD 8 July 1943, CT no. 448 from Cape Town, 12 July 1943.

26. Ibid., DZ1 to AD4, 23 July 1943; HS 3/16 DZ1 to DZ9, 24 July 43;

AABPA R29535, Trompke, Lourenço Marques Nr. 552 of 9 June 1943.

27. Ibid., Trompke, Lourenço Marques Nr. 422 of 21 April 1943 and Nr. 452 of 30 April.

28. PRO HW 1/1762, Portuguese Ambassador in London to Ministry for Foreign Affairs, Lisbon, 21 June 1943, Ministry for Foreign Affairs Lisbon to Portuguese Ambassador in London, 23 June 1943; Llewellyn Woodward, *British Foreign Policy in the Second World War* (London 1975) vol. 4, p. 53; Muggeridge, *Infernal Grove* pp.179–80.

29. Kim Philby, *My Silent War* (London 1968) p.58; PRO HS 3/24, *Ref.No.1526* From W. [to SIS] 26 October 1943, Minute no.15 to Major Benham (SOE) [from SIS], 31 October 1943, CT no.544 Capetown 1 November 1943, '*Interrogation of Umberto Campini* held on board the Portuguese vessel S.S. "Angola" at Cape Town on the 4th November, 1943'.

30. PRO HS 3/24, DZ1 to AD7, 16 December 1943; HS 3/84 South African Mission Progress Report No.7, 8 March 1944.

31. US NA Two RG 226 E134 B292 F1675, Ebert to OSS, 30 January 1944, E88 B644, Director OSS to Ebert Lourenço Marques, 11 February 1944; E88 B660 Incoming Midway Lourenço Marques to Director OSS, 10 November 1944.

32. AABPA R101176, Auswaertiges Amt Inland II 365g to Reichssicherheitshauptamt z.Hd.v. SS-Obersturmbannfuehrer Eichmann, 3 March 1944; PRO HS 3/84, WS to CD, 25 May 1943.

THE VENONA SECRET

CHRISTOPHER ANDREW

No historian of the Second World War nowadays fails to acknowledge the role of signals intelligence (SIGINT). The ULTRA intelligence which derived from the phenomenal success of Anglo-American codebreakers in breaking high-grade enemy ciphers hastened the Allied victory over both Germany and Japan. By contrast, the important role of codebreaking in the Cold War has passed almost unnoticed, due both to a surprising lack of curiosity among contemporary historians and to the unavailability until recently of all postwar SIGINT files.

Though the total volume of SIGINT available to the superpowers during the Cold War was much greater than during the Second World War, Soviet high-grade cipher systems, based on the theoretically unbreakable one-time pad, were far less vulnerable than those of Nazi Germany and Imperial Japan.[1] In the immediate aftermath of the Second World War the failure to produce a Soviet ULTRA led to what a later enquiry described as 'a sense of frustration and anti-climax' in US SIGINT agencies.[2] American and British cryptanalysts, however, had some successes against Soviet traffic, most of which are still classified. The first great SIGINT secret of the Cold War, VENONA, was not declassified until 1995–6.

VENONA was the final codename given to almost 3,000 intercepted Soviet intelligence and other classified telegrams for the period 1940 to 1948, which, as the result of errors in Soviet cipher production, used the same one-time pads more than once and thus became vulnerable to cryptanalytic attack. Most were decrypted, in whole or in part, by American codebreakers with some assistance from the British in the late 1940s and early 1950s.[3] Though the decrypts provided important information on Soviet espionage in regions of the world as far apart as Scandinavia and Australia, the largest and most important groups concerned intelligence operations in the United

States. VENONA revealed that over two hundred Americans were working as Soviet agents during and sometimes after the Second World War, and that the leadership of the American Communist Party was hand-in-glove with the KGB.

Every section of the wartime administration of Franklin D. Roosevelt was penetrated by Soviet intelligence. Had the ailing Roosevelt died in 1944, as seemed quite possible, he would have been succeeded by his then vice-president, Henry Wallace. We now know that the men Wallace had already selected to be his Secretary of State and Secretary of the Treasury, Larry Duggan and Harry Dexter White, were both Soviet agents, codenamed respectively FRANK and JURIST. The US Office of Strategic Services (OSS) was the most penetrated major intelligence agency of the Second World War, perhaps of the twentieth century. Thanks to the Soviet agents in the top-secret laboratory at Los Alamos near Santa Fe, which designed and built the world's first atomic bomb, the first Soviet atomic bomb, successfully tested in 1949, was an exact copy of the American original produced just over four years earlier. Detailed research on the Soviet intelligence operations revealed by VENONA will take some years to complete.[4]

Like ULTRA, VENONA was also remarkable for the extraordinary secrecy which surrounded it. ULTRA had been more closely guarded than any previous intelligence source in British or American history, revealed only to six of Churchill's ministers and probably to even fewer members of the Roosevelt administration. VENONA, however, was more secret still, so secret in fact that even President Harry S. Truman, Roosevelt's successor, was never informed of it. Until almost the end of the Truman administration, the decrypts, the most important intelligence available on Soviet espionage, were also kept from the Central Intelligence Agency and the National Security Council, both founded by Act of Congress in July 1947. So far as is known, no other intelligence secret of comparable importance in the history of the Cold War was concealed from so many of those with the prime responsibility for American security.

In both Britain and the United States the tight restrictions on access to SIGINT during and after the Second World War reflected in part the lessons of past experience. Carelessness in the handling of decrypts between the wars had led to the discovery by the Soviet Union in 1927 that its diplomatic ciphers had been broken by the British, and by the Japanese in 1931 that theirs had been penetrated by the Americans.[5] The small groups privy to ULTRA intelligence in Britain and the United States were rightly convinced that SIGINT was used so successfully in the Second World War largely because the secret was so much better kept. Basking henceforth in the reflected glory of ULTRA, Anglo-American cryptanalysts found it much easier than before the War to persuade those with access to their intelligence to keep secret both their past successes and current operations. The ULTRA secret was not revealed until almost thirty years after the Second World War.

The extraordinary restrictions placed on access to VENONA in the United States, however, cannot be explained simply by the operational requirements of SIGINT agencies. They were due also to the bitter, and at times farcical, internecine rivalries within the US intelligence community at the beginning of the Cold War. J. Edgar Hoover, the autocratic, long-serving director of the Federal Bureau of Investigation (FBI), which was responsible for internal security, had taken a dim view of the founding of the wartime foreign intelligence agency, the Office of Strategic Services (OSS). General William Donovan, the head of OSS, once complained. 'The Abwehr gets better treatment from the FBI than we do'.[6] Hoover similarly regarded the CIA as a dangerous upstart which prevented him achieving his ambition of extending Bureau operations into the field of foreign intelligence.[7]

In the absence of a single SIGINT agency, such as that established in Britain in 1919 with responsibility for both diplomatic and armed service traffic, American cryptanalysis was also plagued for a generation by chronic interservice feuding. 'I have the feeling,' Truman once said ungenerously, 'that if the Army and the Navy had fought our enemies as hard as they fought each other, the war would have ended much earlier.'[8] After Army codebreakers had broken the Japanese PURPLE diplomatic cipher in September 1940, there had been a bitter dispute between the military and naval SIGINT agencies over the production of the MAGIC intelligence derived from it. Following prolonged negotiations the dispute was eventually contained, though not resolved, by an absurd compromise which gave military codebreakers the right to produce MAGIC on even dates and their naval rivals the same privilege on odd dates. Much of the incompetence with which MAGIC was handled before Pearl Harbor derived from this bizarre arrangement. In June 1942 an interdepartmental agreement ended the worst of the confusion by giving, for the first time, sole responsibility for diplomatic as well as military SIGINT to the Army, leaving the Navy in charge only of naval SIGINT. To soften the blow to naval pride, however, diplomatic decrypts were, illogically, supplied to President Roosevelt by his naval rather than his military aide. Throughout the Second World War American military and naval cryptanalysts cooperated more successfully with their British counterparts than they did with each other.[9]

After V-J Day the prewar battles between military and naval crypt-analysts rapidly revived. Faced with the dramatic postwar decline in naval signals, the Navy tried to reclaim its pre-Pearl Harbor share of diplomatic traffic. The Army Security [SIGINT] Agency (ASA) refused to surrender its monopoly of diplomatic decryption simply, so it claimed, for the sake of 'giving the Navy something to do'. Though ASA eventually agreed grudgingly to a (still-classified) compromise, bitter Army-Navy demarcation disputes continued. The creation of an independent US Air Force in October caused further confusion. At the insistence of General Hoyt S. Vandenberg, who became its Chief of Staff in May 1948, the Air Force was given its own independent SIGINT unit.[10]

In August 1948 a committee chaired by Rear Admiral Earl F. Stone, Director of Naval Communications, was ordered to resolve the confusion between the service SIGINT agencies. It failed. After further wrangling, a new Armed Forces Security Agency (AFSA), headed by Stone, was set up in July 1949 to try to coordinate SIGINT operations by the three armed services.[11] AFSA was overseen, but not controlled, by a ten-man Armed Forces Security Agency Committee (AFSAC). Composed of three members from each of the armed services under the chairmanship of the AFSA director, AFSAC was instructed to 'determine and coordinate joint cryptologic military requirements'. Arguably, it only made the existing confusion worse. According to a top-secret report in 1952:

> In place of the two COMINT [communications intelligence] organizations (Army and Navy) that existed during the war, we now have four. . . . AFSA has no authority over the service units, which in turn are independent of each other.[12]

On becoming head of AFSA in 1949, Stone was, to quote a doubtless euphemistic FBI memorandum, 'very much disturbed' to discover that, though ASA had called in the Bureau in an attempt to identify the code-names of the Soviet agents mentioned in the VENONA decrypts, it had failed to inform either the President or the Director of Central Intelligence (DCI). Stone insisted that ASA do so promptly. General Carter W. Clarke, the head of ASA, 'vehemently disagreed'. After what was probably a blazing row, Clarke took his dispute to the Chairman of the Joint Chiefs of Staff, General Omar Nelson Bradley.[13]

Truman had great admiration for and trust in Bradley, and enthusiastically supported his appointment as Army Chief of Staff in succession to Eisenhower in 1948.[14] A year later, however, Bradley was guilty of an extraordinary act of insubordination, siding with Clarke in his dispute with Stone over whether to reveal VENONA to Truman and the CIA. He announced that if the contents of the decrypts ever in his opinion demanded it, he 'would personally assume the responsibility of advising the President or anyone else in authority'. Truman, however, was almost certainly never told.[15] As a result the President remained confused about the nature and reality of Soviet intelligence penetration of the United States. Significantly, in over twelve hundred pages of presidential memoirs, Truman never mentioned the Rosenbergs, Alger Hiss or anyone else publicly accused of being a Soviet agent during his presidency. The ultimate responsibility for Truman's confusion rests with Bradley. The Chairman of the Joint Chiefs appears, on his own authority, to have withheld from the Commander-in-Chief the most important information available to the American intelligence community in the early years of the Cold War on the activities of Soviet intelligence on the territory of the United States.

Bradley, however, was almost certainly less concerned to keep the secret from the President than from the CIA, in particular its head, Rear Admiral Roscoe H. Hillenkoetter, (DCI) from 1947 to 1950. 'Hilly' was frequently Truman's first caller of the day, bringing with him the intelligence briefing which became known as the President's Daily Brief. If Truman were informed of VENONA, he would thus be likely to raise the subject with his DCI. Only by keeping the secret from the President could Bradley be sure that it was kept from the DCI.

Just as Hoover saw the newly-founded CIA as a potential rival, so Bradley seems to have regarded the Agency as an unwelcome threat to the service intelligence agencies and to have resented the fact that, unlike its wartime predecessor OSS, it was not placed under the authority of the Joint Chiefs. Faced with such high-ranking opposition, Hillenkoetter made little attempt to assert his own authority. 'In the hierarchical maze of official Washington,' wrote a sympathetic subordinate, 'his authority scarcely extended beyond the front door. Hillenkoetter's low rank precisely indicated the level of enthusiasm the rank-conscious armed services had for a centralized intelligence system.'[16] As DCI, he was supposed, in addition to directing the CIA, to coordinate the work of the intelligence community as a whole. Hoover and Bradley, among others, ensured that he did not. Hilly proved probably the weakest of all DCIs. A note prepared for Truman at the end of his term of office singled out 'extreme modesty and self-effacing devotion to duty' as Hillenkoetter's most striking 'personal attributes'.[17]

Bradley also seems to have been suspicious of CIA security. Since VENONA revealed that OSS had been comprehensively penetrated by Soviet agents, he must surely have feared that the CIA was likely to be penetrated too. Army intelligence believed that the civilians in the new agency, who were not under military discipline, could not be trusted to keep secrets. Its doubts were encouraged by Hoover. Dr Cleveland Cram, one of the first CIA officials to be 'indoctrinated' into VENONA in 1952, believed that the main opposition to showing the decrypts to the Agency and the White House came not from Bradley but from Hoover.[18]

The decision not to tell the President or the DCI was all the more remarkable in view of the fact that, as Bradley and Hoover were well aware, the British had access to all the VENONA decrypts. Deeply impressed by British-American collaboration on ULTRA during the Second World War, Truman had signed on 12 September 1945 a top-secret one-sentence memorandum, providing for the peacetime continuation of the wartime SIGINT alliance:

> The Secretary of War and the Secretary of the Navy are hereby authorised to direct the Chief of Staff, U.S. Army, and the Commander in Chief, U.S. Fleet, and Chief of Naval Operations to continue collaboration in the field of communication intelligence between the United States Army and Navy and the British, and to extend, modify or discontinue this collaboration, as determined to be in the best interests of the United States.[19]

Still-classified British-American agreements of March 1946 and June 1948 (the latter known as the UKUSA agreement), also involving

Australia, Canada and New Zealand, divided the world up into spheres of SIGINT influence assigned to each of the five powers, and provided for extensive sharing of the intelligence obtained.[20] Liaison officers at ASA from the British SIGINT agency, the Government Communications Headquarters (GCHQ), were informed of the initial VENONA breakthrough even before the FBI. By 1948, according to a CIA/NSA study, 'there was complete and profitable US-UK cooperation' on the project.[21]

GCHQ kept the British foreign intelligence agency, the Secret Intelligence Service (better known as SIS or MI6), and the Security Service (MI5) fully briefed on VENONA. As well as collaborating closely with GCHQ, the chief American cryptanalyst working on the VENONA project, Meredith Gardner, had regular meetings with the SIS and MI5 representatives in Washington, Peter Dwyer and Geoffrey Patterson, both of whom provided information on individuals referred to in the Soviet telegrams to assist the process of decryption.[22] Ironically, Dwyer had to be careful not to mention the decrypts in his meetings with CIA officers. Though the relevant British files have yet to be declassified, there is no reason to doubt that the British Prime Minister, Clement Attlee, and some of his senior ministers were briefed on VENONA. Until November 1952 the British government and intelligence community were thus better informed on Soviet espionage in the United States than the President and the DCI.

Unlike Truman, Dwight D. Eisenhower, who succeeded him as President, had almost certainly been informed of the VENONA project from the outset. The Second World War had turned Ike into a SIGINT enthusiast. Soon after his arrival in Britain as commander of American military forces in June 1942 he had been briefed personally on ULTRA by Churchill during a visit to Chequers. At the end of the war he declared that ULTRA had been 'of priceless value' to him and sent his 'heartfelt admiration and sincere thanks' to British cryptanalysts at Bletchley Park 'for their very decisive contribution to the Allied war effort'.[23] As Army Chief of Staff from 1945 to 1948, Eisenhower was doubtless anxious to be informed of progress in breaking Soviet codes.[24] Like his successor Bradley, he must surely have been kept abreast of ASA's progress on VENONA.[25]

The handling of the VENONA secret changed significantly as a result both of the Korean War and the election of Eisenhower as President. The Korean War exposed the confusion caused by the rivalry and lack of coordination between the four SIGINT agencies to a degree which embarrassed even the agencies. According to a CIA study, 'the responsible military authorities were themselves disgusted by the infighting . . . and by the inefficiencies inherent in the existing [SIGINT] set-up'.[26] Largely as a result of the initial infighting, SIGINT failed to provide advance warning of the North Korean invasion of the South on 25 June 1950. Incredibly, North Korea was not specifically targeted until after the invasion began.[27]

SIGINT targeting – the choice of priorities for signals interception and cryptanalysis – was supposed to be coordinated by the United States Communications Intelligence Board (USCIB), established in July 1948 to represent the six SIGINT consumers: the three armed services, State, the CIA and the FBI. Since USCIB decisions had to be reached unanimously, however, it was largely ineffective.[28] During the seven months before the North Korean invasion, according to a later enquiry, 'the various intelligence agencies were becoming increasingly concerned . . . about the possibility of a Soviet move against South Korea, and yet this concern was never directly communicated to AFSA through the mechanism of the USCIB Intelligence requirements lists'. The minutes of the monthly meeting of the USCIB Watch Committee on 12 April 1950 record that:

> A report relayed by CinCFE [General Douglas MacArthur] stated that the North Korean Peoples' Army will invade South Korea in June of 1950. Representatives of the Department of the Army undertook to ask for further information on this subject.

By the time the invasion began two and a half months later Military Intelligence had still not provided the promised 'further information'.[29] Had North Korea been targeted, it is difficult to believe, given the success of SIGINT operations after the outbreak of war, that there would not have been some warning of the massing of over 90,000 North Korean troops and 150 T-34 tanks at 'jump-off points' north of the 38th parallel before the invasion began.

By the time the Korean battle front stabilized into a military stalemate in the summer of 1951, SIGINT, supported by aerial reconnaissance, provided a reliable means of monitoring the deployment of enemy forces. General Walter Bedell 'Beetle' Smith, who became DCI in October 1950, had a far stronger personality and a much better grasp of SIGINT than his ineffective predecessor, Rear

Admiral Hillenkoetter. During the Second World War Smith had served as Eisenhower's chief of staff, with access to ULTRA. From 1946 to 1949 he served as ambassador in Moscow.[30] Smith was the first non-graduate from West Point or any other military school to have been promoted to four-star general. His rise through the ranks was marked by constant slights from Omar Bradley and other West Pointers.[31] As DCI, however, 'Beetle' stood no nonsense from the better-educated service intelligence chiefs. According to a senior CIA officer who served under him:

> Bedell Smith put us on our feet originally because of his tremendous prestige as Eisenhower's G-3 at the end of World War II. He established our position in relation to the military. He treated the generals and the admirals who were G-2s and A-2s [army and air force intelligence chiefs] and ONI [Office of Naval Intelligence] representatives as schoolboys. He'd make fun of them in front of us all. It was embarrassing sometimes.[32]

Smith was outraged by the lack of cooperation between military and air force SIGINT units in Korea as well as by the inability of AFSA to impose its inadequate authority on the service agencies. By the later months of 1951 he was privately threatening that, unless the State and Defense Departments agreed to a major SIGINT overhaul, he would set about it himself, relying on his authority as DCI to coordinate the work of the intelligence community.[33] In a more restrained memorandum of 10 December 1951, 'Beetle' emphasized 'the unique value' of SIGINT and declared himself 'gravely concerned as to the security and effectiveness with which the Communications Intelligence activities of the Government are being conducted'. By the time Smith drafted this memorandum he had, almost certainly, already won Truman's support for a major SIGINT overhaul by impressing on him, probably for the first time, the damage done by the existing system. The President formally approved the DCI's memorandum on 13 December.[34] At a meeting chaired by Truman the same day in the Oval Office, attended by Smith, Bradley, representatives of State and Defense, and the executive secretary of the NSC, James S. Lay, Jr., the terms were agreed of a high-level investigation into the running of SIGINT.[35] On 28 December a committee to conduct the investigation was appointed, headed by the New York lawyer, George A. Brownell, formerly special assistant to the Secretary of the Air Force, and containing senior representatives of State, Defense and the CIA.[36]

The Brownell Committee submitted its report on 13 June 1952. Its unusual rapidity (by Washington standards) was due largely to the joint insistence of Smith, Dean Acheson, the Secretary of State, and Robert A. Lovett, Secretary of Defense since September 1951, on rapid reform; to the support of the President; and to a shame-faced awareness by the service intelligence agencies of the damage done by their infighting during the early stages of the Korean War.[37] The Brownell report emphasized the 'vital importance' of SIGINT and detailed the confusion and inadequacy of its existing management:

> The Director of AFSA is obliged to spend much of his energy on cajolery, negotiation and compromise in an atmosphere of interser-vice competition. He has no degree of control, except by making use of such techniques, over the three COMINT units operated by the three Services. In fact, he is under the control of the three Service units, through their representation on AFSAC. His only appeal is to the same three services sitting as the Joint Chiefs of Staff.

The Brownell Committee recommended giving AFSA the effective authority over the service SIGINT agencies it had hitherto lacked, abolishing AFSAC, and giving a strengthened USCIB, chaired by the DCI, greater power to oversee the coordination of SIGINT with other intelligence activities.[38] On 24 October Truman signed a top-secret presidential memorandum putting into effect the main recommen-dations of the committee, with one significant addition. In keeping with its enhanced authority, AFSA was renamed the National Security Agency (NSA).[39]

With the DCI chairing the board responsible for setting SIGINT priorities, it was no longer possible to withhold VENONA from the CIA. The first small group of Agency officers was briefed on the decrypts in November. Cleve Cram, the last survivor of that group, was astonished to discover that Robert Lamphere of the FBI, with whom he had been in regular contact for the past few years on counter-intelligence matters, had been the FBI's chief liaison with ASA and AFSA on VENONA since 1948.[40]

The date of NSA's foundation, 4 November 1952, was deliberately chosen to keep it out of the news. All other events that day were over-shadowed by the election of the Republican candidate, Dwight D. Eisenhower, to succeed Truman as President of the United States. No one apparently wished to go through the embarrassment of revealing to Truman, during his last two months in office, the existence of the VENONA decrypts which had hitherto been kept from him.[41] As the first SIGINT enthusiast to enter the Oval Office, however, Eisenhower was almost certainly kept well-informed. As President, he poured resources into NSA, giving it the largest and most advanced bank of computers in the world. Before long, both its budget and its personnel outstripped those of the CIA. For more than two decades, however, even its existence was unknown to the vast mass of the American people. Those in the know in Washington joked that NSA stood for 'No Such Agency'.[42]

The unprecedented secrecy surrounding VENONA failed in its main object – to prevent Moscow discovering that some of its top-secret telegrams were being decrypted. In 1950 AFSA was shocked to discover that one of its employees, William Weisband, had been a Soviet agent ever since he joined the wartime army SIGINT agency in 1942.[43] The son of Russian immigrants to the United States, Weisband was employed as a Russian linguist and roamed around first ASA, then AFSA, on the pretext of looking for projects where his linguistic skills could be of assistance. Cecil Phillips, one of the cryptanalysts who worked on VENONA, remembers Weisband as 'very gregarious and very nosy':

> He would come around and ask questions about what you were doing. . . . He was never aggressive. If you said, as I often did, 'Nothing important,' or 'I'm doing something as dull as hell,' he would wander off. . . . I never heard him offer a political thought. He was around everywhere all the time. He cultivated the senior officers.

Meredith Gardner recalls Weisband looking over his shoulder at a critical moment in the project late in 1946, just as he was producing one of the first important decrypts, a telegram from the New York residency to Moscow of December 1944 listing some of the scientists who were developing the atomic bomb.[44] Soon afterwards Weisband made contact with Soviet intelligence.[45] Thus it was that the VENONA secret was communicated to Moscow almost six years before it reached either the President or the CIA. From 1950 onwards, following Weisband's arrest,[46] Bradley and Hoover must have been aware that the secret they were keeping from Truman and the Agency was known to Stalin.

Moscow, however, had no means of predicting which of its top-secret telegrams would be decrypted or which of its agents would be successfully identified from the decrypts. It therefore depended on Weisband to provide as much information as possible on the progress made by Gardner and his colleagues. After Weisband's arrest, the main Soviet source of intelligence on the VENONA project was probably Kim Philby, who was posted to Washington as SIS liaison officer in the autumn of 1949. Before leaving London, Philby was fully briefed on VENONA. In September 1949 he was able to report to Moscow that the atom spy successively codenamed REST and CHARLES, referred to in a number of the decrypts, had been identified as Klaus Fuchs, thus enabling Moscow to warn those of its American agents who had dealt with Fuchs that they might have to flee through Mexico. Among those who made their escape were Morris and Lona Cohen, who later reappeared in Britain using the aliases Peter and Helen Kroger and were convicted of espionage in 1961.[47] After his death in 1995 Morris Cohen was posthumously declared Hero of the Russian Federation by President Boris Yeltsin.

Soon after his arrival in Washington Philby was taken to AFSA by his predecessor Peter Dwyer and introduced to Gardner. On this, as on a number of previous visits, Dwyer provided information which helped Gardner fill in gaps in one of the decrypts. Gardner still vividly recalls the meeting:

> I was very much pleased [with the progress on the decrypts] and so was Dwyer, of course. Philby was looking on with no doubt rapt attention but he never said a word, never a word. And that was the last I saw of him. Philby was supposed to continue Dwyer's visits, but helping me was the last thing he wanted to do.[48]

Despite discontinuing collaboration with Gardner, Philby regularly received both reports on and the text of VENONA decrypts during his time in Washington.[49] The decrypts which most concerned him were, almost certainly, those which referred to an agent codenamed HOMER operating in Washington at the end of the war. Though VENONA initially provided only vague clues to the agent's identity, Philby quickly realized that HOMER was his former Cambridge contemporary Donald Maclean, who had worked as a Soviet spy in the British foreign service since 1935 and had been stationed at the Washington embassy from 1944 to 1947. Philby was informed by

Moscow Centre that 'Maclean should stay in his post as long as possible' and that plans would be made to rescue him 'before the net closed in'.[50] The net did not begin to close until the winter of 1950–1. By the end of 1950 the list of suspects had narrowed to thirty-five. By the beginning of April 1951 it had shrunk to nine.[51] A few days later a telegram decrypted by Gardner finally identified HOMER as Maclean. It revealed that in June 1944 HOMER's wife was expecting a baby and living with her mother in New York,[52] information which fitted Melinda Maclean but not the wife of any other suspect.

Having learned from his MI5 colleague in Washington, Geoffrey Patterson, that Maclean would be placed under surveillance for some weeks before being called in for interrogation, Philby realized that there still remained a breathing space in which to warn Maclean that he had been identified as a Soviet agent and to arrange for his escape to Moscow. The warning was conveyed by Guy Burgess, who had been recruited as a Soviet agent in 1934 after being talent-spotted by Philby. Since the summer of 1950 Burgess had been working as second secretary at the Washington embassy, lodging with Philby and his wife at their home on Nebraska Avenue.[53] In April 1951 Burgess was ordered home in disgrace after a series of escapades had aroused the collective wrath of the Virginia State Police, the State Department and the British ambassador. Soon after his return to London on 7 May Burgess warned Maclean, then head of the American desk in the Foreign Office, in person, and delivered a further warning to his Soviet controller, Yuri Modin, via his friend and fellow-agent, Anthony Blunt. Moscow rapidly concluded that 'HOMER *must* agree to defect'. Burgess was persuaded to accompany Maclean by being given the impression that he would be free to return to London once Maclean had been successfully exfiltrated. In reality, the Centre believed that Burgess had become a liability and was determined to get him to Moscow, by deception if necessary, and keep him there. 'As long as he agreed to go with Maclean,' wrote Modin later, 'the rest mattered precious little. Cynically enough, the Centre had . . . concluded that we had not one but two burnt-out agents on our hands.'[54]

Meredith Gardner recalls his sense of shock on hearing the dramatic news that Maclean and Burgess had defected on 25 May:

I thought, 'Just think of that! I made them do it!' I didn't really feel self-important but I was impinging on the real world more than when I was just a scholar and studying philology.[55]

Gardner's discovery of HOMER's identity, followed by the double defection, brought almost to a close the careers as Soviet agents of five young Cambridge graduates recruited in the mid-1930s who later became known in the KGB as the 'Magnificent Five': Kim Philby, Guy Burgess, Donald Maclean, Anthony Blunt and John Cairncross.[56] Burgess's flight immediately cast suspicion on his friend Philby, who was recalled from Washington and forced to resign from SIS, though it was another twelve years before he too fled to Moscow. Blunt, Deputy Director of the Courtauld Institute and Surveyor of the King's Pictures, who had shared a flat with Burgess for several years, also came under suspicion. So did Cairncross, the 'Fifth Man', some of whose papers were discovered in Burgess's flat.[57]

Though American and British security procedures failed miserably to prevent Moscow learning of the VENONA decrypts, they were remarkably successful in keeping the secret within the United States and Britain. The secrecy had both short-term and long-term consequences. SIGINT from any source was considered far too secret to be mentioned in court, even in secret session.[58] Though VENONA probably identified more Soviet agents than any other Western intelligence operation of the Cold War, it therefore led to very few convictions. It was possible to mount successful prosecutions against Soviet agents identified in the decrypts only if they could be persuaded to confess or if alternative evidence could be discovered from non-SIGINT sources. Among the few who admitted their guilt when confronted by the evidence against them (though they had no idea it was based on SIGINT) were two of the atom spies in Los Alamos: the German-born British physicist Klaus Fuchs and the American Technical Sergeant David Greenglass, who was recruited by his wife's brother-in-law Julius Rosenberg. Fuchs confessed to espionage in January 1950 and was sentenced two months later, after a trial at the Old Bailey lasting only an hour and a half, to fourteen years' imprisonment. Greenglass made his confession in June 1950 and also implicated Julius Rosenberg, whom VENONA had identified as the organizer, with some assistance from his wife Ethel, of a highly successful Soviet spy-ring in New York, producing a wide range of scientific and technological intelligence. When the Rosenbergs' trial opened in March 1951 Greenglass was the chief witness for the prosecution. Unlike Fuchs, the Rosenbergs were sentenced to death, though the execution was not carried out until June 1953.[59]

VENONA also disclosed the presence at Los Alamos of a third

Soviet agent, Theodore 'Ted' Hall, who was probably even more important than Fuchs. A precociously brilliant Harvard physicist recruited for work on the atomic project in 1944 at the age of only eighteen, Hall was probably the youngest major spy of the twentieth century, given the appropriate, if somewhat transparent, codename MLAD ('Young').[60] Unlike Fuchs and Greenglass, however, Hall had no intention of confessing.

In the early spring of 1950, alerted by the references to Hall in VENONA, the FBI placed him and his wife Joan, then living in Chicago, under round-the-clock surveillance, intercepting their correspondence and (almost certainly) telephone calls, and regularly rummaging through their garbage. FBI Agent Bob McQueen, who was in charge of the investigation, recalls that a year's surveillance produced no evidence against Hall, save for unsurprising confirmation that he was 'a rebel of sorts'.[61] The Halls were constantly on their guard, fearing that their apartment was bugged. 'We never talked at home,' Joan Hall recalls. 'If we wanted to talk about this business we went for a walk.' In the hope of obtaining a confession, McQueen 'invited' Hall for questioning at the FBI field office in Chicago on Friday 16 March 1951 in order to give him 'an opportunity to explain his connection with a matter pertaining to the security of the United States'. To increase the emotional impact of the occasion, McQueen had deliberately chosen a date in the middle of the Rosenbergs' trial. When Hall telephoned his wife from the FBI office to say he was being questioned, Joan Hall recalls thinking, 'God, this is it!'

According to Hall, his FBI questioners told him, 'We know what you did'. Hall, however, remained calm and became increasingly doubtful that the FBI had adequate evidence against him. He was also encouraged to find his questioners 'quite provokable':

> I really got them provoked at one point. I said I wasn't very happy talking with them because I'd read a lot about them framing people and playing various nasty tricks. This really got their hackles up and they said, 'The FBI doesn't frame people'.

Hall left the FBI office at 5.21 p.m. after almost three hours' questioning, but agreed to return on the following Monday morning, 19 March. On this occasion, according to the official record, Hall stayed only sixteen minutes before announcing that he had nothing further to say and getting up to leave. He expected to be stopped and handcuffed before he reached the lift, but, to his surprise, was allowed to leave the FBI building without being challenged.[62]

Apart from Ted Hall, very few of the Soviet agents identified in the VENONA decrypts have described their questioning by the FBI. It is reasonable to suppose, however, that most interrogations reached a similar impasse. The FBI was frustrated by its inability either to use SIGINT evidence to mount a prosecution or to obtain confessions from those implicated by it. MI5 faced the same problem in Britain. Had Maclean's nerve equalled that of Hall and had he been prepared to stonewall his British interrogators rather than flee to Moscow, it would almost certainly have been impossible to convict him of espionage. Burgess, who was not even under suspicion at the time of his defection, could certainly have escaped prosecution. Soviet intelligence was anxious to exfiltrate both of them largely because it wrongly supposed that confessions would have been forced out of them in London by methods similar to those which would have been used in Moscow. The British failure to prosecute the other three of the Magnificent Five, Philby, Blunt and Cairncross, was due not, as is often alleged, to an establishment cover-up but to the failure of long-drawn-out attempts to assemble a case against any of them which met legal standards of evidence.

The prolonged refusal to declassify the VENONA decrypts left a generation and more of liberal Americans, including some prominent historians and political scientists, with a distorted understanding of the early Cold War.[63] The fact that in Britain the atom spies Fuchs and Alan Nunn May admitted their espionage, and that Burgess, Maclean and Philby defected to Moscow, made the reality of Soviet espionage relatively uncontentious. Their nearest American equivalents, by contrast, neither confessed nor defected. The outrageous exaggerations and inventions of Senator Joseph McCarthy's self-serving anti-Communist witch-hunt in the early 1950s made liberal opinion in the United States sceptical of the reality of the Soviet intelligence offensive. The evidence of Elizabeth Bentley and Whittaker Chambers, who had worked as couriers for Soviet intelligence in the United States before and during the Second World War and were able to identify a series of Soviet agents, was widely ridiculed. VENONA provides compelling corroboration for both.[64]

For many American liberals it became an article of faith that Julius and Ethel Rosenberg, like Alger Hiss, a Soviet agent in the State Department found guilty of perjury for denying his involvement in espionage, were the innocent victims of Cold War show trials.

218

VENONA leaves no doubt that all were guilty, though that does not, of course, justify the death sentences passed on the Rosenbergs. It also reveals that after Hiss (Agent ALES) attended the Yalta conference in February 1945 as a member of the US delegation, he went on to Moscow where he was warmly congratulated on his work as an agent and awarded a Soviet decoration.[65] It is easy to imagine the rejoicing in Moscow in April 1945 when Hiss was appointed acting Secretary-General of the United Nations 'organizing conference' at San Francisco.

The revelation of the VENONA secret also has large implications for the history of postwar international relations. Just as the classification of ULTRA led most historians of the Second World War to ignore entirely for almost thirty years the role of SIGINT in hastening victory over Germany, so the even longer classification of post-war SIGINT files has led to a failure for almost half a century to recognize its role in the Cold War. Most histories of American foreign policy over the last half century do not even mention NSA. Henceforth any historian who mentions VENONA will find it hard to ignore the broader significance of SIGINT.

By the standards of the Cold War, VENONA was a rather small-scale operation, never involving as many as a hundred people. Though the decrypts produced by other, much larger SIGINT operations of the 1950s remain classified, it is already clear that some were of considerable importance. A declassified CIA study concludes that SIGINT became 'critically important' during the Korean War. We now know also that during the Suez crisis British-American code-breakers were able to decrypt the diplomatic traffic of all Middle Eastern states except (probably) Israel. The British Foreign Secretary, Selwyn Lloyd, congratulated the cryptanalysts on the 'excellence' as well as the 'volume' of the intelligence they were producing.[66]

Those who study the Cold War now face a difficult but interesting challenge: either to seek to take account of the role of SIGINT or to explain why they consider it unnecessary to do so.

NOTES

1. Cipher systems based on the one-time pad involve the addition of random numbers by the sender to each cipher group which are subtracted

219

by the receiver before beginning decipherment. Provided that the numbers are randomly generated, known only to the sender and receiver, and used once only, the system is theoretically unbreakable.

2. Brownell Committee Report, 13 June 1952, p.17. (This important analysis of the postwar development of US SIGINT has attracted remarkably little attention from historians of the Cold War and US foreign policy. References are to the version of the report declassified in 1981: George A. Brownell, *The Origin and Development of the National Security Agency* [Laguna Hills, California: Aegean Park Press, 1981].)

3. The VENONA decrypts, together with some explanatory material, are accessible on the NSA website: http://www.nsa.gov:8080/. Roger Louis Benson and Michael Warner (eds), *VENONA: Soviet Espionage and the American Response, 1939–1957* (Washington, D.C.: National Security Agency/Central Intelligence Agency, 1996) provide a valuable introduction to, and a selection of, the decrypts.

4. Early research on the VENONA decrypts was assessed in the BBC radio documentary, 'VENONA', written and presented by Christopher Andrew (producers: Mark Burman and Helen Weinstein), first broadcast on Radio 4 on 18 March 1998. The first published research to make use of the VENONA decrypts includes articles by several authors in *Intelligence and National Security* in 1997–8; Joseph Albright and Marcia Kunstel, *Bombshell: The Secret Story of America's Unknown Atomic Spy Conspiracy* (New York: Times Books, 1997); and Allen Weinstein and Alexander Vassiliev, *The Haunted Wood: Soviet Espionage in America – The Stalin Era* (New York: Random House, 1999). Weinstein and Vassiliev were also given exclusive access to KGB files which frequently corroborate, and in some cases amplify, the evidence of the VENONA decrypts.

5. Christopher Andrew, 'Codebreakers and Foreign Offices: The French, British and American Experience', in Christopher Andrew and David Dilks (eds), *The Missing Dimension: Governments and Intelligence Communities in the Twentieth Century* (London, Macmillan, 1984), pp.45–51.

6. John Ranelagh, *The Agency: The Rise and Decline of the CIA* (London: Weidenfeld and Nicolson, 1986), p.114.

7. Athan G. Theoharis and John Stuart Cox, *The Boss: J. Edgar Hoover and the Great American Inquisition*, paperback edition (New York: Bantam Books, 1990), pp.230–2.

8. Clark Clifford, *Counsel to the President: A Memoir*, paperback edition (London: Anchor Books, 1992), p.146.

9. Christopher Andrew, *For The President's Eyes Only: Secret Intelligence and the American Presidency from Washington to Bush* (New York/London: Harper Collins, 1995), pp.104–21, 123–4, 136–7.

10. Brownell Committee Report, pp.17–18. Philip S. Meilinger, *Hoyt S.*

Vandenberg (Bloomongton and Indianapolis: Indiana University Press, 1989), p,.124.

11. Brownell Committee Report, pp.18–19, 27.

12. Brownell Committee Report, p.3. The word SIGINT, already in use within the British intelligence community at the end of the Second World War, did not become current in the United States until the late 1950s. The interception and decryption of messages was referred to by American crypt-analysts as communications intelligence or COMINT. With the development of electronic intelligence (ELINT) during the 1950s, SIGINT was adopted as a general category which included both COMINT and ELINT. Even the word SIGINT remained classified for another two decades. George Bush was the first President to use the term in public.

13. H.B. Fletcher to D.M. Ladd, [FBI] Office Memorandum, 18 Oct. 1949. This important memorandum, which reports General Omar Bradley's decision not to inform Truman of the VENONA decrypts, was declassified late in 1997 as the result of a determined campaign by Senator Daniel Patrick Moynihan as Chairman of the Commission on Reducing and Enforcing Government Secrecy. Though there was already strong circumstantial evidence that Truman was not told, it required Moynihan's tenacity to obtain this memorandum. FBI agents asked by the Commission to search for written evidence were, Moynihan recalls, 'never heard from again'. Only after a personal appeal from Moynihan to FBI Director Louis J. Freeh was the document produced. Daniel Patrick Moynihan, *Secrecy: The American Experience* (New Haven: Yale University Press, 1998), pp.69–73; the FBI memorandum is reproduced on p.72.

14. Robert J. Donovan, *Conflict and Crisis* (New York: W.W. Norton & Co., 1977), pp.338–9.

15. Moynihan, *Secrecy*, pp.69–73. Benson and Michael Warner (eds), *VENONA*, p.xxiv. Though it is, as usual, impossible to prove a negative conclusively, those with access to still classified files in the intelligence archives and the Truman Library have found no indication that Truman was told. Both the evidence cited by Moynihan and Truman's evident ignorance of the VENONA revelations when commenting on Soviet espionage indicate that he was not.

16. Russell Jack Smith, *The Unknown CIA*, paperback edition (New York: Berkley Books, 1992), p.51.

17. Undated memo on Hillenkoetter, filed with Truman to Hillenkoetter, 10 Oct. 1950; Official File, Harry S. Truman Library, Independence, Missouri.

18. Interviews by Christopher Andrew with Dr Cram, September 1996. Because CIA employed very much stricter vetting procedures than OSS, it does not appear to have been penetrated by Soviet agents in the early Cold War. So far as is known, the KGB achieved no major penetration of the Agency until its recruitment of Aldrich Ames in 1985.

19. Truman, Memorandum for the Secretaries of State, War and the Navy, 12 Sept. 1945, Naval Aide Files, box 10, file 1, Harry S. Truman Library. Bradley J. Smith, *The Ultra-Magic Deals* (Novato, California: Presidio, 1993), p.212.

20. Christopher Andrew, 'The Making of the Anglo-American SIGINT Alliance, 1940–1948', in James E. Dillard and Walter T. Hitchcock (eds), *The Intelligence Revolution and Modern Warfare* (Chicago: Imprint Publications, 1996).

21. Benson and Michael Warner (eds), *VENONA*, p.xxii,n45. GCHQ has released no details of British participation in VENONA. Internal evidence in the decrypts, such as British rather than American spelling and a distinct British numbering system, shows, however, that a minority of the Soviet telegrams were decrypted by GCHQ cryptanalysts.

22. Information from Meredith Gardner and interview with Gardner broadcast in the BBC Radio 4 documentary 'VENONA'. Gardner later became NSA liaison officer with GCHQ in Cheltenham.

23. Andrew, *For the President's Eyes Only*, pp.199–200.

24. Truman's authorization of British-American peacetime SIGINT collaboration on 12 September 1945 identifies the Army Chief of Staff (Eisenhower) as one of those involved in implementing this collaboration.

25. During the interval between retiring as Army Chief of Staff in 1948 and becoming President in 1953, however, Ike does not appear to have received detailed briefings on the latest VENONA revelations. He told his cabinet in November 1953, for example, that he had seen no proof that Harry Dexter White had been a Soviet agent – evidence that he had either not seen or had forgotten the evidence of the VENONA decrypts. Stephen E. Ambrose, *Eisenhower*, vol.2: *The President* (New York: Simon and Schuster, 1984), pp.138–9.

26. Ludwell Lee Montague, 'General Walter Bedell Smith as Director of Central Intelligence', vol.5, p.55; DCI Historical Series, DCI-1 (Declassified Documents Reference System, 1991, no.60).

27. Interview by Christopher Andrew with Dr Louis Tordella (who served with AFSA during the Korean War and later became Deputy Director of NSA from 1958 to 1972), April 1992.

28. Interview by Christopher Andrew with Dr Louis Tordella, April 1992.

29. Brownell Committee Report, pp.40–3.

30. Andrew, *For The President's Eyes Only,* pp.187–9.

31. Peter Grose, *Gentleman Spy: The Life of Allen Dulles* (London: André Deutsch, 1995), pp.309, 334.

32. Ranelagh, *The Agency*, pp.190–1.

33. Interview with Dr Louis Tordella, April 1992.

34. Smith, 'Proposed Survey of Communications Intelligence Activities', 10 Dec. 1951; approved by Truman, 13 Dec. 1951; PSF 250, File Central Intelligence, HSTL.

35. James S. Lay, Jr., 'Proposed Survey of Communications Intelligence Activities', 13 Dec. 1951, ibid.

36. Montague, 'Bedell Smith', vol.5, pp.54–5.

37. Brownell Committee Report, p.55.

38. Brownell Committee Report, part 5.

39. 'Communications Intelligence Activities', 24 Oct. 1952, SRH-271, RG 457, National Archives, College Park, Maryland.

40. Interviews by Christopher Andrew with Dr Cram. Extracts from Dr Cram's recollections were broadcast in the BBC Radio 4 documentary 'VENONA'. Dr Cram died in January 1999.

41. Truman's continuing ignorance of VENONA is indicated by a variety of circumstantial evidence. A diary entry by him in February 1953, for example, makes clear his conviction that Harry Dexter White had never been a Soviet agent (Ambrose, *Eisenhower*, vol.2, p.139). Truman could scarcely have been convinced of White's innocence had he seen the references to him in the VENONA decrypts as a Soviet agent.

42. James Bamford, *The Puzzle Palace* (Boston: Houghton Mifflin, 1982).

43. Benson and Warner (eds), *VENONA*, pp.xxviii, 167–70. KGB files show that Weisband had been recruited as a Soviet agent in 1934; Weinstein and Vassiliev, *The Haunted Wood*, p.291.

44. Interviews with Cecil Phillips and Meredith Gardner broadcast in the BBC Radio 4 documentary, 'VENONA'.

45. In 1945 Soviet intelligence broke contact with Weisband as part of the security measures imposed after the defection of Elizabeth Bentley. Contact was resumed in 1947. Weinstein and Vassiliev, *The Haunted Wood*, p.291.

46. Because of lack of usable evidence, Weisband was never prosecuted for espionage. After his suspension from AFSA on suspicion of disloyalty, he was convicted of contempt for failing to attend a federal grand jury hearing on Communist Party activity and sentenced to a year's imprisonment (Benson and Warner (eds), *VENONA*, p.xxviii).

47. Benson and Warner (eds), *VENONA*, pp.xxvii–xxviii.

48. Interview with Meredith Gardner broadcast in the BBC Radio 4 documentary, 'VENONA'. Claims that Philby made further visits to AFSA and looked over Gardner's shoulder as he decrypted VENONA telegrams are inaccurate.

49. Benson and Warner (eds), *VENONA*, p.xxvii.

50. Kim Philby, *My Silent War*, paperback edition (London: Panther Books, 1969), pp.152–4.

51. Robert Cecil, *Divided Life* (London: Bodley Head, 1988), p.118.

52. VENONA, 3rd release, part 1, pp.240–1. VENONA identifies Maclean more clearly than the rest of the Magnificent Five largely because he was the only one to be stationed in the United States during the period covered by the decrypts. Only 29 of the telegrams exchanged between Moscow and the

London NKVD/NKGB residency, mostly dating from 1945, were decrypted in whole or in part. Though these contain a number of references to Philby (STANLEY), Burgess (HICKS), Blunt (JOHNSON) and Cairncross (LISZT), none is sufficiently specific to identify any of the four without further evidence. VENONA, 5th release, part 1, pp.242–82.

53. Yuri Modin, the former controller of the 'Magnificent Five' (Philby, Burgess, Blunt, Maclean and Cairncross), confirms that the plan to warn Maclean that he had been identified as a Soviet agent was worked out not by the Centre but by Philby and Burgess. Yuri Modin, *My Five Cambridge Friends* (London: Headline, 1994), p.199.

54. Modin, *My Five Cambridge Friends*, ch.7. John Costello and Oleg Tsarev, *Deadly Illusions* (London: Century, 1993), pp.338–9.

55. Interview with Meredith Gardner broadcast in the BBC Radio 4 documentary, 'VENONA'.

56. On the careers of the Magnificent Five see, inter alia, Christopher Andrew, 'Cambridge Spies: the "Magnificent Five", 1933–1945', in Sarah J. Ormrod (ed), *Cambridge Contributions* (Cambridge University Press, 1998).

57. Christopher Andrew and Oleg Gordievsky, *KGB: The Inside Story of its Foreign Operations from Lenin to Gorbachev*, paperback edition (London: Sceptre, 1991), pp.402–8. John Cairncross was unable to come to terms with most of his career as a Soviet spy and subsequently published remarkably unreliable memoirs (*The Enigma Spy* [London: Century, 1997]) which represent an almost textbook case of psychological denial. The account of his career in Andrew and Gordievsky, *KGB*, is confirmed and amplified by recently released material from his KGB file: Nigel West and Oleg Tsarev, *Crown Jewels: The British Secrets at the Heart of the KGB Archives* (London: HarperCollins, 1998), chs.9–10; Michael Smith, 'The humble Scot who rose to the top but then chose treachery', *Daily Telegraph*, 12 Jan. 1998.

58. Even had it been decided to use VENONA decrypts as part of the prosecution case, the complexity of the process by which they were produced would have made them difficult to use in evidence.

59. The decrypts which identified Fuchs, Greenglass and the Rosenbergs are in VENONA, 1st release.

60. On Hall's career, see Albright and Kunstel, *Bombshell*. Hall himself is understandably unwilling to enter into detail about the information he passed from Los Alamos, but says that his main motive was to prevent the United States acquiring a nuclear monopoly and becoming a danger to world peace.

61. Interview with FBI Agent Bob McQueen broadcast in the BBC Radio 4 documentary, 'VENONA'. Though Mr McQueen has no precise recollection of the bugging of the Halls' telephone, it is almost certain that

this took place, given the other methods of FBI surveillance.

62. Interviews with Ted and Joan Hall broadcast in the BBC Radio 4 documentary, 'VENONA'.

63. Moynihan, *Secrecy*.

64. I have found no major point on which VENONA contradicts the evidence of Bentley and Chambers; there is much that it directly corroborates.

65. VENONA, 1st release, pp.22,26,31,36–7,46–55; 3rd release, part 3, p.207. Moynihan, *Secrecy*, pp.146–8. Weinstein and Vassiliev, *The Haunted Wood*, chs.2,9,12.

66. Christopher Andrew, 'Intelligence and International Relations in the Early Cold War', *Review of International Studies*, 24, pp.321–30.

Addendum While this volume was in production, two further studies of the Soviet intelligence operations revealed by VENONA were published: John Earl Haynes and Harvey Klehr, *Venona: Decoding Soviet Espionage in America* (New Haven: Yale University Press, 1999); and Nigel West, *Venona: The Greatest Secret of the Cold War* (London: HarperCollins, 1999).

THE ITCH AFTER THE AMPUTATION?

The Purposes of British Intelligence as the Century Turns: An Historical Perspective and a Forward Look

PETER HENNESSY

The historical profession and the practitioners of the craft of intelligence have a good deal in common. Loftily expressed, we are both in the business of reducing the gap between uncertainty and knowledge. It took a biologist, however, to make me appreciate this linkage more fully.

In the summer of 1998, in conversation with Professor Arnold Feinstein, the subject arose of what exactly contemporary history is. As it was a Saturday night in West London and a jolly party was going on all around us, I broke the habits of a lifetime and offered a flippant definition. 'It's gossip-with-footnotes,' I replied.

The snatch of conversation that followed was so intriguing that I wrote it down as soon as I reached home:

AF: Gossip is very important. It has a great deal to do with human consciousness – the need to find out about people who can harm you or bring you pleasure; the need to find out how they are likely to behave. Without this characteristic we would be autistic.

PH: So in that sense intelligence – in the sense of intelligence *services* – is one of the oldest human activities?

AF: Yes. Exactly.[1]

I have to admit that I would not wish the secret vote to be deployed on those people and events which might bring pleasure to Her Majesty's Government (though such persons and possibilities are usually very difficult to find). But it is Professor Feinstein's harm test which must be applied to those activities, operations and capabilities that were funded by £745m-worth of Single Intelligence Vote money in the 1999–2000 financial year.[2] Put baldly, there are – and always will be – certain nasty and dangerous people, places, practices and possibilities which remain beyond the reach of open observation and easily available sources (more of which in a moment).

But history is powerfully involved in current activities in another sense. As Sir Percy Cradock put it soon after relinquishing the chair of Whitehall's Joint Intelligence Committee, history has dealt the United Kingdom 'certain cards . . . and the skill in the game is making use of those cards and playing them as well, as forcefully, as cleverly as we can'.[3] Shortly after the publication of the Blair Government's 1998 Strategic Defence Review,[4] one of its chief framers said quite simply (albeit privately): 'The SDR was driven by history.'[5] In between Sir Percy's words in 1992 and those of the top defence figure six years later a particularly thoughtful senior officer in the Secret Intelligence Service, MI6, wondered aloud (after a discussion of what Douglas Hurd called the UK's appetite for punching heavier than its weight in world affairs[6]) whether Britain's retention of its capacity for global intelligence reach was not merely 'the itch after the amputation?'[7]

I would not go quite as far as the former Deputy Chief of SIS, Sir Gerry Warner, who, when asked by Sir Robert Fellowes, then Private Secretary to the Queen, as he left a lunch at the old MI6 headquarters in Century House, 'What shall I tell Her Majesty her Secret Intelligence Service is for?' replied, 'Please tell her it is the last penumbra of her Empire.'[8] But I do recognize the centrality of past history to current practice and future expectations of the UK's intelligence and security capabilities. As Geoffrey Smith put it, traditionally we have been 'a diplomatic trading nation as well as an economic trading nation',[9] and it is arguable that being ahead of the game in knowledge terms is the most cost effective way of buying influence for a cash and kit-strapped nation with appetites beyond its means. It could be with the UK, at last a genuinely post-imperial nation which no longer equates might with the possession of overseas territory, that we are all Baconians now in understanding that 'knowledge itself is power'.[10]

Interestingly, the 1998 Strategic Defence Review was quite explicit in rejecting what Percy Cradock called the option of 'casting aside' the hand which history has dealt current ministers.[11] One of the primary purposes of the review was to sustain a capacity deep into the twenty-first century 'to go to the crisis' and 'to project power more flexibly round the world,' as the Defence Secretary, George Robertson, put it.[12]

Mad or not, British policy-makers still cannot contemplate a place out of the midday sun of international influence. Crudely put, this means remaining a nuclear-tipped power with a seat on the UN Security Council, underpinned by just enough weaponry of sufficient sophistication, backed by a willingness to pay what the former U.S. Defense Secretary, Robert Macnamara, called 'the blood risk',[13] in any serious military front-line the United States cares to erect on land, at sea or in the air. (Mr Macnamara was polite enough to avoid mentioning the Vietnam War in which he was deeply involved and the British were not.) These aspirational and policy 'givens', explicit or implicit, transmit 'givens' of their own to the British intelligence community.

The past has its pitfalls as a guide, however, because of its allure. In the UK context (despite the Philbys, the Blakes and the Bettaneys and the palpable lack of timely, JIC-promoted intelligence on the Falklands in 1982 so vividly revealed by the Franks Report of 1983[14]), the overall impression of intelligence remains that of a dangerous and skilful craft at which its British practitioners have excelled. In short that we have a special aptitude for that part of the 'great game' which does not require a diaspora of north-west frontiers and a large territorial empire to sustain it. It is a belief that the overseas friends of British intelligence have done much, and continue to do much, to promote.

A recent example of this flowed from the pen of Ray Seitz, the State Department career officer whose spell in Grosvenor Square made him one of the most successful US Ambassadors to the Court of St James in living memory. 'To be an Anglophile,' he wrote in his champagne case of a memoir, *Over Here*,

> You need imagination, because imagination is a fundamental part of British life. The British like to pretend, which is one reason why they make such good writers, actors and spies. There always seems to be a little bit of make-believe about the place. For the British, the show

does go on – the play is the thing – and they seem to prize few things so much as a good performance.[15]

The men and women of what used to be called the Intelligence Branch of the Secret Intelligence Service conform pretty closely to that shrewd piece of Seitzery. And though their exploits and the paper trail of 'CX' reports left by them remain protected by the very highest classification levels, the public has a certain sense of their swash and buckle thanks to a very rich domestic spy literature which stretches from Buchan's Hannay to Le Carré's Smiley.

I have always thought it intriguing that that especially early version of global technological enterprise, the film industry, should for its 'great spy' character seize on a member of Her Majesty's 'last penumbra', James Bond of MI6, and remain wedded to him throughout a period in which the British intelligence effort (in terms of numbers and resources) was constantly dwarfed by its American and Russian counterparts. When it comes to celluloid swash and buckle, the Brits undoubtedly remain supreme. And such a global image has its practical uses. As a former 'C' put it of his service, 'When we make the final approach and ask someone to help the British as an agent, as often as not they almost stand to attention.'[16]

But who is to say that this very powerful combination of historical influences, impressions and sheer romance exerts negligible sway not just on new recruits into the UK's intelligence networks but also on tyro ministers, a select number of whom go from piecing together their picture of the world from the newspapers and the electronic media to the best and newest material the clandestine agencies, the Cabinet Office and the Defence Intelligence Staff, the DIS, can provide?

Ministers are usually genuinely and quickly impressed with what they receive on the 'opaque five per cent' (usually the nastier, harder targets which hostile states go to great pains to protect) as opposed to the 95 per cent of information which is thought to be available from open sources. And even on breaking stories which, once they have broken, will be of an intensely public kind, ministers generally appreciate the value-added by the country's intelligence reach. As one insider put it: 'Today's SIS report is tomorrow's diplomatic report and the day after's newspaper report. But those two days can be crucial.'[17]

Yet the impression caught on the velcro of the nation's collective memory of derring-do allied to great technical proficiency of the Bletchley Park wartime codebreaking variety leads to huge and unattainable expectations. Each time the headlines rail against this or that real or imagined 'intelligence failure', it is as if the newsdesks of the nation and the readers or viewers of their product expect the Government Communications Headquarters, GCHQ, to have every inner sanctum of every tyrant wired-up for sound, SIS to have an agent-in-place in every private office or bedroom of any note and the Security Service, MI5, to have a tail on every nasty operating on the inviolate soil of the United Kingdom. It was never like that (despite the successes of Ultra and the Double-Cross system during the Second World War), never will be – and never can be. The Foreign and Commonwealth Office and Her Majesty's Treasury are not subject to the same expectations, let alone the Department of Education and Employment or the Ministry of Agriculture. But the number of young women coming before the Civil Service Selection Board who express an interest in MI5 (over half in recent years[18]) suggests that even among the finer products of institutionalized enlightenment (the British universities) the secret world retains a very definite pulling power.

M.R.D. Foot straddles like no other the jagged intersection of the historical and intelligence professions. A good part of his intellectual life has been devoted to the study of this terrain – so much so that he has a walk-on part, in exactly this guise, in John Le Carré's *A Perfect Spy*.[19] So he is the natural first stop for anyone interested in discerning the mixture of perpetual purposes (allowing for the 'Second Coming' or any intervening 'Rule of the Saints', of course) and changing patterns of the UK's intelligence effort as the centuries turn. Michael, too, is as aware as anybody of the fluidity insiders attribute to that combination of an end to the Cold War (in its 1944–1989 varieties at least) and the explosive, cumulative effect of technological advances on global intelligence competition.

Our conversation about it took place in a spare half-hour before an MA Examination Board meeting down the Mile End Road in London's East End in the early summer of 1998.[20] Michael's definition of the perpetual purposes of the British intelligence and security services was 'to keep the administration aware of dangers to the country's freedom from economic, military and subversive threats (in which I include the drugs trade) and from terrorism.' Like anyone with a sense of the Treasury's traditional scepticism about the cost

231

implications of any activity (and in Great George Street you do find people who are utterly immune to swash and buckle, the glories of a great past or the panache of a Hannay or a Bond), Michael appended an immediate view that 'The impact of the disappearance of the USSR should have been the occasion of an increase in the intelligence budget now we no longer have that single enemy against whom it was so easy to organize everything.'

On the economic side, Michael observed that 'The world economy, like the sea, is one.' The knock-on effects of collapses are considerable and intelligence should 'provide the material the *Financial Times* is not allowed to know'. The military front is unknowable but the proliferation of weapons-of-mass-destruction (including the nuclear-bomb-in-the-suitcase) had to be given primary attention. Subversion could still come from Left or Right (though Michael is 'much less uneasy' than he was about the danger from the Left). On Irish terrorism Michael (in June 1998) hoped 'the cease-fire lasts but suspect it won't'. He was especially intriguing on the unforseen. He wanted a twin-track approach here rather more formalized than the JIC's existing system of inquests and 'crisis lists'.[21] Michael urged the creation of a 'Catastrophes Unit' which would include an 'Historical Section' tasked to look back on matters which 'intelligence did not foresee'.[22]

If I had been putting pen to paper in the autumn of 1988, I would have recorded that about 80 per cent of the UK's intelligence and security effort went on coping with the activities of the Soviet Union and the Warsaw pact on its own terrain and other people's. Now 80 per cent of it is devoted to non-Russian affairs[23] (though insiders say the two most prominent intelligence lacunae in 1996–98 were the failure to predict the magnitudes of the Far Eastern and Russian financial, economic and political crises[24]).

It is also quite sobering to recall that MI5, which spent over 40 per cent of its budget in 1997–98 on terrorism of the Irish or the international kinds,[25] only began to develop a counter-terrorist capacity in 1967, initially in response to threats from the Middle East.[26] (It only acquired the lead on Northern Irish-related terrorism from Special Branch in 1992.[27]) By 1997–98 a tiny 0.3 per cent of MI5's budget was devoted to countering domestic subversion and this was largely absorbed by the pension costs of retired agents.[28] One third of the Security Service's resources was pitted against domestic subversion in the 1970s.[29] During the Cold War years MI5 reckon they

had about 95 per cent of the Communist Party of Great Britain identified and on their files,[30] and from recently declassified JIC papers for
1956, especially the one dealing with the CPGB's secret discussions
with its Soviet counterpart in May and June of that year, it is quite
plain that they really did have that Party and its Headquarters in
Covent Garden wired-up-for-sound.[31]

On the SIS and GCHQ fronts, targets and priorities have been
similarly transformed since the end of the Cold War with about 15
per cent of resources now allocated to the former Soviet Union.[32]
(Though the targets here remain serious enough – the safety and
command-and-control of nuclear weapons; the overall condition of
the region for stability rather than deterrence purposes; the likely
impact of the 'millennium bug', though worries here are, if anything,
more acute about the control systems of nuclear power stations than
nuclear weapons installations.[33]) Intelligence insiders agree with the
applicability of Michael Foot's maritime metaphor to such matters.
As one senior member of the UK Intelligence community put it: 'It *is*
like the sea. It *is* one.'[34]

The ending of the great half-a-century stand-off with the Soviet
Union has brought with it not just the requirement of 'unlearning the
past 50 years'[35] and the operational modes and thought patterns of
the Cold War which, as Michael Herman has put it, 'was in a special
sense an intelligence conflict' in which, as never before, had 'the
collection of intelligence and its denial to the adversary been such
central features of an international rivalry.'[36] Developments since
the fall of the Berlin Wall in November 1989 (or the failure of the
counter-coup in Moscow during August 1991 when then – and only
then – did the Assessments Staff of the British Joint Intelligence
Committee crack open the champagne to celebrate the end of the
Cold War[37]) have, naturally, led to substantial rethinks and reorgani-
zation inside the UK's Intelligence community.

What is well known on the inside but not fully appreciated on the
outside is that, as the century ends, 'the Russians are still spying on
the UK as if the Cold War hadn't ended, though the consequences
don't matter quite so much'.[38] What is scarcely appreciated at all
beyond the practitioners' net is the degree to which so-called 'friend-
to-friend espionage' has increased. As an insider explained: 'It's
not just economic and industrial, it's political. It's the whole gamut.
After all, there is an analysis which says the next century is going to
be the Pacific century. It is state-to-state this activity so you have

to penetrate. It's not so dangerous as the old activities against the Soviet Union, but it's more varied and complex because you can be a friend and foe at the same time.'[39]

Ministers' clearly want information on these areas of vexing ambiguity. It would be fascinating to know, quarter by quarter, how the half-dozen or so papers produced each week by the JICs Assessments Staff break down into subject areas and categories. Though I suspect the *really* delicate friend/foe material is kept out of the weekly *Red Book* of JIC intelligence summaries which goes to the Queen (the longest continuous reader of the volume and recipient of the No.1 copy since 1952[40]) and selected ministers. Plainly there is a spectrum of intelligence gathering and analysis in terms of both difficulty and sensitivity as well as range and reach.

So what would an early twenty-first century menu of British intelligence yield look like in the light of certain 'givens'? The first given, for the purposes of this chapter, is that the UK intelligence effort will be of roughly the same organizational configuration (the unpublished elements of 1997–98 Comprehensive Spending Review included consideration of a merger between MI5 and MI6 but this was rejected,[41] rightly in my view) and resourced at about the same levels in real terms (i.e. people and funds). The 1998 resources' picture was something like this:

- MI5. Strength 1,860; Budget £140m.[42]
- MI6. Strength c.1,800; Budget c.£180m.[43]
- GCHQ. Strength c.4,500; Budget c.£430m.[44]
- DIS. Strength c.450; Budget c.£50m.[45]

There are other 'givens' that need to be noted, starting with the general philosophy of what is both justifiable and necessary for the intelligence and security services of an open society to attempt and here the new parliamentary oversight arrangements established by the Intelligence Services Act 1994 have been of value. The 1997–98 annual report from the Intelligence and Security Committee, under the former Conservative Defence Secretary, Tom King, provided a particularly good and timely overview of the UK's intelligence effort in the aftermath of the Strategic Defence Review and the examination of the Single Intelligence Vote as part of the Comprehensive Spending Review.[46]

A Ditchley Foundation Conference on 'The Future of Intelligence in Democracies' held in October 1997 accepted two 'iron laws' and offered five 'consensual givens'. They were as follows:

IRON LAWS

1: That every human invention since the wheel had eventually spread round the world and it was idle to believe that weapons of mass destruction would be the first and sole exception.

2: That human nature had changed little if at all since primitive man converted himself into a hunter-gatherer.

CONSENSUAL GIVENS

1: That special intelligence capabilities would be necessary to reduce the number of secrets possessed by potential threateners of national security.

2: That the acquisition of such 'secrets' would diminish thereby the opacity and danger of the 'mysteries' that would remain.

3: That the value-added material which only secret sources and methods could provide would enable customers to check the public positions of potential adversaries against reality and to calibrate more effectively the indications of risk and menace which could be gleaned from open sources.

4: That certain aspects of 'peacekeeping', not least the maintenance of the nuclear taboo that had held since August 1945, depended to a large degree on secret capacities.

5: That successful counter-terrorism depended upon top-flight intelligence frequently pooled with other members of a constellation of intelligence 'clubs'.[47]

There are other more colloquial ways of delimiting a consensus on justifiable targets and priorities: weapons of mass destruction and the capabilities and intentions of those who possess them or are seeking to; terrorism; the international drugs trade (the last two are often brigaded together as 'drugs and thugs' by those in the intelligence trade). Magnitudes here are already considerable. There are around two dozen countries which give concern on the proliferation front;

235

there were about 400 terrorist attacks per year in the late 1990s; the international drugs trade now surpasses the oil industry in annual turnover.[48]

So how might the consensual areas appear on a page of British intelligence priorities?

■ Weapons-of-mass-destruction (WMD). There are sufficient states with sufficient reach to bring nuclear, chemical or biological destruction to the UK home base for this to be of primary concern for the foreseeable future.

■ Terrorism

(a) state-sponsored (which could be linked to WMD capabilities).

(b) non-state-sponsored eg. Middle Eastern or North African groups. Any recrudescence of terrorist activity in Ireland, North or South.

■ An International Drug Trade of a magnitude capable of dominating the politics and economics of some countries, seriously contaminating certain regions and of bringing social and criminal harm to all societies.

Around the edge of this consensus is serious crime (which now absorbs 2.5 per cent of MI5's resources and is permitted by the Security Service Act 1996[49]). There are those who argue that this should have remained solely a police function, though I would not be among them. Here, too, in terms of its existence on the margins of consensus, lies the gathering of political and economic intelligence on friendly rivals in the games of trade and influence. I would not be unduly squeamish here either. Better a knowledge-war than conflicts of other kinds. Here, too, I am with Palmerston who observed famously of the U.K. in 1848 that: 'We have no eternal allies, and we have no perpetual enemies. Our interests are eternal and perpetual, and those interests it is our duty to follow.'[50]

If the UK through its political class continues to opt-in to the influence business it will need more than just preventive intelligence about the misfortunes nations, groups or events might visit upon it. It will need knowledge of an extra special kind to prime its decision-takers and to trade with its allies. I am convinced, in this context, of the paramount importance of the continuation of the intelligence alliance with the United States especially and those other nations whose representatives enhance the JIC table in the Cabinet Office of a Wednesday afternoon. (The Americans have been there since 1951; the Canadians since 1958; the Australians and the New Zealanders arrived in 1969, though the latter were asked to leave when they went non-nuclear in the 1980s and denied berths to US warships carrying nuclear weapons.[51])

The US/UK special intelligence relationship is of immense value to Britain. As a very senior figure in the British intelligence community put it in the late 1990s:

> 'It's organic. It exists at all levels – acquisition, product, analysis (particularly cryptography). It is the most enduring, the deepest and the broadest of the UK-US special relationships. It is quite clear that the intelligence area is the part that's really special.
>
> 'There are one or two areas of exception, but it's virtually the same machine. The intelligence relationship is still unique in the sense that we can bring expertise and capacity, not just in particular areas but across the whole board. Nobody else can actually give the Americans serious help in every area of this business. And it's continuous – an every moment relationship.'[52]

Such a view is corroborated on the US side. As Joe Nye, Dean of Harvard's Kennedy School of Government, has put it, British intelligence, in his experience, 'had more influence on American intelligence than did any other country'. As Chair of the National Intelligence Council in Washington:

> 'I often read UK reports. . . . I found the British reports concise, well focused, well informed and well written. They were particularly good as a check against American parochialism. Even when I disagreed with some judgements, it was extremely useful to have an alternative point of view that I respected because of the quality of the people and resources devoted to many key areas.'[53]

Joe Nye also stressed the value of the UK's retention of 'a broad global perspective similar to ours', whereas other intelligence allies focused 'on a single region or a few issues'.[54]

I cannot see any 'intelligence club' surpassing the US/UK one. For both historical, practical and technical reasons it will remain *the* intelligence relationship for Britain even if the European Union manages to develop something approaching an integrated foreign and defence policy.

Where should there be an element of re-examination and re-appraisal? Perhaps in the mechanics – the means of converting raw material into finished product and conveying it to Whitehall customers, both ministerial and official. The UK's Joint Intelligence Committee system of *agreed* assessments is the envy of all the insiders I have ever talked to in Washington. Some domestic customers regard it, however, as overcooked and unduly polished. They reckon they need the regular roughage of SIGINT and HUMINT, decode and CX report, to avoid constipation.[55]

It is very difficult for those outside the loop to judge this. Perhaps the turn-of-the-century is the moment for another look at all the linkages and transmission belts – a review comparable to 1957 when the JIC, post-Suez, was removed from the Chiefs of Staff and given to the Cabinet Office[56] or 1968 when Sir Burke Trend (then Secretary of the Cabinet) and Sir Denis Greenhill (then Chairman of the JIC) created the Cabinet Office Assessments Staff to give the JIC a bigger all-source analysis capability.[57] The centre is still very small – not much more than 30 people in all.[58] It was last examined seriously in the late 1970s[59]. The Quinlan review of intelligence provision 1991–92, out of which came the combined budget – the Single Intelligence Vote – did not cover this aspect,[60] the 'high table' of British intelligence, as Percy Cradock likes to call it.[61]

Finally, what is the justification for the whole enterprise as the century turns? On the money side, just one serious conflict avoided thanks to timely and accurate intelligence would pay for the whole of the UK's intelligence effort for several years. The capital costs arising out of the Falklands War (quite apart from the battle bills themselves) reached £2.6 billion over the first five post-invasion years[62] – the equivalent, at mid-1980s prices, of about three years-worth of total British intelligence activity. And if prevention fails and British forces are deployed in action, what GCHQ, in collaboration with the United States' National Security Agency, can provide truly comes into its own as a reducer of the 'blood price'.

But the overriding justification for clever, timely and honest intelligence is that it is a great force-multiplier for a nation brimming neither with surplus weaponry nor cash, yet which aspires to legitimate and, one hopes, decent and beneficial influence in a nasty world. The intelligence yield can help mightily to keep ministers not only well-briefed but illusions-free. As the Chief of SIS, Sir Maurice Oldfield, put it in March 1974 when summoned by his new minister, the Foreign Secretary, Jim Callaghan, to be asked what his job was for, 'My job, Secretary of State, is to bring you unwelcome news.'[63] It has not been – and cannot be – better put than that.

NOTES

1. Conversation with Professor Arnold Feinstein, 20 June 1998.
2. *Modern Public Services Britain: Investing in reform*, Cm 4011, (HMSO, 1998), p.102.
3. Sir Percy was speaking on the BBC Radio 4 *Analysis* programme, 'Out of the Midday Sun?' first broadcast on 23 July 1992. The text of the programme is reproduced in Peter Hennessy, *Muddling Through: Power, Politics and the Quality of Government in Postwar Britain*, (Gollancz, 1996), pp.150–67.
4. *The Strategic Defence Review*, Cm 3999, (HMSO, 1998).
5. Private information.
6. Lord Hurd used this phrase in a speech at the Royal Institute of International Affairs in 1993. See *The Financial Times*, 4 February 1993.
7. Private information.
8. Sir Gerry has given me permission to attribute this remark.
9. Geoffrey Smith is author of *Reagan and Thatcher* (Bodley Head, 1990). He delivered this judgement during a seminar at the Institute of Historical Research, 30 January 1991.
10. Francis Bacon, 'Of Heresies' in his *Religious Meditations*, (Humfrey Hooper, 1597).
11. Sir Percy was speaking on 'Out of the Midday Sun?'
12. *The Strategic Defence Review*, p.2.
13. Mr Macnamara was talking during the build-up to the first Gulf War and expressed his gratitude for Britain's unique willingness to pay the blood price. Peter Hennessy and Caroline Anstey, *Moneybags and Brains: The Anglo-American 'Special Relationship since 1945*, Strathclyde/*Analysis Paper No.1*, (Department of Government, University of Strathclyde, 1990), pp.28–9.
14. The Franks Report is most easily found in the Pimlico edition with an 'Introduction' by Alex Danchev. Lord Franks et al, *The Franks Report: Falkland Islands Review*, (Pimlico, 1992).
15. Raymond Seitz, *Over Here*, (Weidenfeld, 1998), p.10.

16. Private information.
17. Private information.
18. Private information.
19. John Le Carré, *A Perfect Spy*, (Coronet edition, 1987), p.484.
20. Conversation with Professor M.R.D. Foot, 22 June 1998, before a meeting of the Summer Examination Board of the MA in Contemporary British History Programme, Queen Mary and Westfield College, University of London.
21. Private information.
22. Conversation with Professor M.R.D. Foot, 22 June 1998.
23. Private information.
24. Private information.
25. *MI5. The Security Service*, Third Edition, (Home Office, HMSO, 1998), p.9.
26. Private information.
27. *MI5. The Security Service*, Third Edition, p.14.
28. Ibid.p.19.
29. Private information.
30. Private information.
31. Public Record Office, CAB 158/25, JIC (56) 95, 3 September 1956, 'Discussions in Moscow between the British Communist Party and CPSU representatives, May/June 1956'.
32. Private information.
33. Private information.
34. Private information.
35. Private information.
36. Michael Herman, 'The Role of Military Intelligence since 1945', a paper delivered to the Twentieth Century British Politics and Administration Seminar at the Institute of Historical Research, 24 May 1989.
37. Sir Percy Cradock, *In Pursuit of British Interests: Reflections on Foreign Policy Under Margaret Thatcher and John Major*, (John Murray, 1997), p.121.
38. Private information.
39. Private information.
40. PRO, PREM 13/1343, 'Correspondence with Cabinet Office on Joint Intelligence Committee current assessments'. Anonymous JIC official to Michael Palliser, 31 October 1966.
41. Private information.
42. *MI5 The Security Service*, Third Edition, p.9.
43. Private information.
44. Private information.
45. Private information.

46.Intelligence and Security Committee, *Annual Report 1997–98*, Cm 4073, (HMSO, 1998).
47.Peter Hennessy, 'The Future of Intelligence in Democracies: Scope, Justification and Control', Ditchley Conference Report No.D97/12 (Ditchley Foundation, 1997), p.1.
48.Private information.
49.*MI5: The Security Service*, Third Edition. Annex 1.
50.Quoted in John Dickie, *Inside the Foreign Office*, (Chapmans, 1992), p.42.
51.Private information.
52.Private information.
53.Joseph S. Nye Jr. to Peter Hennessy, 7 July 1998.
54.Ibid.
55.Private information.
56.PRO, PREM 11/2418, 'Middle East 1957–58', Brook to Macmillan, 6 December 1957 and private information.
57.Private information.
58.Private information.
59.Private information.
60.Private information.
61.Cradock, *In Pursuit of British Interests*, p.40.
62.Michael Herman, *Intelligence Power in Peace and War* (CUP, 1996), p.302, fn67. For late 1990s estimates of the cost of 'Fortress Falklands' (£3.6 billion 1982–97; £65m per annum in the late 1990s) see 'Portillo pushes for Falklands oil revenue', *The Independent*, 5 January 1997.
63.Private information.

SELECT BIBLIOGRAPHY – 1998

Publications are listed in chronological order by year. Only books, articles and major contributions to compilations and to works by other authors have been listed. Although M.R.D. Foot has published, since 1946, a wealth of short articles, reviews, short notices of books, short contributions and obituaries, these have not been included. Significance, rather than length, has been the guiding principle behind this selection. Unpublished lectures and talks have been omitted.

M.M.F.

1952

—— With J.L. Hammond, *Gladstone and Liberalism* (English Universities Press); 2nd ed. (Methuen), republished: New York (Collier Books), 1966.

—— 'Great Britain and Luxemburg 1867', *English Historical Review*, 1xvij, 264, pp. 352–79 (quoted as *EHR* below).

—— Contributions to: S. Morrison (ed.), *The History of the Times*, vol. IV, chapter VI; pts of chapters III, VII, VIII, XXIII, App. II, App. III.

1954

—— 'Select Bibliography' in: J.A.R. Marriott, *England since Waterloo*, 15th ed. (Methuen).

1956

—— *British Foreign Policy since 1898* (Hutchinson's University Library).

1958

—— Entries on: Aberdeen (4th Earl); Clarendon (4th Earl); Ellesmere; Fane, Julian; Gladstone, W.E.; Granville (1st Earl); Liverpool (Earls of); Lyons (1st Earl); Lytton (1st Earl); Melbourne (2nd Viscount); Palmerston (3rd Viscount) [pt]; Reeve, Henry, in: W. Yust (ed.), *Encyclopaedia Britannica*, (re-printed with some revisions, 1967).

1959

—— Entries on: Croft, Henry Page; Greenwood, Hamar, in: *Dictionary of National Biography 1941–1950*.

243

1960

—— 'La Grande-Bretagne et L'Europe', in: M. Beloff (ed.), *L'Europe du XIXe et du XXe siècle*, Milan (Marzorati), II, 813–38.

—— 'The Origins of the Franco-Prussian War and the Remaking of Germany', in: J.P.T. Bury (ed.), *New Cambridge Modern History*, X, chapter 22.

1961

—— *Men in Uniform*, Institute for Strategic Studies, *Studies in International Security*, III (Weidenfeld and Nicolson).

1964

—— Introduction to J.L. Hammond, *Gladstone and the Irish Nation* (unaltered reprint) (F. Cass).

1966

—— *SOE in France* (HMSO); 2nd impression (revised) (HMSO), 1968; 3rd impression (HMSO), 1976.

1967

—— Entries on: Anglesey (1st Marquess); Bentinck, Lord George; Bryce (1st Viscount); Canterbury (1st Viscount); Carnarvon (4th Earl); Cavendish, Lord Frederick; Cowley (1st Earl); Cranbrook (1st Earl); Derby (14th–17th Earls); Devonshire (8th Duke); Dufferin (1st Marquess); Eyre, Edward John; Fawcett, Henry; Forster, W.E.; Gorst, Sir J.E.; Goschen (1st Viscount); Hammond, Edmund; Harney, G.J.; Morley, John; Playfair, Lyon; Rosebery (5th Earl); Selborne (2nd Earl), in: W.E. Preece (ed.), *Encyclopaedia Britannica*, Chicago.

1968

—— 'Triumph of the [French] Resistance', in: B.H. Liddell Hart (ed.), *History of the Second World War*, V, xi.

—— Ed: *The Gladstone Diaries*, I, II, 1825–1839 (Oxford University Press).

1969

—— 'Morley's Gladstone: a reappraisal', *Bulletin of the John Rylands Library*, li, 2.

—— 'Reflections on SOE' [Percival lecture], *Memoirs and Proceedings of the Manchester Literary and Philosophical Society*, CXI (1968–69), 5.

—— 'Copyright and Learned Journals', *The Author*, LXXX, 3.

1970

—— 'Writing Secret History', *The Author*, LXXXI, 2.

—— Introduction to and two chapters on 'Special Operations', in: M.R. Elliott-Bateman (ed.), *The Fourth Dimension of Warfare* (Manchester University Press); reprinted in *The Interservice Journal*, I, San Francisco, 1982.

1971

—— 'Civil and Military Relations', *RUSI Journal*.

—— 'Officials and Secrets', *The Author*, LXXXII, 4.

—— Entry on: Cope, Sir Alfred William, in: *Dictionary of National Biography, 1951–1960*.

1972

—— Prefatory note to: J.R. Western, *Monarchy and Revolution* (Blandford Press).

1973

—— Ed: *War and Society. Historical essays in honour and memory of J.R. Western 1928–1971* (Paul Elek).

—— 'The IRA and the Origins of SOE', in: M.R.D. Foot, (ed.), *War and Society* [see above]; reprinted in *The Interservice Journal*, I, San Francisco, 1982.

—— Foreword to L.B. Oatts, *The Emperor's Chambermaids* (Ward Lock).

1974

—— Ed. *with* H.C.G. Matthew, *The Gladstone Diaries*, III–IV (Oxford University Press).

—— 'Revolt, rebellion, revolution, civil war: Irish experience', in: M.R. Elliott-Bateman, J. Ellis and T. Bowden (eds.), *Revolt to Revolution* (Manchester University Press).

1975

—— 'Sir Winston Churchill', in: H. van Thal (ed.), *The Prime Ministers*, II (Allen & Unwin).

1976

—— *Resistance, an analysis of European Resistance to Nazism, 1940–1945* (Eyre Methuen); 2nd impression (revised) (Eyre Methuen), 1977; paperback ed. (Granada: Paladin), 1978.

1977

—— 'Resistance, War and Revolution', in: G.W. Keeton and G. Schwarzenberger (eds.), *The Year Book of World Affairs*, XXXI (Stevens & Son) [Lectures given at King's College, London, 1973].

—— *With* Baudot, M [and others], *Encyclopédie de la guerre 1939–1945*, Paris, Tournai (Casterman); USA ed. *The Historical Encyclopedia of World War II*, New York (Facts on File), 1980.

—— 'History slice by slice', *Economist* (Jan).

1978

—— *Six Faces of Courage* (Eyre Methuen); Revised ed. (Magnum), 1980; Part reprinted as: 'The Face of Courage', in: J.E. Lewis (ed.), *The Mammoth Book of True War Stories*, 1992.

—— 'Subcontinent set free', *Economist* (Jan).

1979

—— With J.M. Langley, *MI 9* (Bodley Head); 2nd ed. revised, Boston and Toronto (Little, Brown), 1980.
—— 'Gladstone and Panizzi, *British Library Journal*, V, i.
—— Foreword to: J.C. Masterman, *The Double-Cross System in the War of 1939–1945* (Granada).

1980

—— 'Open Secrets', *Economist* (March).

1981

—— 'Spies and Cucumbers', *Economist* (Jan).
—— 'Was SOE any good?' *Journal of Contemporary History*, XVI, 1.
—— Foreword to J. Garlinski, *The Swiss Corridor* (Dent).
—— Entries on: Browning, Boy and Hambro, C, in: *Dictionary of National Biography 1961–70*.

1982

—— 'Dusting off 1951's archives', *Economist* (Jan).
—— 'The Road from Phoenix Park', *Economist* (May).

1983

—— 'Pleasures of hindsight', *Economist* (Jan).
—— 'Mr Gladstone and his Publishers', in: R. Myers and M. Harris (eds.), *Author/Publisher Relations during the Eighteenth and Nineteenth Centuries*, Oxford (Oxford Polytechnic Press).

1984

—— *SOE. An outline history of the Special Operations Executive, 1940–1946* (BBC publications); reprinted 1985; (slightly) revised ed., Frederic, Md. (Universities Publications of America), 1986; revised ed. (Mandarin), 1990; reprinted (Mandarin), 1993; Czech translation, Brno, 1997.
—— 'That was 1953, that wasn't', *Economist* (Jan).

1985

—— 'The Gladstone Diaries', in: P.J. Jagger (ed.), *Gladstone, Politics and Religion* (Macmillan).
—— 'Retrospect', in: D. Hawkins, *War Report D-Day to VE-Day* (BBC publications).

1986

—— 'In Eden's day', *Economist* (Jan).
—— 'Les Britanniques et la résistance armeé en France', in: *Les Armées françaises pendant la seconde guerre mondiale 1939–1945*, Paris (Ecole nationale supérieure de technique).

—— 'British bid to armed French resistance: II 1940–1944 and the secret services', in: *Franco-British Studies*, II [Lectures delivered May 1984].

—— 'The Hawarden Kite', in: *The University of Leeds Review 1986–87*, XXIX [lecture delivered Dec. 1985]; reprinted in: *Journal of Liberal Democrat History*, XX (1998).

—— Entries on: Churchill, P.M.; Mockler-Ferryman, E.E.; Nicholls, F.W.; Palmer, R.C., 3rd Earl of Selborne, in: *Dictionary of National Biography 1971–1980*.

1987

—— 'The year of lost Empire', *Economist* (Jan).

—— 'Uses and abuses of intelligence', *Intelligence and National Security*, II (i).

—— A Comparison of SOE and OSS', in: K.G. Robertson (ed.), *British and American Approaches to Intelligence* (Macmillan).

1988

—— 'Voices of Silence', *Economist* (Jan).

—— 'Comrades-in-Arms', *History Today* (Dec).

—— Foreword to: W.J. Casey, *The Secret War against Hitler*, Washington.

—— Foreword to: R. Slowikowski, *In the Secret Service* (Windrush Press).

1989

—— 'Almost the last post', *Economist* (Jan).

—— *Churchill and the Secret Services*, Toronto (Churchill Society for the Advancement of Parliamentary Democracy).

—— 'Tyrants and the human cost', *William and Mary Tercentenary Journal*.

'Underground Warfare' [and several other shorter contributions], in: N. Frankland (ed.), *The Encyclopaedia of Twentieth-Century Warfare* (Mitchell, Beazley).

—— Foreword to: Sir Peter Tennant, *Vidsidan ar kniget*, Stockholm.

1990

—— *Art and War* (Headline/Imperial War Museum).

—— Ed: *Holland at War against Hitler: Anglo-Dutch Relations 1940–45* (F. Cass).

—— 'The *Englandspiel*' in: M.R.D. Foot (ed), *Holland at War against Hitler* [see above].

—— 'What use was resistance?', in: J.P.B. Jonker, A.E. Kersten and G.N. van der Plaat (eds.), *Vijftig jaar na de inval*, 's-Gravenhage.

—— 'De Gaulle et les services secrets pendant la guerre', *Espoir*, 71.

—— 'Stay-behind parties', *History Today*, XL.

—— 'George Blake', in: K. Robbins (ed.), *Biographical Dictionary of British Political life in the Twentieth Century* (Blackwell).
—— Entries on: Montagu, E.E.S. and Sporborg, H.N., in: *Dictionary of National Biography, Supplement 1981–1985*.
—— Foreword to: L.R. Shoemaker, *The Escape Factory*, New York (St Martin's Press).

1991
—— *Open and Secret War, 1938–1945*, Austin (Faculty Seminar on British Studies, University of Texas).
—— 'Finance and the 1914 War', *Modern History Review*, III.

1992
—— 'Gulf War', *Annual Register 1991*.
—— 'Dieppe: Triumph out of disaster', *History Today*, XLII.
—— 'OSS and SOE: an equal partnership?', in: G.C. Chalou (ed.), *The Secrets War. The Office of Strategic Services in World War II*, Washington (National Archives and Records Administration).
—— Contribution to: J.D. Sainsbury (ed.), *The F Section Memorial Valençay* (Hart Books).

1993
—— Entries on: Amery, John; Dansey, Sir C.E.M.; Holland, J.C.F.; Meinertzhagen, R.; Murphy, W.; Szabo, V.R.E., in: C.S. Nicholls (ed.), *Dictionary of National Biography, Missing Persons*.

1994
—— 'Resistance', in: B. Pitt (ed.), *Fiftieth Anniversary of D-Day* (Imperial War Museum).
—— 'Britische Geheimdienste und deutscher Widerstand 1939–1945', in: K-J Müller and D.N. Dilks (eds.), *Grossbritannien und der deutsche Widerstand 1933–1944*, Paderborn (F. Schöningh).
—— 'What use are secret services?', in: H.P. Peake and S.H. Halpern (eds.), *In the Name of Intelligence: essays in honor of Walter Pforzheimer*, Washington (NIBC Press).
—— 'The British secret services and Northern Europe', in: *la Résistance et les Européens du Nord*, Brussels (Centre de recherches et d'études historique de la seconde guerre mondiale), Paris (Institut d'histoire du temps présent).
—— 'Normandy D-Day', *Mars and Minerva*, VIII.

1995
—— Consultant editor of and contributions to: I.C.B. Dear (ed.), *The Oxford Companion to the Second World War* (Oxford University Press).
—— 'Eisenhower and the British', in: G. Bischof and S.E. Ambrose,

Eisenhower: a centennial assessment, Baton Rouge (Louisiana State University Press).

—— 'Great Britain and the French Resistance', in: D. Dutton (ed.), *Statecraft and Diplomacy in the Twentieth Century* (Liverpool University Press).

—— 'Open and Secret War 1938–1945', in: W.R. Louis (ed.), *Adventures with Britannia* (I.B. Tauris).

1996

—— 'The Liberation of France and Restoration of Democratic Government', in: G. Bennett (ed.), *The End of the War in Europe 1945* (HMSO).

—— 'Le SOE et le maquis', in: F. Marcot (ed.), *La Résistance et les Français, lutte armée et maquis*, Paris (Annales littéraires de l'Université de Franche Conté) [lecture at Colloque, Besançon, 1995].

—— Entry on: Wynne, Greville Maynard, in: *Dictionary of National Biography 1986–1990*.

—— Contributions (on 'Resistance'; 'Ruses'; 'Special Operations'; 'Terrorism') to: R. Cowley and G. Parker (eds.), *The Reader's Companion to Military History*, Boston, New York (Houghton Mifflin).

—— Contribution to Appendix 'Belsen Testimonies: The Camp and its liberation' of: J. Reilly (ed.), *Belsen in History and Memory, Journal of Holocaust Education*, V, 2–3; republished (F. Cass), 1997.

—— Introduction to G. Zembsch-Schreve, *Pierre Lalande* (Leo Cooper).

1997

—— Foreword to: Sir Peter Wilkinson, *Foreign Fields* (I.B. Tauris).

1998

—— 'Et Fachoda?' *Modern History Review*, IX, 3.

—— 'The Young Panizzi', *British Library Journal*, XXIII, 2.

—— Contribution to: G. Cowell (comp.), *SOE A British Contribution* (Special Forces Club).

INDEX

Agents have been indexed under their real names. Cover names are in italics. Names of operations and circuits/networks are in small caps. Entries in foreign languages are also in italics. Military ranks have only been given where they were needed for identification.

252

254

256

Kell, Vernon, 153, 165
Kershaw, Ian, xv
Kesselring, A., 13
KGB (Committee of State
    Security – USSR), 204,
    216
Kim Il Sung, 58–60
King
    Log, 107
    Stork, 107
King, E.J., 42, 53
King, Tom, 234
Kitchener, Sir Herbert (later,
    1st Earl), 153
Knežević,
    Nikola, 101
    Radoje, 101
    Živan, 98–102
Knopf, (publisher), 76
Kojić, Slavko, 100
Kolko, Gabriel, 78
Koppe, Wilhelm, 86–90,
    92–4
Korea, xv, 51, 57–65, 209,
    211–12, 219
    North, 58–60, 62, 210
    South, 58–9, 210
Kragujevac, 99
Kraljevo, 99
Kramer, Rita, 131
Kroger, Helen, see Cohen, L.
Kroger, Peter, see Cohen, M.
Ku Klux Klan, 76

Labrador, see Creel, R.
Lalatović, Mirko, 101
Lamirault, Claude, 172, 175
Lamphere, Robert, 212
Lancaster, (bomber), 111
Landes, Roger, 130
Lang, Fritz, 140
Lange, Herbert, 93
Langley, J.M., 106
Languedoc, 136
Lapin Blanc, Le, see Yeo-
    Thomas, F.F.E.
Laski, Harold, 30
Lattre de Tassigny, J. de, 38
Lawlor, Sheila, 75
Lay, James, S., Jr., 211
LEBÉ-NORD, (resistance
    network), 174
Le Carré, John, 230–1
Lecco, 8, 14

Ledger, C.K., 187, 190–1
Ledier, Marie, 147
Legrand, see Morier, H.
Leidenburg, Justus, 186
Leipzig, 87
Levin, Anna, 193
Lewis, C.S., 23
LIBERTÉ/JULIETTE,
    (operation), 177
Lika, 101
Lindemann, Sir Frederick, 1st
    Viscount Cherwell, 39
Lisbon, 4–5, 100–2, 179–81,
    198
Litzmannstadt, see Lodz
Livingstone, Goodhue, 188
Ljubliana, 41
Lloyd, Selwyn, 219
Local Defence Volunteers, see
    Army, British – Home
    Guard
Lockhart, Guy, 174–6
Lodz, 86, 90, 92
Loire, 176
London, xxiii–xxiv, 2–5,
    26–9, 57, 62, 97–102,
    120, 124–5, 130, 161,
    172, 181–2, 189,
    191–2, 194–5, 197,
    214–15, 218, 227, 231
    British Museum, xxi
        Library, xxii
    Bush House, 28
    Courtauld Institute, 216
    Imperial War Museum,
        xxiv
    Lambeth Palace Library,
        xxii
    Public Record Office, 28,
        119
    University
        Senate House, 22
    Westminster, 64
    Whitehall, xvii, xxiv, 19,
        64, 121, 125, 127,
        129, 159, 162, 188,
        228, 238
    Wimbledon, 21
Longford, Lord, see
    Pakenham, F.
Los Alamos, 204, 216
Lourenço Marques, 185–93,
    195–8
Loustaunau-Lacau, Georges,
    179

Lovett, Robert A., 212
Low Countries, see
    Netherlands
Lowe, Peter, xv
Loyettes, 176–7, 180
Ludecke, Fritz, 164
Luftwaffe, 182
Lugano, 8
Lukacs, John, xv
Lumsden, Sir Herbert, 53
Lyons, 7, 175–6, 180
Lysander(s), xvii, 169–70,
    172–8, 180–2

Mabillon, John, 71
MacArthur, Douglas, xiii, xv,
    51–66, 210
Macartney, C.W., 28
McCaffery, J., 4, 7, 14–16
McCairns, James, 177–8, 182
McCarthy, J.R., xvii, 78, 218
Mackenzie, Compton, 121
Mackinnon, Donald, xix
Maclean,
    Donald, 214–16, 218
    Melinda, 215
MacMahon, Maurice, 180–1
Macmillan, H., 108, 127
Macnamara, Robert, 229
Macon, 175–6
McQueen, Bob, 217
Madagascar, 186, 188–9
Maddox, Robert, 78, 82
Madeleine, see Inayat Khan,
    N.
Madrid, 4, 179
Magenta, Duc de, see
    MacMahon, M.
Maho, see Hentic, P.
MAGIC, (intelligence), 205
Malakand Field Force, 152
Mallaby, C.R.D., xiv, 1–16
    (passim)
Malory, Sir Thomas, 107
Malta, 98, 101, 103
Manchester, xxii–xxiv,
    19–20
Manchuria, 61, 63
Manna, Alfredo, 192–6, 198
Manuel, André, 174
Mao Tse-tung, 60
Maoist, 141

257

259

261

Versailles, 72, 74, 80
Vichy, 3, 34, 37, 138, 142–3,
    145, 172, 175, 179,
    181–2
Victor Emmanuel III, King of
    Italy, 6
Vidor, King, 140
Vienna, 41, 161
Vietnam, 80, 229
Vistula, 88
V-J Day, 206
Vojvodina, 101
Volta Mantovana, 10

Wackherr, Robert, 177
Wake Island, 61
Wallace, Henry, 204
Walters, Anne-Marie, 122
War
  Boer, 153–4
  1914–18, 21, 27, 35–6,
    55, 72–4, 76–7,
    79–81, 84, 136–7,
    152, 154–64
    (*passim*), 166, 186
  1939–45, xiii, 27, 30,
    73–5, 79–81, 105,
    108, 111, 115, 120,
    145, 151–2, 164,
    166, 169, 171, 183,
    186, 203–6, 208–9,
    211, 218–19, 231
  Cold, xvii, 56–7, 78, 80–1,
    203–5, 207, 216,
    218–19, 231–3
  Twentieth-century, xv, 72,
    76
  Cabinet, 34, 38–40
  Council, 156–7

Office, 120–1, 123–4,
    153–4
  Room, 158–9
Ward, Irene, Dame, 125, 127
Warner, Sir Gerry, 228
Warsaw, 90, 232
Warthe
  (river), 84
  (district), *see* Warthegau
Warthegau, (*Reichsgau
    Wartheland*), xv, 84–94
Washington (DC), 21, 37,
    44, 52, 54–7, 61–4, 81,
    98, 190, 208–9, 211,
    213–16, 237–8
Waterloo, Battle of, 72
Webster, Charles, 27
Wegerer, Alfred von, 72
Wehrmacht, see Army,
    German
Weimar Republic, 28
Weisband, William, 213–14
Werz, Luitpold, 186, 194,
    197–8
West, Nigel, *see* Allason, R.
Western, John, xxii–xxiii
Wheeler-Bennett, John, xx
WHEELWRIGHT, (circuit), 122
'Whippy', *see* Nesbitt-Dufort,
    J.
Whipsnade Zoo, 172
White, Ralph, xvi–xvii
White Rabbit, see Yeo-
    Thomas, F.F.E.
Whitney, Courtney, 63
Whittall, Edward, 161–2
Wilhelmshaven, 160
Wilkinson, Gerald, 53
Willert, Sir Arthur, 21–3,
    25–6

Williams, William A., 78
Willoughby, Charles, 57, 61
Wilson, Sir Arthur, 159
Wilson, Duncan, 29
Winchester, xx, xxiv, 107
Winterbotham, Frederick,
    181
Wireless, xvi, 2–5, 7, 11,
    97–103 (*passim*), 125,
    154, 160, 163, 169–71,
    176–7, 181, 186, 190
Wohlhynia, 83
Wolff, Karl, 12–16
Wolverton, 25
Woods, Christopher, xiv
W/T (Wireless Telegraphy),
    see wireless

XX (Double Cross)
    Committee, 171, 231

Yalta, 81, 219
Yeats, W.B., 115
Yeltsin, Boris, 214
Yeo-Thomas,
    Barbara, 177
    F.F.E., 121–2, 130, 177–8
Yorkshire, 157–8
Young, Courtney, 194
YTHS, 97–9, 102–3
Yugoslavia, 2–3, 19, 100–1,
    103, 112
    Government in exile, 98,
    102–3

Zanin, Don Mario, 8, 14
Zeebrugge, 155
Zitelmann, Rainer, 73
Zurich, 15